Second Edition

TEACHING DISABILITY SPORT

A Guide for Physical Educators

Ronald W. Davis, PhD
Texas Woman's University

Human Kinetics

Library of Congress Cataloging-in-Publication Data

Davis, Ronald W., 1950-
    Teaching disability sport : a guide for physical educators / Ronald W.
Davis. -- 2nd ed.
        p. cm.
    Rev. ed. of : Inclusion through sports, c2002.
    Includes bibliographical references and index.
    ISBN-13: 978-0-7360-8258-7 (hard cover)
    ISBN-10: 0-7360-8258-1 (hard cover)
    1. Physical education for people with disabilities.   2. Mainstreaming in
education.   I. Davis, Ronald W., 1950- Inclusion through sports.   II. Title.
    GV445.D344 2010
    796.04'56--dc22

                                    2010025117

ISBN-10: 0-7360-8258-1 (print)
ISBN-13: 978-0-7360-8258-7 (print)

This book is a revised edition of *Inclusion Through Sports,* published in 2002 by Human Kinetics.

The Web addresses cited in this text were current as of July 2010, unless otherwise noted.

Acquisitions Editor: Scott Wikgren; **Developmental Editor:** Melissa Feld; **Assistant Editor:** Rachel Brito; **Copyeditor:** Patsy Fortney; **Indexer:** Dan Connolly; **Graphic Designer:** Joe Buck; **Graphic Artist:** Yvonne Griffith; **Cover Designer:** Bob Reuther; **DVD Face Designer:** Susan Rothermel Allen; **Photographer (cover):** St. Petersburg Times/Zuma Press/Icon SMI; **Art Manager:** Kelly Hendren; **Associate Art Manager:** Alan L. Wilborn; **Illustrator:** © Human Kinetics; **Printer:** Sheridan Books

Printed in the United States of America   10 9 8 7 6 5 4 3 2 1

The paper in this book is certified under a sustainable forestry program.

Human Kinetics
Web site: www.HumanKinetics.com

United States: Human Kinetics
P.O. Box 5076
Champaign, IL 61825-5076
800-747-4457
e-mail: humank@hkusa.com

Canada: Human Kinetics
475 Devonshire Road Unit 100
Windsor, ON N8Y 2L5
800-465-7301 (in Canada only)
e-mail: info@hkcanada.com

Europe: Human Kinetics
107 Bradford Road
Stanningley
Leeds LS28 6AT, United Kingdom
+44 (0) 113 255 5665
e-mail: hk@hkeurope.com

Australia: Human Kinetics
57A Price Avenue
Lower Mitcham, South Australia 5062
08 8372 0999
e-mail: info@hkaustralia.com

New Zealand: Human Kinetics
P.O. Box 80
Torrens Park, South Australia 5062
0800 222 062
e-mail: info@hknewzealand.com

E4790

To all the professionals who once taught, are teaching, and will be teaching children with disabilities in the area of physical education.

To my mentors, who remain very special to me and have influenced my professional development: Dr. Lane Goodwin, Dr. Jean Pyfer, Dr. Claudine Sherrill, and Dr. Ron French.

A special dedication to my colleagues who have supported me and encouraged my efforts: Dr. Michael Ferrara, Dr. Cynthia Piletic, and Dr. Timothy Davis.

To my family: my wife, Janelle; sons, Matthew L. Davis, Cpt. (USAF), Timothy A. Davis, Lt. (U.S. Army); and daughter, Molly (first team ESPN Academic All-American, 2009), whose support has motivated me to complete this project.

Finally, I thank God for His grace and for working in my life to change me. Much has happened in the world since 2002 and we have much to be concerned about but much more to be thankful for. God bless America.

Contents

Part I Program Planning 1

1 ABC Curriculum Model Overview 3

2 Assessment 7

3 Implementation Planning, Teaching, and Evaluating . . 13

4 Implementing Disability Sport 25

Part II Disability Sports, Skills, and Activities 33

Inclusion Index

- Wheelchair Basketball
- Sitting Volleyball
- Goalball
- The Slalom (Track)
- Indoor Wheelchair Soccer
- Boccia
- Wheelchair Tennis

	Sports in general physical education	Disability sports			
Invasion games	**Basketball**				
	Passing	Wheelchair Basketball	Indoor Wheelchair Soccer	Sitting Volleyball	Goalball
	Dribbling	Wheelchair Basketball	Indoor Wheelchair Soccer		
	Shooting	Wheelchair Basketball	Indoor Wheelchair Soccer	Goalball	
	Ball movement	Wheelchair Basketball	The Slalom (Track)		
Net games	**Soccer**				
	Passing	Indoor Wheelchair Soccer	Indoor Wheelchair Soccer	Sitting Volleyball	Goalball
	Dribbling	Indoor Wheelchair Soccer	Indoor Wheelchair Soccer	The Slalom (Track)	
	Throwing in	Indoor Wheelchair Soccer	Goalball		
	Blocking	Indoor Wheelchair Soccer	Goalball		
	Volleyball				
	Serving	Sitting Volleyball	Wheelchair Tennis		
	Bumping/passing	Sitting Volleyball	Goalball		
	Setting	Sitting Volleyball			
	Blocking	Sitting Volleyball	Goalball	Indoor Wheelchair Soccer	
	Tennis				
	Forehand	Wheelchair Tennis			
	Backhand	Wheelchair Tennis			
	Serve	Wheelchair Tennis	Sitting Volleyball		

Inclusion Index

	Sports in general physical education	Disability sports		
Court games and track events		**Track and field**		
	Sprinting			
	Relay			
	Throwing			
Target games		**Bowling**		
	Throwing			

Game Finder

Game	Page number	Skill	Organizational pattern	On DVD
Wheelchair Basketball: Low-Functioning Students				
Gauntlet I	63	Bounce stop	One on one	💿
Gauntlet II	63	Bounce stop	Small group	💿
Gauntlet III	64	Bounce stop	Large group	💿
Give and Go	59	Passing	Small group	
Hanging On	58	Passing	One on one	
Pass and Shoot (Shooting)	60	Shooting	Small group	
Pass and Shoot (Dribbling)	62	Dribbling	Small group	
Reaching Out I	67	Ball retrieval	One on one	
Reaching Out II	67	Ball retrieval	Small group	
Reaching Out III	68	Ball retrieval	Large group	
Right Back at You	61	Dribbling	One on one	
Shot's Away	60	Shooting	One on one	
Spinning Wheels I	65	Bounce spin	One on one	
Spinning Wheels II	65	Bounce spin	Small group	
Spinning Wheels III	66	Bounce spin	Large group	
Triangle and Go I	59	Passing	Large group	💿
Triangle and Go II	61	Shooting	Large group	💿
Triangle and Go III	62	Dribbling	Large group	💿
Wheelchair Basketball: Moderate- to High-Functioning Students				
At the Hoop	72	Shooting	Large group	
Call It Out	70	Passing	Large group	
Crossover	76	Bounce spin	One on one	
Down and Back	78	Ball retrieval	Small group	
Giddy Up	79	Ball retrieval	Large group	💿
In the Bucket	72	Shooting	Small group	
On the Move I	73	Dribbling	Small group	
On the Move II	74	Dribbling	Large group	
Reach for It	78	Ball retrieval	One on one	
Remember Me	70	Passing	Small group	
Spin City I	77	Bounce spin	Small group	

Game	Page number	Skill	Organizational pattern	On DVD
Wheelchair Basketball: Moderate- to High-Functioning Students (continued)				
Spin City II	77	Bounce spin	Large group	
Spinning the Ball	71	Shooting	One on one	
Stationary	73	Dribbling	One on one	
Stop the Music I	75	Bounce stop	One on one	
Stop the Music II	75	Bounce stop	Small group	
Stop the Music III	76	Bounce stop	Large group	
Target Toss	69	Passing	One on one	
Indoor Wheelchair Soccer: Low-Functioning Students				
Bump and Go I	97	Dribbling	One on one	
Bump and Go II	98	Dribbling	Small group	
Bump and Go III	99	Dribbling	Large group	
Capture It	95	Passing	Large group	
Charge!	96	Shooting	One on one	
Keep It Out I	101	Blocking	One on one	
Keep It Out II	102	Blocking	Small group	
Keep It Out III	103	Blocking	Large group	
Knock It Off I	99	Throw-in	One on one	
Knock It Off II	100	Throw-in	Small group	
Knock It Off III	101	Throw-in	Large group	💿
Pass It On I	94	Passing	One on one	
Pass It On II	94	Passing	Small group	
Rebound	96	Shooting	Small group	
Score It	97	Shooting	Large group	
Indoor Wheelchair Soccer: Moderate- to High-Functioning Students				
Call It Out	105	Passing	Large group	
Feed and Go (Shooting)	107	Shooting	Small group	
Feed and Go (Blocking)	112	Blocking	Small group	
Feed and Go Plus 1 (Shooting)	107	Shooting	Large group	
Feed and Go Plus 1 (Blocking)	112	Blocking	Large group	
Feed Me	106	Shooting	One on one	
On the Move I	108	Dribbling	Small group	
On the Move II	109	Dribbling	Large group	

(continued)

Game Finder *(continued)*

Indoor Wheelchair Soccer: Moderate- to High-Functioning Students *(continued)*				
Game	Page number	Skill	Organizational pattern	On DVD
Partner Pass	105	Passing	Small group	
Pick a Spot	110	Throw-in	Small group	
Pick a Spot With D	111	Throw-in	Large group	
Pin Block	112	Blocking	One on one	
Reach Back	110	Throw-in	One on one	
Stationary	108	Dribbling	One on one	
Target Toss	104	Passing	One on one	
Sitting Volleyball: Low-Functioning Students				
Keep It In	132	Blocking	Large group	
Over It Goes	135	Serving	Large group	DVD
Right Back at You	131	Blocking	One on one	
Roll and Block	132	Blocking	Small group	
Serving Cone	133	Serving	One on one	DVD
Serving Line	134	Serving	Small group	
Table Target Pass I	127	Passing	One on one	DVD
Table Target Pass II	128	Passing	Small group	DVD
Table Target Pass III	128	Passing	Large group	DVD
Tarzan Attack I	129	Attack-hit	One on one	
Tarzan Attack II	130	Attack-hit	Small group	
Tarzan Attack III	130	Attack-hit	Large group	
Sitting Volleyball: Moderate- to High-Functioning Students				
Clean the Kitchen	143	Serving	Small group	
Just the Three of Us	142	Blocking	Large group	
Pass It Up	136	Passing	One on one	
Put 'Em Up	140	Blocking	One on one	
Rip It	140	Attack-hit	Large group	
Serving Math	144	Serving	Large group	
The Wall	141	Blocking	Small group	
Throw It Over I (Attack-Hit)	138	Attack-hit	One on one	
Throw It Over I (Serve)	142	Serving	One on one	
Throw It Over II (Attack-Hit)	139	Attack-hit	Small group	
Up and Over I	137	Passing	Small group	
Up and Over II	137	Passing	Large group	

Game	Page number	Skill	Organizational pattern	On DVD
Wheelchair Tennis: Low-Functioning Students				
Balloon Backhand	159	Backhand	Small group	
Delivery Service	161	Serving	Small group	
Guest Server	162	Serving	Large group	
Strike It Rich I (Forehand)	156	Forehand	One on one	⊙
Strike It Rich II (Backhand)	159	Backhand	One on one	⊙
Strike It Rich III (Serve)	161	Serving	One on one	⊙
Tabletop Tennis	157	Forehand	Small group	
Tarzan Tennis	158	Forehand	Large group	
Zigzag Tennis	160	Backhand	Large group	
Wheelchair Tennis: Moderate- to High-Functioning Students				
Mixed Doubles Plus 1	166	Forehand	Large group	
Mixed Doubles Plus 1	166	Backhand	Large group	
Reverse and Go	164	Forehand	Small group	
Reverse and Go	164	Backhand	Small group	
Serving the Reverse and Go	165	Serving	Small group	
The Serving Chair	167	Serving	Large group	
Wall to Net	163	Forehand	One on one	
Wall to Net	163	Backhand	One on one	
Wall to Net	163	Serving	One on one	
Goalball: Low-Functioning Students				
Don't Go There I	182	Blocking	One on one	
Don't Go There II	182	Blocking	Small group	
Don't Go There III	183	Blocking	Large group	
Here I Am	184	Passing	One on one	
Remember Me I	184	Passing	Small group	⊙
Throw It Out I	180	Throwing	Small group	
Throw It Out II	181	Throwing	Large group	
Up It Goes	180	Throwing	One on one	
Zigzag Relay	185	Passing	Large group	⊙
Goalball: Moderate- to High-Functioning Students				
Block It	189	Blocking	Small group	
Four Square	189	Blocking	Large group	
Here I Am	190	Passing	One on one	

(continued)

Game Finder (continued)

Game	Page number	Skill	Organizational pattern	On DVD
Goalball: Moderate- to High-Functioning Students (continued)				
Remember Me II	190	Passing	Small group	
Slide Over	188	Blocking	One on one	DVD
Step to Throw I	186	Throwing	One on one	
Step to Throw II	186	Throwing	Small group	
Step to Throw III	187	Throwing	Large group	
Work It Across	191	Passing	Large group	
Slalom: Low-Functioning Students				
Circle Up	205	360-degree turn	One on one	
Giant Slalom I	208	Figure-eight turn	Small group	
Giant Slalom II	209	Figure-eight turn	Large group	
Grand Reverse	203	Reverse turn	Small group	
Reverse and Go	204	Reverse turn	Large group	
Reverse, Turn, and Go	206	360-degree turn	Large group	DVD
Ring Masters	206	360-degree turn	Small group	
Tap and Go	202	Reverse turn	One on one	DVD
The Weave	207	Figure-eight turn	One on one	
Boccia: Low Functioning Students				
Block Party	228	Blocking	Large group	
Build a Fort	226	Blocking	One on one	
Clearing the Way	229	Defeating the block	One on one	
Crossing the Atlantic	223	Throwing (ramp, long, and short)	One on one	
Four Corners I	230	Defeating the block	Small group	
Four Corners II	231	Defeating the block	Large group	
In the Zone	224	Throwing (ramp, long, and short)	Small group	
Not in My House	227	Blocking	Small group	DVD
Ramp Attack	225	Throwing (ramp, long, and short)	Large group	DVD

Boccia: Moderate- to High-Functioning Students				
Game	Page number	Skill	Organizational pattern	On DVD
Around the World	233	Throwing (long and short)	Small group	
Boccia Math	232	Throwing (long and short)	One on one	
Carpet Blocker	235	Blocking	One on one	
Even or Odd	239	Defeating the block	Small group	
Gate Blocker	236	Blocking	Small group	
In or Out	240	Defeating the block	Large group	
Side Pocket/Corner Pocket	238	Defeating the block	One on one	
Tic-Tac-Toe	234	Throwing (long and short)	Large group	
Tic-Tac-Toe With a Block	237	Blocking	Large group	

Foreword

Dr. Ron Davis has served as the president of the National Consortium for Physical Education and Recreation for Individuals with Disabilities and is widely recognized for his expertise in disability sport. In this second edition of *Teaching Disability Sport*, Dr. Davis shares what he has learned over the past 30 years from working with students and athletes with disabilities, and he shows how to communicate this wisdom to future physical educators.

In this edition, Dr. Davis uses disability sport as a means of accomplishing three goals. First, he highlights how students with disabilities desire and derive the same benefits from sport as students without disabilities; in order for students with disabilities to achieve these benefits, they need to learn in physical education the prerequisite skills for their sports. Second, Dr. Davis demonstrates how disability sport can be used as an inclusion model for modifying games and sports so that all students can participate and learn how to accommodate each other. Finally, he illustrates how disability sport can be infused into the general physical education curriculum with the use of the achievement-based curriculum model.

While this book will be extremely valuable for adapted physical educators, it has been specifically targeted to general physical educators and the professionals who train those educators. Dr. Davis recognizes that the majority of students with disabilities in our schools have mild and moderate disabilities, and those students are typically included in general physical education classes. This places general physical educators in the leadership role and requires them to modify their curriculum so it addresses the needs of students both with and without disabilities.

In *Teaching Disability Sport*, Dr. Davis provides teachers with the tools for making these curricular revisions in the form of the ABC model and the resources to assist general physical educators so that they can teach disability sport. The book is organized into two parts. Part I addresses program planning and explains how to use the ABC model. The first three chapters in part I highlight what teachers need to do to address the needs of their students with disabilities, such as modifying their curriculum, assessing student needs, and creating IEPs. Each of the chapters illustrates how the needs of a student named Tony, who has a mild learning disability and cerebral palsy, are addressed. Part I ends with a chapter on implementing a disability sport and presents an innovative tool called the inclusion index, which helps teachers identify the common elements between the disability and traditional versions of various sports.

Part II focuses on disability sports, skills, and activities. A chapter on wheelchair basics details how to teach students five essential wheelchair skills for participating in all wheelchair sports. The remaining chapters in part II focus on the categories (invasion, net, court) of disability sport (e.g., basketball, soccer, volleyball, tennis, goalball, slalom, and boccia) and provide detailed information on how each sport is played. This is followed by a review of the basic skills that are required for participating in the sport, including task analyses of each of the skills. Functional profiles are then presented and modifications discussed to address the needs and abilities of students at each functional level. Finally, games are presented to address the different skills and functional profiles that have been identified. These chapters are complemented by extensive tables, figures, and graphics to illustrate the skill components and the organizational patterns of the games. In addition, a DVD shows select games from each chapter being taught in a general physical education class. The goal of the DVD is to illustrate some of the game progressions and to provide teachers with some concrete examples that can then be modified to address their unique needs.

This book is a valuable contribution to the professional literature and exemplifies Dr. Davis' vision of addressing the physical education needs of students with disabilities by facilitating their inclusion through disability sport, which in turn will expand their sport and recreational opportunities and educate others about the universal value of sport for all students. The practical nature of the content should make this resource ideal for all physical educators working with students with disabilities and for those professionals preparing future physical educators.

Luke E. Kelly
University of Virginia

Preface

Sport is understood, respected, and practiced around the world; it is universal. Whether you are watching the Super Bowl or a game of wheelchair basketball, the common ground is that you are watching sport. Sport, to include disability sport, can be taught to students with and without disabilities in your physical education classes. This new edition is written from the perspective of teaching within an inclusive physical education setting (i.e., those with and without disabilities). Your students can receive several benefits from participating in disability sport in an inclusive physical education setting: (a) improved social interactions between students with and without disabilities (e.g., dialoguing about upcoming tournaments, individual player performances, and team standings in both disability and traditional sport); (b) the recognition that classmates are more alike than different; (c) an increasing respect for the athleticism required in disability sport (e.g., wheelchair basketball, wheelchair soccer, goalball); and (d) improved health and fitness for all. By implementing the suggestions and activities in this book, you will not only improve appropriate programming for students with disabilities, but also expand your curriculum for all students.

The second edition of this book addresses students enrolled in physical education teacher education (PETE) preparation programs, as well as teachers and coaches currently working with students and players. Based on feedback from professionals directing PETE programs in higher education, more attention has been given to including disability sport content in the pedagogy of physical education. Originally this book was titled *Inclusion Through Sports* and was written for those grassroots professionals who served students with disabilities in general physical education. This second edition, now titled *Teaching Disability Sport: A Guide for Physical Educators*, is a textbook to be used by PETE programs that offer a disability sport course or an emphasis of disability sport within methodology courses.

The second edition is also meant to serve as a supplemental book for introductory adapted physical education courses. This new edition is written using pedagogy content from PETE elementary and secondary methodology courses with practical applications from over 150 games and activities.

It is my desire to use the body of knowledge within disability sport as a resource in preparing PETE students to teach students with and without disabilities. The philosophical belief that sport is universal remains central to this edition. Learning about disability sport, and how to teach it, will help you improve your programming for students with and without disabilities.

SPORT SKILLS

The disability sports selected for this book are for students with physical or sensory impairments and were chosen, in part, based on their popularity. These sports have competitions at the national or international level, or both. By learning about these sports in your PETE preparation, you will be able to infuse this information into your teaching curriculum and teach students with and without disabilities skills they can use throughout their lifetimes.

The sport-specific skills associated with these disability sports are task-analyzed to their simplest forms to help you address the needs of students with disabilities. For example, consider the task of shooting a basketball. All students require some functional level of grasp and release to shoot a basketball. A student with a disability in your class, however, may not have the functional ability to grasp and release. In chapter 6, two of the games suggested in the games-by-skill-level index for low-functioning students are Hanging On and Shot's Away. These activities will help you address functional grasping and releasing for a student with a disability within your basketball unit and are presented with several class formats to help you attend to all students in the class.

STATEMENT FROM THE GOVERNMENT ACCOUNTABILITY OFFICE (GAO)

In 2010 the GAO released findings in a report concerning physical education (PE) and participation in athletics for children with disabilities. The results indicated that the schools currently provide students with and without disabilities similar opportunities to participate in PE but face challenges when serving students with disabilities, especially regarding teacher preparation. The report indicated that general PE teachers need more training opportunities to work with students with disabilities. District and school officials whom GAO interviewed cited a lack of information on ways to expand athletic opportunities and lack of clarity regarding schools' responsibilities. According to this report, education has provided little information or guidance on PE or extracurricular athletics for students with disabilities, and some states and districts the GAO interviewed said more would be useful. It is my belief that the second edition of this text provides assistance and offers answers to these concerns (GAO, June 23, 2010).

ORGANIZATION

The second edition is organized into two parts: part I, Program Planning, and part II, Disability Sports, Skills, and Activities. Part I addresses the pedagogy of disability sport, and part II provides practical activities for playing the disability sport using modifications as needed (adapted sport) in your physical education classes.

Part I: Program Planning

This book is written to be used as a primary text for a PETE disability sport course. Students reading this book should have had, or be currently enrolled in, an elementary or secondary PETE methodology course. PETE students should be familiar with curriculum designs and categories, and they should have a background in teaching styles and class formats. The purpose of this book is not to be a primary methodology text, but rather, to use basic methodology content as supplemental to teaching disability sport.

Chapter 1 presents the achievement-based curriculum (ABC) by Kelly and Melograno (2004) and serves as a guide for the remainder of part I. The ABC curriculum model was selected because of its systematic approach to teaching and the fact that it can be implemented to address a school program, an entire class, or one student. All of the components of the ABC model follow a logical process and should guide you through the implementation of disability sport content. The components of the ABC model are program planning, assessing, implementation planning, teaching, and evaluating. Chapter 1 focuses on planning, and each of the remaining ABC components are addressed in chapters 2, 3, and 4.

Chapter 2 (Assessment) provides a brief explanation of the legislative responsibilities of the general physical educator serving students with disabilities. Assessment information is included to help the PETE student and the professional currently teaching in the field to better understand the assessment process and the use of the individualized education program (IEP). A sample assessment and IEP are provided to help you develop goals and objectives for lesson plans using the activities in part II of the book. Assessment, according to the ABC model, also involves the systematic process of observing students to determine their needs for learning.

Chapter 3 focuses on implementation planning, teaching, and evaluating. A template of a unit plan is also provided to help with implementation and addresses curriculum delivery, class format, teaching style, activity name, prompts and cues, and activity modifications. In addition, I offer my own theoretical model to help with teaching and modification decisions. Activity modification during teaching is also discussed.

Coaches of athletes with disabilities should also be able to use the information in chapter 3. This chapter parallels the process of creating a sound coaching plan. Coaches must consider the same steps when implementing long- and short-term seasonal plans and deciding how best to teach the skills of the game and conduct player and team evaluations. Seasonal plans should consist of goals and objectives for players that are developed from skill assessments, game performances, and coaches' observations. Coaches can use the unit planning template for teachers as a coaching plan, and modify the lesson plan template to use as a practice plan. All the activity suggestions for each skill within each sport can be used for drills at practice and can be included in the overall coaching plan.

Chapter 4 provides planning templates for applying the ABC model. You will see the inclusion index and templates for an assessment instrument, an IEP, and a unit teaching plan that you can duplicate to help you work through the ABC model.

Part II: Disability Sports, Skills, and Activities

Part II presents many of the activities included in the first edition of this book. The sports and activities remain organized in four subparts (wheelchair basics; invasion games; net games; and court, field, and target games). You can use each of the seven chapters on sports to write effective lesson plans.

- *Teaching or coaching wheelchair basics.* Chapter 5 is about mobility skills generic to wheelchair sports. Teaching students with disabilities basic wheelchair mobility skills might be very appropriate for some students and athletes and can provide valuable lessons to use at any point in your curriculum or practice plans. Wheelchair mobility skills such as self-propulsion, stopping, and performing a stationary or moving pivot are essential for students and athletes who use manual wheelchairs. Information about wheelchair selection and operation, and fitting a student properly for a wheelchair, is presented in appendix A.

- *Invasion games.* Invasion games feature teamwork and some type of offensive strategy to invade a defended goal area. The defense must react to an offensive attack near the defended goal area. Chapters 6 and 7 present the invasion games of wheelchair basketball and indoor wheelchair soccer, respectively.

- *Net games.* Net games are played on a court using a net to separate two teams or individuals. The net becomes part of the offensive and defensive strategies. Chapters 8 and 9 describe sitting volleyball and wheelchair tennis, respectively. Skills similar to those required in traditional volleyball and tennis are presented, with specific disability sport modifications regarding court size and game rules.

- *Court, field, and target games.* The last section of part II presents games played indoors or outdoors on flat surfaces. Chapters 10, 11, and 12 address goalball, slalom, and boccia. Goalball is played by people who are blind or visually impaired, and the slalom sport is for people with severe disabilities who use power (battery-operated) wheelchairs. The slalom offers a unique activity to infuse into your track unit. Boccia is a new sport added to this second edition. It can be played indoors or outdoors. The game is played competitively by people with cerebral palsy indoors on a court using leather boccia balls. Players with severe disabilities use ramps to roll the ball onto the court. Chapter 12 presents only the indoor game.

STATEMENT ON INCLUSION

Physical education is meant to address three domains of learning: psychomotor, cognitive, and affective. The inclusion suggestions in each of the activities in the sport chapters of part II are designed to address all three domains. I believe that teachers can include students with disabilities by implementing psychomotor modifications. For example, you can shorten base paths or lower nets for students with movement limitations or minimal upper-body strength. But you should not assume that physical modifications address all three learning domains; unless you provide specific tasks that are designed to emphasize all three domains, you will not fully accomplish inclusion. You should be aware that modifications can negatively affect students without disabilities. Your activities should provide opportunities for students with and without disabilities to share in the decision-making process for all modifications. In addition, putting the student with a disability in a decision-making role will help to address the affective domain of learning and promote a more comprehensive inclusion setting.

SUMMARY

This book is about expanding your professional skill sets as a PETE student or future or current teacher or coach by using disability sport to teach students with and without disabilities. The foundation of knowledge for this text is from the field of disability sport. Suggestions of game, equipment, and rule modifications are presented as pedagogical information. The ABC model is presented as a guide to help you plan, assess, implement, teach, and evaluate units and activities for all students, especially those with disabilities, in general physical education settings. Sample planning and assessment instruments are provided on the DVD to help you address student and program goals and objectives. A unit planning template is also provided on the DVD to help you manage and evaluate your program curriculum. Over 150 games and activities are cross-referenced to functional profiles (low, moderate, and high) of students with disabilities. You have the choice of how much and which disability sports to include in your curriculum. Following this systematic process (ABC) should improve your teaching, students' progress, and program effectiveness. The suggestions in this edition will move you from planning to teaching while keeping the scope and sequence of your curriculum accountable with the built-in mechanisms for program and student evaluations.

How to Use the DVD-ROM

D VD icons have been placed throughout the book to indicate which activities are demonstrated on the DVD (see also the contents below). You can view the video clips to get a sense of how the activities are performed, or show them to students to see how others have successfully completed the activities. DVD icons are also used in the book to indicate reproducible forms that are available as PDF files on the DVD.

You can view the video content either on a television with a DVD player or on a computer with a DVD-ROM drive. The PDFs on this DVD-ROM can only be accessed using a DVD-ROM drive in a computer (not a DVD player on a television). To access the PDF, follow these instructions:

Microsoft Windows

1. Place DVD in the DVD-ROM drive of your computer.
2. Double-click on the My Computer icon from your desktop.
3. Right-click on the DVD-ROM drive and select the Open option from the pop-up menu.
4. Double-click on the Documents and Resources folder.
5. Select the PDF file that you want to view or print.

Macintosh

1. Place DVD in the DVD-ROM drive of your computer.
2. Double-click the DVD icon on your desktop.
3. Double-click on the Documents and Resources folder.
4. Select the PDF file that you want to view or print.

Note: You must have Adobe Acrobat Reader to view the PDF files.

DVD Contents

- Wheelchair Basketball
  - The Game
  - Triangle and Go
  - Gauntlet
  - Giddy Up
- Indoor Wheelchair Soccer
  - The Game
  - Knock It Off
- Sitting Volleyball
  - The Game
  - Table Target Pass I
  - Table Target Pass II
  - Table Target Pass III
  - Serving Cone/Over It Goes
- Wheelchair Tennis
  - The Game
  - Strike It Rich
- Goalball
  - The Game
  - Remember Me I
  - Zigzag Relay
  - Slide Over
- Slalom
  - The Game
  - Tap and Go
  - Reverse, Turn, and Go
- Boccia
  - The Game
  - Ramp Attack
  - Not in My House

Acknowledgments

I would like to thank the following professionals for contributing their reviews, critiques, and professional opinions on their respective sports in this book. I sincerely appreciate their efforts.

Sport	Professional
Wheelchair basketball	Ronald Lykins, University of Missouri wheelchair basketball coach
Indoor wheelchair soccer	David Stephenson, indoor wheelchair soccer coach, Houston, TX
Sitting volleyball	Denise Van De Walle, volleyball coach, Bowling Green University
Wheelchair tennis	Randy Snow, wheelchair tennis player, coach, author (deceased 2009)
Goalball	John Potts, USOC sports director, USABA goalball
Slalom	Bill Wilkie, USCPAA coach
Boccia	Jeff Jones, director, BlazeSports America, Atlanta, GA
	Cathy Drobny, technical committee, BlazeSports America, Topeka, KS
	Gina McWilliams, coordinator, BlazeSports America, Grand Prairie, TX
	Mary Knudsen, adapted physical educator, Crowley, TX

I wish to thank the following people for contributing their expertise in the teaching of adapted physical education classes and for demonstrating the skills presented in the book and on the DVD.

Sport or activity	Individual
Wheelchair basketball	Patty Cisneros, USA 2000 Paralympic wheelchair basketball team
	Karen Wake, USA 2000 Paralympic wheelchair basketball team
Indoor wheelchair soccer	Michael Gillam, Ball State University
	Amanda Campbell, Ball State University
Sitting volleyball	Molly Davis, Burris Middle School, Muncie, IN
	Lauren Kaminsky, Burris Middle School
	Nadia Tabari, Burris Middle School
Wheelchair tennis	Tim Davis, Burris Middle School
Goalball	Dr. Thomas Weidner, Ball State University

Sport or activity	Individual
Slalom	Hector Garcia, Ball State University
Wheelchair fitting	Matthew Davis, Burris High School and Indiana Academy
	Molly Davis, Burris Middle School
Wheelchair mobility	Tim Davis, Burris Middle School
Boccia	Tanner Lowry, Strickland Middle School, Denton, TX

DVD	Individual
	Dr. Linda Hilgenbrinck, Joanne Keeler, Cathy Webb, graduate APE students from Texas Woman's University and students from Strickland Middle School in Denton, TX
Teaching	David Martinez, Cherokee County School District, GA
	Dr. Luis Columba, SUNY-Cortland
	Dr. Michelle Grenier, University of New Hampshire
Logistics	Beverly and Elwood Nelson for the use of their beautiful cabin in the north woods of Minnesota

PART I

Program Planning

Chapter 1

ABC Curriculum Model Overview

Let's meet Tony: Tony is a fifth-grade student with mild learning disabilities and cerebral palsy (CP) with moderate to high function in his upper body. He uses a manual wheelchair for ambulation. Tony has been active in recreational activities outside of school (i.e., swimming and basketball). He has participated in general physical education during elementary school, but now as he prepares for middle and high school, he wants to focus more on sports and competition. Tony is able to dribble a basketball but lacks certain motor and fitness skills, which affects his ability to pass and shoot. His local community recreation center has a wheelchair basketball league for players in the eighth grade and up, and Tony wants to play in that league by the time he reaches the eighth grade. What would you do if Tony were placed in your general physical education class as a fifth-grader? How would you address his needs? What would be your plan to help Tony achieve his goal? How would you systematically approach this scenario? Let's see how using the achievement-based curriculum (ABC) model might help Tony achieve his goals and help you improve your teaching.

The purpose of this chapter is to provide an overview of the achievement-based curriculum (ABC) model; specific applications are presented in subsequent chapters. The ABC model by Kelly and Melograno (2004) is a procedural model to help physical education teachers use a systematic approach to reaching achievable program, class, or student goals. The ABC model is a process model that helps teachers move across five components to address their teaching goals and objectives for all students. The model provides an overall mechanism for reviewing, evaluating, and updating teaching. It does not dictate what content should be taught, nor how it should be taught; it simply helps teachers choose the best program for all their students.

I chose the ABC model because of its logical progression and components that provide a clear framework for accountability. Using the ABC model as a guide keeps you focused on appropriate goals and objectives for your students and your physical education program. The two components I appreciate the most are assessment and implementing the plan.

The assessment chapter (chapter 2) reviews two categories of testing (norm referenced and criterion referenced) that will help you focus on your student's needs within a motor task. You can implement the criterion-referenced testing during an activity and thus minimize your assessment time.

The ABC model is a top-down approach, which means that the amount of content to be taught is dictated by the amount of time available for instruction (Kelly & Melograno, 2004). The ABC model stresses the importance of considering instructional time before implementing your overall curriculum (or plan). Calculating instructional time is very important and helps you determine how many objectives would be realistic given the frequency of class offerings (e.g., 50 minutes per day, three days per week, and 15 weeks per semester).

Given that Tony has some mild learning disabilities and limited motor function, learning and mastering all the content in a secondary general physical education (GPE) program is a concern. Because Tony has several individual movement and motor differences from his typically developing peers, a suitable GPE programming alternative might be to reduce his content and identify specific areas that would help him reach his goals. The ABC model helps you consider the individual differences of *all* your students and their ability to interact with classmates and in activities within the physical education classroom.

The ABC model does result in more record keeping; you must know the student's current skill levels, the skill levels he hopes to achieve, how to get him there, and how to evaluate his accomplishments. Implementing the five components of the ABC model will help; they are program planning, assessing, implementation planning, teaching, and evaluating.

PROGRAM PLANNING

The first step in the ABC model is program planning. At this point you need to determine what you have taught, what you need to teach, and how much time you have available. To help Tony reach his goals of participating in secondary GPE and playing competitive wheelchair basketball, you must become familiar with his elementary GPE; in other words, what skill sets is he bringing to your class? In addition, you must understand the similarities and differences between traditional and wheelchair basketball. You will need to improve your knowledge of the sport, including skills to be taught, and then determine where this information can be infused into your curriculum. An inclusion index is provided in chapter 4 to help you determine the overlap of sports in a general curriculum and disability sports. The inclusion index should be used during your planning process. A full explanation of how to use the inclusion index is presented in chapter 4.

Much of part II of this book focuses on the specifics of each disability sport by providing a summary of the sport, rules, and suggested activities. As you begin to plan, consider the amount of time available, the equipment needed, your location, and student abilities; from there you should consider setting goals and objectives for your program and deciding how you will reach them.

Your planning should consider progression, sequence, and scope (elementary to secondary) when possible (Thomas, Lee, & Thomas, 2008). When considering *progression,* think about the difficulty of the tasks and what skills students or athletes need to master. *Sequence* refers to planning from year to year and requires that you consider the depth of your program. The *scope* of the planning gets at the heart of this text; scope addresses the content of the program, its breadth and depth. Are you willing to continue to use disability sport from elementary to secondary physical education?

The target population of this book is upper elementary through high school students and athletes. I suggest beginning to use disability sport around the fourth grade and continuing into high school. For example, in the fourth grade you should consider teaching wheelchair basics (pushing, stopping, and pivoting techniques) because these skills form the basis of all wheelchair sports. In grades five through seven, you can implement sport-specific skills such as passing and catching, dribbling, and retrieving a ball. From grades eight through twelve, you should focus on the context of a specific game—in Tony's case, wheelchair basketball. The in-depth scope includes understanding rules, formations, strategies, and game play to help Tony reach his goal of playing competitive wheelchair basketball in the community league.

ASSESSING

Content must be simplified and broken down into attainable units, but it must also match the skill sets of the student. You must be able to assess all your students—those with and without disabilities. The assessment component of the ABC model should help you determine student performance levels before considering program direction and content.

The assessment process is a key component within special education placement, and as a PETE student or teacher in the field, you should be familiar with this process from your introduction to adapted physical education course. Legislation and the assessment process are discussed in depth in chapter 2. A meaningful lesson is the result of a good assessment process, which helps you identify specific objectives, select appropriate games and activities, and develop activities that address the strengths and weaknesses of your student(s). Much of this process is captured in the individualized education program (IEP). The IEP should be thought of as a management plan based on assessment results and put in place to identify specific objectives for the student with a disability within the lesson plan. As a general physical educator in training or currently teaching in the field, you should be actively involved with the IEP process. If you are not, seek assistance from the special education classroom teacher or adapted physical educator.

IMPLEMENTATION PLANNING

Once you have assessed Tony, you can identify his programming needs to improve his skill performance. Begin by planning instructional approaches and focus on how and what you need to teach. This is called implementation planning (Kelly & Melograno, 2004). Implementation planning is based on the results of the assessment. The activities associated with this component include developing and implementing key teaching templates (i.e., unit and lesson plan templates). You must be able to identify strengths and weaknesses from the assessment score sheets (e.g., in basketball—passing, dribbling, and shooting). Chapters 2 and 3 provide specific examples of moving from assessment to teaching, and chapter 4 provides unit and lesson plan templates.

TEACHING

Using the first three ABC components, you should be ready to teach. Having planned, assessed, and implemented, you should be ready to present activities that engage students and maximize learning. Teaching a class composed of students with and without disabilities can be challenging and will require you to consider how to use various types of curriculum delivery, class formats, teaching styles, and modifications to reach your objectives. In short, you need to know how to manage your teaching environment to provide desirable student outcomes. You also need to evaluate the impact of your lessons on your students. Specifics about teaching students with and without disabilities in the same setting are discussed in chapter 3. What will be needed to teach Tony and the remainder of the students without disabilities during future GPE curriculum activities? As he continues on into high school, what instructional modifications will need to be made to help him succeed? These questions are answered in chapter 3.

EVALUATING

As you reach the end of a unit, you need to evaluate student performance and program effectiveness. The ABC model reminds you that you should always be monitoring student progress. Data from initial and post assessments will help. In addition, teacher aides, peer tutors, and assistive technology can help you improve your teaching by helping you evaluate your program effectiveness. Teacher aides (paraeducators) can be taught to record and maintain data files on student performances. They can also provide you with the students' background information, classroom programming, and other academic goals that can be supported in physical education.

Peer tutors can be taught to administer simple checklists using task analysis data sheets. These students can work directly with the student(s) with a disability during class activities, which would minimize your logistical concerns if you are teaching large classes. Although paper-and-pencil recording of assessment results might be the simplest to implement, electronic recording (i.e., using personal digital assistants, or PDAs) might facilitate report writing. Data recorded using a handheld PDA could easily be transferred into an electronic report at the conclusion of any unit and presented as documentation of students' performances and program effectiveness.

As you progress through your lessons, you will likely need to make changes based on your observations of student performances, student engagement (i.e., environmental interactions), and task difficulty. Use these observations to modify any or all of the ABC components (program planning, assessing, implement planning, teaching, or evaluating).

You might discover that you ran short of time for each lesson in the basketball unit. In this case, your modification would be to reduce content and reconsider class formats (e.g., use small group instead of large group activities). Instead, you might discover that you have made a poor equipment selection: students with low functional profiles were unable to throw regulation-sized balls during a softball unit, resulting in less-than-successful performances. Your response would be to modify the activity by changing to lighter balls (e.g., Nerf) for this activity. Keep in mind that all modifications affect *all* students, those with and without disabilities.

SUMMARY

The purpose of this chapter is to provide an overview of the ABC curriculum model. As previously mentioned, I chose the ABC model as framework for this second edition because I believe it provides a logical progression and uses components that offer a clear framework for accountability. The ABC model of planning, assessing, implementation planning, teaching, and evaluating is a reasonable guide for keeping you focused on the scope and sequence of your physical education program while addressing appropriate goals and objectives for your students. Remember that blank forms for assessments, IEPs, and unit and lesson plans are located on the DVD.

Chapter 2

Assessment

You met Tony in chapter 1. He is a student with a mild learning disability and cerebral palsy (CP) who is currently enrolled in your general fifth-grade physical education class. Tony uses a manual wheelchair and has a desire to play competitive basketball by the time he reaches eighth grade and continue on through high school and beyond graduation. To address these goals, you need to assess Tony's motor performance so that you can implement a teaching plan that addresses his needs. This assessment information should help you plan a program that has an appropriate scope and sequence of activities. This chapter will help you consider Tony's background, opportunities in the community, and logistics while you assess his motor and fitness skills.

You need to consider the preliminary assessment information outlined in this chapter as you implement the ABC process. In the top-down ABC model, you consider two things: the student's ecological (environmental) opportunities, and the skills the student specifically needs to successfully participate in the activity (in this case for Tony, community-based wheelchair basketball).

To facilitate future sport and recreational opportunities for Tony, and contribute to his overall assessment process, you might need to ask a series of questions from the following categories:

- *Background.* What is the type and severity of Tony's disability; in other words, what degree of cerebral palsy (CP) does he lives with? What are the dos and don'ts associated with appropriate physical education programming for Tony? Several types of CP affect people in various ways (spasticity, athetoid, ataxia, mixed) during a motor or fitness task. Suggested readings are also included at the end of the book.

- *Opportunities.* What sport or recreational opportunities presently exist in the community or will exist once Tony completes high school? Look into programming at your local YMCA or community recreation center. Most of these facilities have Web sites or publish flyers that list their programs. In our story, Tony has evidently located such a program, which should help you determine specifics about the program (i.e., leadership, schedule of activities, locations).

- *Logistics.* What are the logistical and transportation concerns related to participating in a sport or recreational activity outside of school? In planning for Tony, you need to ask, Where is the program? And, How will Tony get there? To answer these questions, you need to consider a collaboration between his parents and school-based service personnel (i.e., physical or occupational therapists). As you conduct Tony's ecological assessment, begin to turn your attention to the skills he will need to perform the activity in your physical education curriculum.

- *Skills needed.* What opportunities exist in the current physical education curriculum to help Tony develop appropriate sport, recreational, and leisure skills for the future? Which of these skills does he need to participate successfully in the future?

These questions will help you focus on your curriculum and the opportunities that exist within your educational setting. You must decide which skills you will need to emphasize within your current curriculum and how you will teach them. To address skill performance, you need to assess the motor and fitness skills Tony will need to achieve his educational goals and objectives. Of course, you should be assessing all of your students, but Tony's process might require a little more detail to determine the best educational placement to help him achieve his long-range (top-down) goal of playing competitive basketball. You should have a clear understanding of the special education placement process (including the individualized education program, or IEP) as you consider Tony's skills assessments. You may find that you need some help from an adapted physical educator.

EDUCATIONAL PLACEMENT DECISIONS

Educational placement decisions regarding students with disabilities in physical education need to be based on a comprehensive assessment. Your assessment must consider the student's physical and motor fitness and fundamental motor skills, and the skills needed to participate in individual and group games, sports, aquatics, and dance. The Individuals With Disabilities Education Act of 2004 (IDEA, PL 108-446) mandates that such assessments be conducted by a highly qualified (effective) professional, which historically has been an adapted physical educator. If a trained adapted physical educator is not available in your school or school district, as the general physical educator, you will likely complete this assessment. Having addressed preliminary assessment information and identified the skills you want to assess, you should use an instrument that will provide the information to teach. Two categories of assessments are generally taught in PETE preparation programs: norm referenced (formal) and criterion referenced (informal). The next section offers a brief overview of these two categories.

CATEGORIES OF ASSESSMENTS

Norm-referenced assessments are considered *product* related, or interested in a number (e.g., percentile, percentage), and are administered with strict guidelines. Usually each item on a norm-referenced test has very specific instructions (e.g., *Place your feet squarely against the sit and reach box, lean forward at the waist, with arms and fingers extended and touch as far forward as you can, no bouncing*). Modifications are not allowed. The results are scored as a number and converted to a standard score for comparison to other students of similar gender, grade level, or age.

Criterion-referenced assessments are interested in *process,* or the quality of the movement; that is, how the student performs the test item. The students' performances are usually compared to a set of descriptors or criteria. Checklists or task analysis assessment tools also fall into the category of criterion-referenced or curriculum-embedded criterion-referenced assessments. Curriculum-embedded criterion-referenced assessments can offer immediate feedback on where to start teaching.

For example, the following criteria might be used to assess throwing a ball using an overhand motion for a student in your class *without* a disability:

- Stands with side orientation to the target.
- Holds ball in throwing hand.
- Brings ball back with throwing arm, elbow bent.
- Rotates trunk at waist in preparation to throw.
- Brings ball backward, forward, and overhead, and rotates trunk toward direction of target upon ball release.
- Releases ball, follows through, and shifts weight to maintain balance.

With each analysis of the movement, you compare the student without a disability with the criteria to see how well she performs the skill. After five trials you note that the student demonstrates trunk rotation in only one of the five trials. This information helps you decide where to begin instruction and what you should emphasize (e.g., trunk rotation).

CREATING YOUR OWN ASSESSMENT USING THIS TEXT

Conducting a criterion-referenced assessment for a student *with* a disability is the same process as just described for students *without* disabilities. For example, you could use such an assessment to assess Tony's wheelchair basketball skills to determine whether he might be able to play in a recreational league following high school graduation. After responding to the previous set of questions (background, opportunities, logistics, skills needed), you determine the essential basketball skills Tony would need upon graduation. In part II, chapter 6, on wheelchair basketball, you learn that numerous skills are specific to wheelchair basketball (pass, dribble, shoot, bounce stop, bounce spin, and ball retrieval). You can now task-analyze each skill to establish a criterion-referenced assessment.

For example, the chest pass, as presented in chapter 6, has six key teaching points, or criteria:

1. Eyes on target
2. Two hands on ball
3. Elbows flexed in preparation
4. Elbows extend at ball release
5. Thumbs point downward
6. Follow through

By transferring these criteria to an assessment checklist and adding a quantitative measure, you can develop an assessment instrument to use for Tony. The results will help you determine where to begin teaching so you can start him toward the goal of playing in a recreational league.

Figure 2.1 illustrates how the teaching points presented in part II, chapter 6, for the chest pass can be used as criteria to develop an assessment instrument.

To use this instrument, place an X if the student has accomplished the task, a slash (/) if you believe the student is in transition and attempting the task, and a zero (0) if the student cannot perform the task. Remember to allow five trials before filling in this assessment (see figure 2.2 for a completed score sheet for Tony). Repeat the assessment for the other wheelchair basketball skills or any other sport skill. Remember, you are trying to choose the skills that will allow Tony to participate in wheelchair basketball safely and successfully now and in the future. Some students with disabilities might be able to accomplish only the pass and shoot, whereas others might be able to accomplish the pass, dribble, shoot, and bounce stop. All students are unique, and each brings a unique set of abilities. Once you have assessed, you are ready to contribute to the IEP by writing present-level statements, annual goals, and short-term objectives.

Student's name: _____

Chest pass	Trials 1–5					Comments
Eyes on target						
Two hands on ball						
Elbows flexed in preparation						
Elbows extend at ball release						
Thumbs point downward						
Follow through						

Key: X = accomplished   / = with assistance   0 = not accomplished

Figure 2.1   Sample blank basketball assessment score sheet.

Student's name: *Tony* _____

Chest pass	Trials 1–5					Comments
Eyes on target	X	X	X			*Needed verbal cues to keep eyes on target.*
Two hands on ball	X	X	X	/	/	*Needed verbal and PA to hold the ball correctly.*
Elbows flexed in preparation	/	X	X	X	/	*Needed PA to hold the ball correctly in prep.*
Elbows extend at ball release	0	/	/	/	/	*Extension limited.*
Thumbs point downward	0	0	0	/	/	*Extension limited.*
Follow through	/	/	/	/	/	*Needed reminders to follow through.*

PA = physical assistance

Figure 2.2   Basketball assessment score sheet for Tony.

WRITING THE IEP (PRESCRIPTION) AND BEGINNING IMPLEMENTATION PLANNING

To become more involved with the IEP process, you need to know the three basic components of an IEP: (a) the present-level statement, (b) the annual goal, and (c) short-term objectives. These components are central to the IEP document and the educational placement in the least restrictive environment (LRE). Using examples from chapter 6, Wheelchair Basketball, let's look at how you could apply each of these IEP components in Tony's case (see the completed IEP in figure 2.3 at the end of this section).

Present Level of Performance

The present-level performance statement is written based on an assessment of what the student can do. Notice that the emphasis is on the word *can*. The present-level performance statement should not tell someone what the child *can't* do, but rather, what he or she is able to accomplish at the present time. Here is an example of how to write a present-level statement using the information from Tony's assessment (see figure 2.2).

Since Tony is a fifth-grader with CP who uses a manual wheelchair, he has moderate functioning and the potential to play recreational wheelchair basketball. You notice that Tony has some difficulty performing the skill of chest passing (target skill). The more familiar you become with Tony, the more you notice that he has difficulty with arm extension upon release and follow-through. Using the assessment instrument in figure 2.2, you could write the following present-level statement for Tony:

> *Present-Level Statement: Tony can pass a regulation ball with both hands with his eyes on the target while performing a chest pass from his wheelchair in three out of five trials and attempts full arm extension on release and follow-through.*

Annual Goals

Annual goals look at the big picture but include information that is observable and measureable (quantified). Continuing with Tony's IEP, his annual goal statement might read as follows:

> *Annual Goal Statement: Tony will improve his chest pass in wheelchair basketball by keeping his eyes on the target, bending his elbows in preparation, and fully extending his arms during release and follow-through in five out of five trials.*

Short-Term Objectives

Short-term objectives are the stair steps leading to the annual goal and should also be written in a measurable context (again, quantifiable). Although the concept of *measureable* is often left to interpretation by each school district, generally, measurements of distance, weight, or time are acceptable in physical education.

Components	Criteria
Present level of performance	*Tony is able to keep his eyes on the target in four out of five trials and is able to hold a basketball with two hands with assistance in three out of five trials.*
Annual goal	*Tony will improve his chest pass in wheelchair basketball by keeping his eyes on the target, bending his elbows in preparation, and extending his arms during release and follow-through in five out of five trials.*
Short-term objectives	*1. Tony will be able to complete four of five attempts of the chest pass with arms fully extended on release and follow-through.* *2. Tony will be able to complete five of five attempts of the chest pass with arms fully extended on release and follow-through.*

Figure 2.3 Sample IEP using the three components.

Some measurement statements are written as a percentage of accomplishments (e.g., three of five trials, or 60 percent). Short-term objectives for Tony might be written as follows:

1. Tony will be able to complete four of five attempts of the chest pass with arms fully extended on release and follow-through.

2. Tony will be able to complete five of five attempts of the chest pass with arms fully extended on release and follow-through.

Notice that each short-term objective should move you in the direction of accomplishing the annual goal and improving the present level of performance statement. Thus, in Tony's case, if he completed three out of five correct chest passes and then five out of five correct chest passes, he would be moving toward meeting his annual goal of improving one skill in wheelchair basketball (see the IEP in figure 2.3).

SUMMARY

The purpose of this chapter is to help you learn more about assessment as it relates to a student with a disability in your physical education class. In addition, it can help you communicate with your special education colleagues, contribute to the assessment process of students with disabilities, and actively engage in IEP development and implementation.

The assessment process is the same for all students, in that you should be constantly documenting performance to address improved performance. Not all assessment processes are established for the purpose of writing an IEP. Once you understand the unique characteristics of all your students, you can focus on teaching lessons that meet the needs of *all* your students. Remember that blank forms for assessments, IEPs, and unit and lesson plans are located on the DVD.

Implementation Planning, Teaching, and Evaluating

Now that you have assessed Tony, you must decide how to teach or implement your plan to move into teaching. The assessment information has given you information on Tony's motor and fitness strengths and weaknesses and allowed you to reach outside the school setting and determine sporting opportunities in the community. As a result of this process, you should have a better understanding of how Tony learns, how he performs in group and individual settings, and how much time it takes for him to master a skill—all the ingredients you need to teach.

IMPLEMENTATION PLANNING

Implementation planning allows you to plan instruction. To do so, you must be familiar with various curriculum models and types of curriculum deliveries. In addition to understanding curriculum models and how you might deliver them, you must consider class formats. Do your students learn well in one-on-one settings, in small groups, or in large groups such as a team game context? Then, prior to implementing your plan, you need to consider how much time is available to accomplish your objectives. As you implement your plan, you must decide whether you are striving for mastery of the objectives, or less than mastery. Kelly and Melograno (2004) suggest that student mastery of a single motor objective could take more than six hours of instructional and activity time. Consider the number of minutes available per week, class, and semester as you implement your plan; this will help you decide on the number of objectives you select to accomplish and evaluate.

As you consider implementing your curriculum model and delivery, and class formats, you must decide which teaching styles will best address student learning. Selection of teaching styles is an individual process involving your skill sets and your students' functional, cognitive, and social levels. Some types of activities lend themselves better to one teaching style than another (e.g., team sports use the command style; movement education uses guided discovery). The choice is yours.

Finally, throughout all your planning implementation, you must include a plan for evaluation. Without a process of evaluation, you will not be able to document student improvement and program effectiveness.

Curriculum Considerations

Many curriculum models can be used in adapted physical education and general physical education programs for all grade levels. Examples of curriculum models within adapted physical education are the achievement-based curriculum (ABC) model, data-based gymnasium, Project Active, Mobility Opportunities Via Education (MOVE), and Moving to Inclusion.

Some of the more common curriculum models in general physical education are the activity-based curriculum, the movement-based curriculum, the concept-based curriculum, and the teaching games for understanding approach (TGFU). The TGFU model creates the following categories for games: invasion, target, net/wall, and field. All the disability sports in part II of this book are arranged in these categories. Wheelchair basketball and indoor wheelchair soccer are invasion games; wheelchair tennis and sitting volleyball are net games; and slalom, goalball, and boccia are court, field, or target games (see the inclusion index in chapter 4). As more students with disabilities are included in traditional education settings, PETE programs need to teach disability sport, and professionals currently teaching need to address disability sport.

As you consider implementing a general physical education curriculum (e.g., activity based, movement based, games for understanding), you will have to think about how to include students with disabilities. You might have to modify your curriculum delivery to address the motor, affective, and cognitive needs of students with disabilities.

The four types of curriculum delivery to consider are same, multilevel, modified, and different (Block, 2007; Collier, 2005).

- *Same.* In a same curriculum, students with disabilities follow the same curriculum as students without disabilities. The objectives are likely to be different for the two groups of students (see the inclusion index in chapter 4).

- *Multilevel.* The multilevel curriculum delivery is generally implemented for students with mild disabilities; it involves minimal activity accommodations to facilitate success. This might require activities in which you address the environmental interactions discussed later in this chapter by modifying the tasks. For example, a student using a wheelchair (considered low to moderate functioning) might be allowed to strike a beach ball from a tall traffic cone to signify a serve in volleyball.

- *Modified.* The modified curriculum is sometimes referred to as an overlapping type of delivery and can be used to address students considered more severely disabled. Essentially, such students work on the same activities as those without disabilities, but for different reasons (objectives). For example, a lesson might include a beanbag-tossing activity designed to promote accuracy for the students without disabilities. However, the student with severe disabilities might have the objective of improving range of motion in the elbow and shoulder as stated in the IEP (same activity, but different purpose). In this case, the curriculums (same and modified) are overlapping (see the inclusion index in chapter 4 and the unit planning template later in this chapter).

- *Different.* Sometimes a student with a disability cannot safely or successfully participate in a multilevel or modified curriculum. In this case, the student would have to take part in activities unrelated to the general curriculum. Consider a student who is blind attending your general physical education class; how would you address the unit on basketball for this student? As this student matures, graduates, and becomes a member of the community, she will be very unlikely to participate in a basketball game. However, she may be able to participate in a goalball league through a community recreation center. Given that scenario, implementing a *different* curriculum delivery would seem very appropriate. During the basketball unit, the student who is blind could be working on various skills within the game of goalball (e.g., throwing, passing, blocking). The casual observer might see the entire class in a basketball unit while one student is practicing goalball skills. One way to minimize *different* curriculums is to consider moving an entire disability sport into your general curriculum or infusing the delivery (i.e., combining disability sports such as sitting volleyball and goalball into your general curriculum and having all students play these sports) and making it a *same* curriculum. If all students learned the sport of goalball, students with and without disabilities would be on common ground and not different. Ponder and discuss the benefits of having an entire class, those with and without disabilities, learn a disability sport together (see the unit planning template in chapter 4).

Class Formats

Class formats are important to address as you plan instruction and consider how to organize students to perform activities. Consider especially how you would use class formats when teaching students with and without disabilities in the same class. Four teaching formats are presented: one on one, small group, large group, and mixed group.

• *One on one.* The one-on-one format promotes skill acquisition and establishes a ratio of one teacher to one student. The format is good for students with low functional ability because it provides highly individualized instructional episodes.

• *Small group.* The small group format allows three to eight students to work with a teacher or teacher aide. Students with and without disabilities can be included in this format, which allows you to provide frequent feedback during instructional time. The small group format can support the achievement of social goals and objectives (e.g., taking turns, waiting, offering congratulations to others).

• *Large group.* Generally considered a format for team games, the large group format includes the entire class (students with and without disabilities). You must make wise decisions about your teaching style (teacher centered or student centered) when implementing a large group format. Also, consider how the student with a disability can share in a decision-making role. Suggestions are included with each of the activities in part II under Inclusion Suggestions.

• *Mixed group.* A mixed group format uses a combination of class formats (one on one, small group, large group; consider the Gauntlet activities in chapter 6 on Wheelchair Basketball). Your decision to use this class format will depend on the number of students with disabilities in your class and the functional profiles of both groups (students with and without disabilities).

Each activity in part II of this book is organized according to the functional level of the student with a disability and the class format. Although the mixed group format is not mentioned in part II, it is implied that this format is a composite of the previous types (one on one, small group, and large group). See the games-by-skill-level indexes for students considered low functioning or moderate to high functioning for each of the sports in part II.

Prompting and Cueing

Implementation planning within the ABC model also requires that you consider prompting and cueing. The terms *prompting* and *cueing* are interchangeable for the purposes of this book. However, some experts consider prompting to be extra information added by the teacher to ensure targeted responses from the student (e.g., physical or verbal). Prompting involves emphasizing the relative information within the task. Cueing is considered preliminary instructions or directions for completing the task.

Prompting can come in the form of verbal, model (visual demonstrations), or physical assists. Students with disabilities often need additional prompting or cueing to understand the relevant dimensions of a task. For example, a student with cerebral palsy might need an additional physical prompt to correctly position his elbow alignment in preparation for shooting a basketball after being given the cue "We will be shooting baskets today." Another example is a student with a visual impairment who needs an additional physical or kinesthetic prompt to improve her release and follow-through after throwing a goalball.

Verbal, model, and physical assists also work for students without disabilities. Demonstrating and physically assisting students to improve their performances have been used extensively for many years. When working with both groups, those with and those without disabilities, use appropriate prompting to help them move toward skilled independent movement.

Teaching Styles

Class organizations and accommodations for students with and without disabilities will be affected by the teaching style you use. Table 3.1 is an abbreviated list and description of teaching styles. For a more complete list and explanations, read *A Teacher's Guide to Including Students With Disabilities in General Physical Education, Third Edition* by Block, 2007.

Teaching styles address how to organize and present the information for the lesson; there is no one best teaching style. You must feel comfortable with the style you have chosen and should take into account how students learn and which physical education domain the lesson is targeting (psychomotor, cognitive, or affective).

According to Mosston and Ashworth (1994), there is a continuum of teaching styles; at one end are the reproductive (teacher-centered) styles, and at the other end are the productive (student-centered) styles. In the reproductive styles, the teacher decides what, when, how, and how long students will perform the activities. Students are expected to reproduce the skill as the teacher directs the lesson (e.g., throwing a goalball precisely as presented). Productive styles allow students to decide what movement patterns work best for them in addressing a movement task (e.g., pushing a wheelchair while dribbling a basketball). Table 3.1 is a brief review of the teaching style spectrum (Mosston & Ashworth, 1994).

Unit Planning Template

The purpose of implementation planning is to help you outline lesson objectives, class time, instructional activities, and class formats or student groupings (Kelly & Melograno, 2004). This chapter offers a unit planning template to help you plan, implement, and evaluate a two-week unit using the activities from part II of this text (see figure 3.1). Remember that the ABC model suggests that content be sim-

Table 3.1   Spectrum of Teaching Styles

Reproductive styles	Teacher centered
Command	Students must follow all the directions provided by the teacher. Generally, all students in the class are doing the same skill in the same manner.
Practice/task	Students work individually, or in small groups, which allows the teacher time to provide individual feedback in various formats (one on one, small group).
Reciprocal	Students work in small groups (at least three in the group) and provide feedback to one another using the criteria the teacher has established; this style can help promote social interactions between students with and without disabilities. Adjustments would need to be made for students with visual, auditory, or cognitive impairments.
Self-check	Students work individually and use the criteria established by the teacher to respond to feedback. Adjustments would need to be made for students with visual, auditory, or cognitive impairments.
Inclusion/invitation	This style allows students to self-select the degree of difficulty of the task. The teacher must provide options for the students so they can move on to more difficult tasks (e.g., create three distances from which to shoot a basketball while seated; allow students to select the distance to start from).
Productive styles	**Student centered**
Guided discovery	The teacher asks a specific sequence of questions that leads the student toward a target skill previously unknown and unaccomplished.
Convergent discovery	Students are challenged to discover the solution to a problem through logical reasoning and critical thinking. There is generally only one correct answer, and the students must come to an agreement to produce the answer. This style would be effective with students with limited mobility skills.
Divergent discovery	This style allows the students to produce multiple responses to a question posed by the teacher. Students must use problem solving, logical reasoning, and critical thinking skills associated with convergent discovery. Here the students consider all the responses that are feasible or possible to address the problem.

plified and broken down into attainable units to match the skill sets of the student. Complete the unit planning template before implementing the two-week unit, and use it afterward to help with student and program evaluation. This document will help you move from planning into teaching and assist with lesson plan development.

Complete each category within the unit planning template: curriculum delivery, class format, teaching style, activity name(s), and prompts plus any modifications needed. Explanations of the various curriculum delivery methods, class formats, teaching styles, and prompts were presented previously in this chapter.

- *Curriculum delivery:* Same (S), multilevel (Mt), modified (MD), different (D)
- *Class format:* One on one (1:1), small group (SM), large group (LG), mixed group (Mix)

- *Teaching style:* Command (C), practice/task (PT), reciprocal (R), self-check (SC), inclusion (I)
- *Activity name(s):* Copy the name(s) only of the activity/activities or game(s) from the sport chapters in part II of this book.
- *Prompt/Cues:* Verbal (V), model (M), physical assist (PA)

Figure 3.1 provides an example of a completed unit planning template using Tony's basketball unit. The games are taken from the wheelchair basketball chapter (chapter 6) in part II of this book. You will use the information from the unit planning template and the activity descriptions from the sport chapters to write your lesson plan (see the next section).

Student of interest: *Tony, fifth grade*   Description: *Moderate cerebral palsy, nonambulatory*

Monday	Tuesday	Wednesday	Thursday	Friday
Curr delivery: Mt Class format: SM Tch style: C and PT Activity name: **Give and Go** Prompts/cues: V and PA; keep eyes on target and extend your arms Modification: Increase distance between players to encourage arm extension	Curr delivery: ____ Class format: ____ Tch style: ____ Activity name: Prompts/cues: Modification:	Curr delivery: D, Mt/MD Class format: 1:1 and SM Tch style: C and PT Activity names: **Hanging On** **Pass and Shoot** Prompts/cues: V, P; extend your arms; concentrate on release Modification:	Curr delivery: ____ Class format: ____ Tch style: ____ Activity name: Prompts/cues: Modification:	Curr delivery: Mt Class format: SM Tch style: PT Activity name: **Remember Me** Prompts/cues: M and PA; extend and follow through Modification: Increase size of circle
Curr delivery: Mt Class format: LG Tch style: PT and R Activity name: **Call It Out** Prompts/cues: V and M Modification: Use different-size balls	Curr delivery: ____ Class format: ____ Tch style: ____ Activity name: Prompts/cues: Modification:	Curr delivery: S, MD Class format: SM and LG Tch style: C and R Activity name: **Partner Pass (from wheelchair soccer)** Prompts/cues: V and M Modification: Increase distance between partners	Curr delivery: ____ Class format: ____ Tch style: ____ Activity name: Prompts/cues: Modification:	Curr delivery: Mt Class format: SM and LG Tch style: C and R Activity names: **Pass and Shoot** **Partner Pass** Prompts/cues: V and PA Modification: Only as needed

Curriculum delivery (Curr delivery): S = same, Mt = multi, MD = modified, D = different; **Class format:** 1:1 = one on one, SM = small group, LG = large group, Mix = mixed group; **Teaching style (Tch style):** C = command, PT = practice/task, R = reciprocal, SC = self-check, I = inclusion; **Prompts/cues:** V = verbal, M = model, PA = physical assist

Evaluation:

Goals accomplished:

Comments:

Figure 3.1   Sample unit planning template for Tony.

TEACHING: WRITING LESSON PLANS

You are responsible for deciding what your students will learn, giving students feedback, and identifying the skills that need continued attention. Lesson plans are used to help you implement and manage your instructional environment. Each chapter in part II contains activities using the following categories that can be used to structure a good lesson plan: class format, organizational pattern, equipment, description, extensions (modifications), and inclusion suggestions. See a sample lesson plan for Tony in figure 3.2; it uses information from the activity Hanging On in chapter 6, Wheelchair Basketball (see page 58).

Objective: Improve grasp and release	**Student's name**: Tony	**Time**: 9:00–9:45 a.m.	**Curriculum(s)**: Different and multi/modified
Activity name: Hanging On	**Class format**: One on one and small group	**Organizational pattern**: Individual with peer assistant; all other students in small group work on passing. Rotate students into one-on-one with Tony. Conclude with large group, modified passing relay activity.	**Equipment**: Small Nerf ball, deflated playground ball, Nerf volleyball, or junior basketball

Description: Give Tony the ball and have him hold it as long as possible. See how long he can hold the ball using one hand. Help him with his grasp as needed. If necessary, he may use two hands.	
Extension: Change the position of Tony's hands and arms (e.g., in front of the body, overhead).	**Inclusion suggestions**: Tony can demonstrate to the class the ability to accomplish the activity and work in the large group setting.

Figure 3.2 Sample lesson plan for wheelchair basketball—passing.

PROGRAM AND STUDENT EVALUATING

Within the ABC model, the components of planning (program and implementation) and assessing (student at the beginning and ending of unit(s) or pre/post) provide the basis for evaluation. Program evaluation addresses whether the students have achieved program goals and objectives, as well as the effectiveness of the program.

You can use the unit planning template to evaluate the unit after it is completed in terms of class format, teaching style, and prompts and cues. You can also review and evaluate the number of times the student with a disability participated in same, different, or multilevel curriculums, and which brought about the greatest degree of success. Conducting a program evaluation can help you determine what variables might be contributing to or restricting student progress. Reviewing the unit planning template following the completion of a unit might help you assess the need for additional equipment, a change of location, or more time to complete the activity.

The same skill-level, criterion-referenced assessment can be used both before and after each unit. For example, according to the assessment chart from chapter 2, Tony's preassessment data indicated that he demonstrated or accomplished skill performance in three out of five trials (60 percent) for eyes on target, two hands on ball, and elbows flexed in preparation during the chest pass. Also during preassessment, Tony needed assistance with at least two of five trials (40 percent) of the remaining three components (elbows extend at ball release, thumbs point downward, and follow through); he did not demonstrate an accomplished (unassisted) performance in any of these skill components.

Tony's postassessment data resulted in the profile in figure 3.3, which reported improvement in all six components of the chest pass. He completed eyes on target and two hands on the ball unassisted 100 percent of the time. He also improved unassisted elbow extension to 80 percent of the time, or four out of five trials, compared to 80 percent of assisted movement in the pretest. This evaluation provides evidence of skill improvement and can serve as documentation when you are considering future activities or grading.

Both program and student performance evaluations can be used to determine the effectiveness of your teaching. They may reveal a need to modify your lessons, manage your time better, or alter other logistical issues. Activity selection and implementation are two of the first points to address in modification.

Student's name: _Tony_

Chest pass	Trials 1–5					Comments
Eyes on target	X	X	X	X	X	_Kept eyes on target 100%._
Two hands on ball	X	X	X	X	X	_No prompts needed; held the ball correctly._
Elbows flexed in preparation	X	X	X	X	/	_Held the ball correctly._
Elbows extend at ball release	X	X	X	X	/	_Increased elbow extension with minimal prompts._
Thumbs point downward	X	X	/	/	/	_Improved release._
Follow through	X	/	/	/	/	_Needed PA minimally._

Figure 3.3 Postassessment data for Tony's chest pass.

MODIFICATIONS AND ENVIRONMENTAL INTERACTIONS

Your teaching skills help you determine the best teaching styles, class formats, prompts, and curriculum deliveries for producing successful lessons for students with and without disabilities. As a PETE student or teacher in the field, you have likely been taught to consider the variables unique to the student, the task, and the environment when determining what and how to teach (Newell, 1986). When teaching students with and without disabilities in the same activity, you must be skilled at modifying the lesson; this section briefly shares my own personal approach to lesson modifications.

Newell (1986) developed a model of interaction using the three variables of student, task, and environment. Student variables include age, body type, gender, culture, motivation level, and disability. Environmental variables include the class setting (indoor or outdoor; pool or gymnasium), lighting, temperature, space, and floor surfaces. Task variables are those considered part of the curriculum, including movement skills required by the student. I suggest that you focus simply on the interaction between the environment and the tasks, before being concerned with the student's skills.

This modified environmental interaction model is dynamic and is presented as two infinitely continuing lines, one vertical, representing the performer's functional ability, and one horizontal, representing the difficulty of the task. The intersection of the two lines creates a four-quadrant environmental interaction (see figure 3.4).

The four-quadrant environmental model represents the potential for dynamic positive (+) or negative (–) interactions. When applying this model to activity selection, consider the potential for your students' success (+) or nonsuccess (–). Your objective, as a teacher, is to change the tasks to result in more successful interactions. For example, a student with high functional ability should experience positive environmental interactions (quadrant +1) with difficult or complex tasks. Likewise, a task considered easy or simple could bring success for a student with lower functional ability identified in quadrant + 3. However, when you select a task that is simple for the student with high functional ability, or a task that is difficult for a student with low functional ability, the environmental interaction will likely not bring success or enjoyment (quadrants –2 and –4). The quadrants are not meant to be sequential (i.e., you must move from quadrant 1 to quadrants 2, 3, and then 4); rather, consider them *starting* points for the student(s) in a task with the goal of moving toward success, or a positive (+) quadrant.

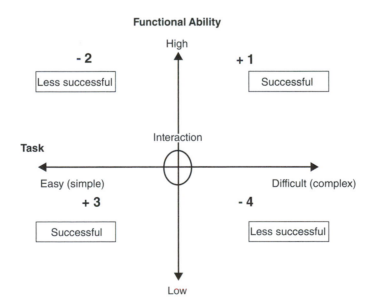

Figure 3.4 Environmental interaction model.

Consider what would happen if you were teaching a basketball unit to a class of students with and without disabilities (see figure 3.5). The student with a disability in this class is moderate to low functioning (see the detailed description in chapter 6) and uses a manual wheelchair. The task for this student, and all the other students, is to shoot a traditional basketball from the traditional free-throw line to a traditional height (i.e., 10 ft, or 3 m) represented by the starting position A within quadrant 4. This environmental interaction would likely not result in success for the student with a disability. You decide to modify the task and change some of the variables for the student with a disability (e.g., allow her to use a Nerf ball and lower the basket). The student using the wheelchair would likely have more success because the task and environment are more closely matched to her abilities, identified by position B in quadrant 3. As the skill and function of this student improve, you could increase the difficulty. Eventually, the student with a disability could shoot a playground ball or a junior basketball to a goal height of 8 feet (2.4 m) and 10 feet (3 m) and experience a successful environmental interaction identified by position C in quadrant 1.

Keep in mind that this model is dynamic; within each quadrant are multiple environmental interactions (changing positions within a quadrant) that can occur for all students. As you consider teaching, evaluating, and modifying, make sure to consider the environmental interactions brought about by your students' functional abilities (those with and without disabilities) and the tasks you have selected. Keep this model in mind as you present the activities suggested in part II of this book. Most of the activities associated with each sport in part II were developed to address the functional abilities of only students with disabilities. Each chapter in part II defines low, moderate, and high student functional profiles for the sport addressed. In addition, activities are presented according to environmental teaching formats (one on one, small group, and large group). All the large group activities are meant to be conducted in inclusive settings (i.e., those that include students with and without disabilities).

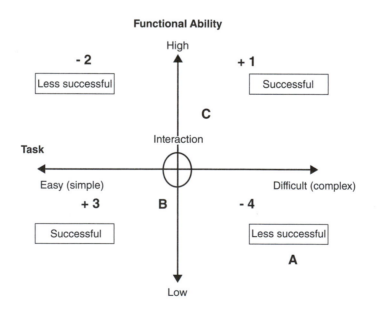

Figure 3.5 Environmental interaction model with basketball.

Because you are unlikely to be able to change or modify the student with a disability, you will need to modify the task. To do so, you must recognize that you can control or change only certain variables within any given activity. Consider the following variables that could be modified in a task as suggested by Kasser and Lytle (2006) and Morris and Stiehl (1999): equipment, rules, organizational pattern, and instruction.

- *Equipment.* Equipment modifications that need to be considered for students with disabilities relate to size, weight, length, grip strength needed, mobility needed, and the vision and hearing functions of the student. In the example from the environmental interaction model, the teacher successfully moved the student through the quadrants by modifying the task of shooting a traditional basketball to a traditional hoop while sitting in a wheelchair (see figure 3.5). The size, weight, and height of the hoop were all modified to create a more successful environmental interaction for this task.

- *Rules.* Rule modifications need to be agreed on and applied to everyone in the class, those with and without disabilities. A problem could occur when special rules are implemented only for students with disabilities and not for those without. Consider this closely when you are addressing tasks that require boundary lines, the need for sequential throws (e.g., throws to bases), and striking pitched objects, and rules related to player fouls or team penalties. Allow all students (those with and without disabilities) to decide what rule modifications are acceptable prior to implementing the game or activity. Allowing everyone to contribute to rule modifications puts all students in decision-making roles, especially those with disabilities.

- *Organizational pattern.* The organizational pattern of a game refers to the positions of the players on the court or field (e.g., five-on-five basketball, eleven on a side in soccer, six on a side in volleyball) and their patterns (e.g., basketball zone versus person to person, baseball infield versus outfield, volleyball front row versus back row).

These organizational patterns might need to be modified to ensure safety and success when students with disabilities are included. A five-on-five game of basketball might not be safe for a student with cerebral palsy (CP) with minimal ambulation skills. A modification of three-on-three half-court may be more successful, or you could try a game of sideline basketball. Remember that students without disabilities will be affected by this modification, so seek everyone's input before implementing it.

Consider the organization modifications you would need to include a student using a wheelchair in a basketball game with students who are ambulatory. Increasing or decreasing the size of the playing area will affect the organizational patterns; again, seek input from all the students in the class before implementing organizational pattern modifications. Lastly, review the information presented earlier for selecting the class format; selecting the appropriate class format can help with modifying game or activity organizational patterns.

- *Instructional modifications.* Much of the information related to instructional modification was mentioned earlier with considerations for prompting, or cueing. You must be familiar with how your students learn (e.g., visual, tactile, kinesthetic, or auditory) and do the best you can to address each student's learning ability. Not all students are verbal learners, and many need additional prompts (e.g., demonstration) to carry out a motor task correctly. The use of picture cards coupled with physical prompts might help certain students perform the task. For kinesthetic learners, you might demonstrate the task and use movement patterning (i.e., hand over hand assistance).

SUMMARY

As you consider how to apply the ABC model using content from disability sport, remember that students with disabilities bring a new set of abilities to your class. As a PETE student or teacher in the field, you have to consider the environmental interactions you will be creating through your activities and how you will organize, teach, and modify your class setting. Your PETE program or your daily teaching will provide you with opportunities to use various teaching styles, class formats, and activity modifications. If you are a PETE student, request to teach disability sport during your preparation courses and begin to apply this information. As a current teacher, consider learning more about disability sport and implementing this content into your curriculum. Remember that blank forms for assessments, IEPs, and unit and lesson plans are located on the DVD.

Chapter 4

Implementing Disability Sport

In applying the ABC model to our fictional student, Tony, you have worked through planning, assessing, implementing the plan, teaching, and evaluating. You have considered his background and his desire, or goal, (top down) to play recreational competitive wheelchair basketball. Through skill assessments you have determined his strengths and weaknesses, and used that information to implement a plan for teaching. As you considered how to teach (curriculum deliveries, teaching styles, available time, environmental interactions, and evaluation), you moved forward with a plan to measure Tony's progress and the effectiveness of your program. Now you need a few tools to help you document Tony's progress and your program's impact as you pursue teaching disability sport. Be mindful that the ABC model has direct application to coaching athletes with disabilities, in addition to teaching students with disabilities in a physical education setting.

This chapter will help you apply the foundational information you now have to the practical aspects of teaching disability sport. It provides the following five working documents:

1. Inclusion index
2. Assessment instrument
3. IEP template
4. Unit planning template
5. Lesson plan template

The ABC model serves as a guide throughout this chapter; the model components are program planning, assessing, implementation planning, teaching, and evaluating. The premise in this chapter is that you are teaching a general physical education class and you have at least one student with a disability in your class (i.e., inclusive setting).

ABC MODEL: PROGRAM PLANNING USING THE INCLUSION INDEX

The inclusion index is a planning aid that will help you identify the common ground between disability sport and traditional sport (i.e., cross-referencing). This index helps you select an activity based on the functional profile of your student with a disability.

Reading the Inclusion Index

The inclusion index (see next page) is organized into three columns: column 1 lists the categories of games from the teaching games for understanding curriculum mentioned in chapter 3 (e.g., invasion games; net games; and court, field, and target games); column 2, titled Sports in General Physical Education, includes the traditional sports of basketball, soccer, volleyball, tennis, track and field, and bowling assumed to be taught in general PETE methods activity courses or in school-based programs (within each traditional sport are skills associated with the sport, such as passing, dribble, shooting, and ball movement in basketball); and column 3, titled Disability Sports, has three or four cross-references between disability and traditional sport-specific skills. Each disability sport is represented by an icon printed at the top of the page, and these show cross-referencing. The icons represent wheelchair basketball, indoor wheelchair soccer, sitting volleyball, wheelchair tennis, goalball, the slalom, and boccia ball.

Using the Inclusion Index

Follow these six steps to use the inclusion index.

1. Locate a sport.
2. Cross-reference a disability sport.
3. Learn about the sport and its skills.
4. Determine the functional level of performance of your student with a disability.
5. Assess the student's skill performance.
6. Select and implement an appropriate game.

Step 1: Locate a Sport

Locate the sport in your current curriculum from the game categories in column 1 of the inclusion index. For example, you are planning to teach several sports from the invasion games category (e.g., basketball and soccer), and you know you have two students with disabilities in your general physical education class. One is Tony, who uses a manual wheelchair, and the other is a student who is visually impaired. Locating the invasion games category in column 1 helps you organize your unit plan to infuse disability sport content into your curriculum. Your next step is to determine which sports have common ground between traditional and disability sport.

Step 2: Cross-Reference a Disability Sport

To cross-reference a disability sport with the traditional sport, simply read across from column 1 and find the traditional sport or sport skill in column 2 (Sports in General Physical Education) that is included in your unit plan. Now, cross-reference the traditional sport or skill to the disability sport or skill using the icons in column 3. Once you have determined the cross-reference to the disability sport or sport skill, refer to the appropriate sport chapter in part II. As you read through each disability sport chapter, consider the curriculum delivery (from chapter 3—same, multilevel, modified, or different) you will use when teaching your unit.

For example, let's say you have decided to teach a basketball unit and are currently working on the skill of passing. Tony is in your class, and you need additional ideas to help him with passing. Turn to chapter 6 and read about the three passes in wheelchair basketball; then read how each can be used in a game or activity. The games and activities are presented according to the student's functional profile and

Find the traditional sport or sport skill

Determine which disability sport teaches those same skills

Locate the game category from your current curriculum

Inclusion Index

Legend:
- Wheelchair Basketball
- Indoor Wheelchair Soccer
- Sitting Volleyball
- Boccia
- Goalball
- Wheelchair Tennis
- The Slalom (Track)

		Sports in general physical education	Disability sports			
Invasion games		**Basketball**				
		Passing	Wheelchair Basketball	Indoor Wheelchair Soccer	Sitting Volleyball	Goalball
		Dribbling	Wheelchair Basketball	Indoor Wheelchair Soccer		
		Shooting	Wheelchair Basketball	Indoor Wheelchair Soccer	Goalball	
		Ball movement	Wheelchair Basketball	The Slalom (Track)		
		Soccer				
		Passing	Indoor Wheelchair Soccer	Indoor Wheelchair Soccer	Sitting Volleyball	Goalball
		Dribbling	Indoor Wheelchair Soccer	Indoor Wheelchair Soccer	The Slalom (Track)	
		Throwing in	Indoor Wheelchair Soccer	Goalball		
		Blocking	Indoor Wheelchair Soccer	Goalball		
Net games		**Volleyball**				
		Serving	Sitting Volleyball	Wheelchair Tennis		
		Bumping/passing	Sitting Volleyball	Goalball		
		Setting	Sitting Volleyball			
		Blocking	Sitting Volleyball	Goalball	Wheelchair Basketball	
		Tennis				
		Forehand	Wheelchair Tennis			
		Backhand	Wheelchair Tennis			
		Serve	Wheelchair Tennis	Sitting Volleyball		

The entire inclusion index can be found on pages viii-ix.

class formats. You might use an activity suggested for a large group class format so you can teach students with and without disabilities together (see chapter 3). Keep in mind that you must assess the skill level of the student(s) with a disability, as discussed in chapter 2. In other words, don't forget to do an assessment before implementing your teaching plan.

Another consideration you might have to make would be for a student who has a visual impairment in your basketball class. You discover from cross-referencing that the skill of passing is required for both goalball (disability sport) and basketball (traditional sport). You would then turn to chapter 10, read about goalball, and then read about the specific skill of passing. Using games to emphasize passing in goalball during a basketball unit might be considered a multilevel or modified curriculum delivery (as discussed in chapter 3), which would be acceptable.

Step 3: Learn About the Disability Sport and Its Skills

Once you have cross-referenced the disability sport or skill with the traditional sport or skill, you need to learn about the disability sport. Chapters 6 through 12 each begins with a narrative about the sport called Description of the Sport followed by a brief overview of the sport in table format. The description of the sport includes the following: field of play, players, equipment, starting the game, game objective, game length, general rules and penalties, rules specific to the sport, and a summary of the sport.

In the next section of each disability sport chapter, called Skills to Be Taught, you will read about and view selected skills deemed important for this sport. Each skill is task-analyzed and supported with an illustration to help with instruction. You are now ready to select games or activities based on the functional profile of your student with a disability. You are not expected to have completed a skill assessment at this point; remember, the inclusion index is part of the planning component of the ABC model. You are still planning *how* you want to teach; specific information regarding *what* to teach must come from the student's skill assessment.

Step 4: Determine the Functional Level of Performance of Your Student With a Disability

Once you are familiar with the disability sport and the skills to be taught, you need to determine your student's functional level of performance and how you will implement the game you selected in an inclusive setting (i.e., students with and without disabilities in the same general physical education class). Each chapter in part II has a student functional profile table that is organized according to functional ability (i.e., low, moderate, and high). These profiles have been operationally defined and modified according to each disability sport's official classification system. The functional profiles are meant to be general guidelines to use in game selection and planning.

Once you have determined the functional profile of your student with a disability, refer to the general game modifications in each chapter so you can address both students with and without disabilities in your lesson.

Step 5: Assess the Student's Skill Performance

Review the information presented in chapter 2, Assessment. A brief review of how to conduct the assessment and write the IEP are included in that chapter along with samples of completed forms. Blank assessment and IEP forms are also included in this chapter and on the supplemental DVD to help you complete this step. Once your skill assessments and IEP are written, you are ready to move on to step 6 and select an appropriate game or activity to address the student's goals and objectives.

Step 6: Select and Implement an Appropriate Game

Each chapter in part II includes two games-by-skill-level indexes that match specific games to the student's functional profile and the teaching class format (see tables 4.1 and 4.2). One is for low functional ability, and the other is for moderate to high

Table 4.1 Games-by-Skill-Level Index for Low-Functioning Students—Wheelchair Basketball

Skills	One on one	Small group	Large group
Passing	Hanging On	Give and Go	Triangle and Go I (Passing)
Shooting	Shot's Away	Pass and Shoot (Shooting)	Triangle and Go II (Shooting)
Dribbling	Right Back at You	Pass and Shoot (Dribbling)	Triangle and Go III (Dribbling)
Bounce stop	Gauntlet I	Gauntlet II	Gauntlet III
Bounce spin	Spinning Wheels I	Spinning Wheels II	Spinning Wheels III
Ball retrieval	Reaching Out I	Reaching Out II	Reaching Out III

Table 4.2 Student Functional Profiles for Indoor Wheelchair Soccer

Functional skill level	Student profile
Low	Severe disabilities in all four extremities; uses an electric or power wheelchair.
Low to moderate	Severe to moderate disabilities in three of the four extremities; can use a manual wheelchair for short distances.
Moderate	Minimal paraplegic (two lower) or hemiplegic (one side) disability; uses a manual wheelchair and can push the wheelchair at a moderate to high level.
High	No neurological or physical disability in the upper extremity or trunk; has some severe disability in at least one lower extremity.

functional ability. Once you have chosen the appropriate index (low or moderate to high), simply find the skill to be addressed (e.g., passing in wheelchair basketball) and cross-reference it with the class format (i.e., one on one, small group, or large group); then pick a game to teach. Remember to keep the interaction model in mind (see chapter 3) as you plan the activity, and be ready to change the environmental interactions as needed once you begin teaching.

SUMMARY

Part I of this book introduces the components of the ABC model to help you apply disability sport content to your general physical education curriculum. Chapters 1, 2, and 3 are foundational, and chapter 4 helps you move from theory to practice. Part II of this book includes many of the sports and skills from the first edition of this text. With an update of rules and the inclusion of a new sport (boccia), this text should serve as a sound reference for teaching students with and without disabilities using sport content. The following blank templates can also be found on the DVD. Use them to plan, implement, and evaluate your own progrram. Remember that blank forms for assessments, IEPs, and unit and lesson plans are located on the DVD.

BLANK TEMPLATES

 ## Wheelchair Basketball Assessment Score Sheet

Student's name: _____

Sport/skill: Wheelchair basketball/chest pass

Chest pass	Trials 1–5					Comments
Eyes on target						
Two hands on ball						
Elbows flexed in preparation						
Elbows extend at ball release						
Thumbs point downward						
Follow through						

Key: X = accomplished   / = with assistance   0 = not accomplished

 ## Wheelchair Tennis Assessment Score Sheet

Student's name: _____

Sport/skill: Wheelchair tennis/forehand

Forehand	Trials 1–5					Comments
Pull back on wheel with dominant hand in preparation						
As ball nears, pull back on nondominant-hand wheel while positioning arm to strike						
Position dominate arm with racket extended back and shoulder rotated away from net						
Swing arm forward on ball contact while pulling nondominant wheel back and turning into the strike						
Contact ball and follow through						

Key: X = accomplished   / = with assistance   0 = not accomplished

 ## Goalball Assessment Score Sheet

Student's name: _____   Sport/skill: Goalball/throwing

Throw	Trials 1–5					Comments
Upright stance with ball resting on dominate hip						
Step forward with nondominant foot while swinging dominant arm back with ball						
Lower body position bending lead leg upon release of ball						
Keep shoulders and hips facing target						
Release ball, and follow through by lifting throwing arm up above shoulder						

Key: X = accomplished   / = with assistance   0 = not accomplished

Assessment Score Sheet

Use this blank assessment to assess any sport skill. The criteria can come from the teaching points in each sport chapter or the captions from drawings of each skill.

Student's name: _____ Sport/skill: _____

Skill	Trials 1–5					Comments

Key: X = accomplished   / = with assistance   0 = not accomplished

 ## Blank IEP (using only three components)

Student's name: _____ Task: _____

Present level of performance	
Annual goal	
Short-term objectives	

Blank Unit Planning Template

Monday	Tuesday	Wednesday	Thursday	Friday
Curr delivery: _____ Class format: _____ Tch style: _____ Activity name: Prompts/cues: Modification:	Curr delivery: _____ Class format: _____ Tch style: _____ Activity name: Prompts/cues: Modification:	Curr delivery: _____ Class format: _____ Tch style: _____ Activity name: Prompts/cues: Modification:	Curr delivery: _____ Class format: _____ Tch style: _____ Activity name: Prompts/cues: Modification:	Curr delivery: _____ Class format: _____ Tch style: _____ Activity name: Prompts/cues: Modification:
Curr delivery: _____ Class format: _____ Tch style: _____ Activity name: Prompts/cues: Modification:	Curr delivery: _____ Class format: _____ Tch style: _____ Activity name: Prompts/cues: Modification:	Curr delivery: _____ Class format: _____ Tch style: _____ Activity name: Prompts/cues: Modification:	Curr delivery: _____ Class format: _____ Tch style: _____ Activity name: Prompts/cues: Modification:	Curr delivery: _____ Class format: _____ Tch style: _____ Activity name: Prompts/cues: Modification:

Curriculum delivery (Curr delivery): S = same, Mt = multi, MD = modified, D = different; **Class format:** 1:1 = one on one, SM = small group, LG = large group, Mix = mixed group; **Teaching style (Tch style):** C = command, PT = practice/task, R = reciprocal, SC = self-check, I = inclusion; **Prompts/cues:** V = verbal, M = model, PA= physical assist

Evaluation:

Goals accomplished:

Comments:

 ## Blank Lesson Plan Template

Objective:	Student name:	Time:	Curriculum(s):
Activity name:	**Class format:**	**Organizational pattern:**	**Equipment:**

Description:

Extension(s):	Inclusion suggestion(s):

PART II

Disability Sports, Skills, and Activities

Chapter 5

Wheelchair Basics

Five basic movement skills are essential for students who use manual wheelchairs. These skills could be taught as part of a physical education class for students with disabilities within the general curriculum. They could also be taught to students without disabilities who are learning a disability sport. The five movement skills are forward propulsion, stopping, backward propulsion, the stationary pivot or spin, and the moving pivot or spin. Each skill is described in this chapter and key teaching points are included. The mainwheel of the wheelchair is referenced as the face of a clock. Therefore, if the teaching suggestion mentions positioning the student's hands at 12 o'clock, that should be interpreted as placing the hands at the top of the mainwheel.

FORWARD PROPULSION

All references to pushing a wheelchair are made from the perspective of the person doing the pushing and not from the perspective of being pushed. Pushing a wheelchair is described in two phases: propulsion and recovery. The propulsive phase is when the person exerts force onto the handrims, driving the wheelchair forward. Using the clock face reference, the propulsion phase is approximately from 12 o'clock to 5 o'clock. The recovery phase begins at the end of propulsion, or between 5 and 6 o'clock. The recovery phase begins as the hands break contact with the handrims and move back up to the beginning of the propulsive phase, or approximately 11 or 12 o'clock.

When teaching the propulsive phase, emphasize starting the hands at top dead center of the mainwheel (figure 5.1*a*). As the student makes contact with the handrims and tires, he should push with the pads of his hands and rest his thumbs on the tires, keeping his fingers slightly curled under the handrim. As the student begins to push, make sure his elbows, shoulders, and hands are in alignment, ready for the elbows to be extended forward with force (figure 5.1*b*). As the elbows are extended, the student flexes his trunk slightly with his shoulders over the tires and drives his hands and elbows forward and down, using trunk flexion to reach forward. As his hands reach forward and downward as far as possible, the student pushes through at least one quarter of the wheel's circumference and gets ready for the recovery phase (figure 5.1*c*). To execute the recovery phase, the student releases his hands from the rims briefly to return to the start position (figure 5.1*d*) and focuses on returning his hands to the rims as quickly as possible (figure 5.1*e*). Remember, hands off the rims means no force is applied, and no force to the handrims means the wheelchair is slowing down, so emphasize maximizing propulsion phases and minimizing recovery phases.

Figure 5.1 Forward propulsion. *(a)* Hand position on tire and rim for forward propulsion. *(b)* Body position to begin forward propulsion. *(c)* Begin recovery phase. *(d)* Recovery phase. *(e)* Reposition hands for next forward propulsion.

STOPPING THE WHEELCHAIR

The second wheelchair mobility skill to learn is stopping the wheelchair with control. All disability sports that use a wheelchair require a high degree of wheelchair control. Players unable to maintain control of their wheelchairs during a game could be penalized or ruled out of control.

To teach proper stopping techniques, start the student from the basic position described in forward propulsion. As the wheelchair is moving forward, the student leans forward as far as possible and grips both wheels simultaneously. As the student secures a solid grip, he pulls back on the wheels simultaneously by wrapping his fingers around the handrims (figure 5.2a). To control the stop, the student leans backward as the pull is made, maintaining an equal pull and balanced sitting positioned (figure 5.2b). People with weak abdominal support should consider using special strapping for support during competition, because sudden stopping could cause the person to fall from the wheelchair.

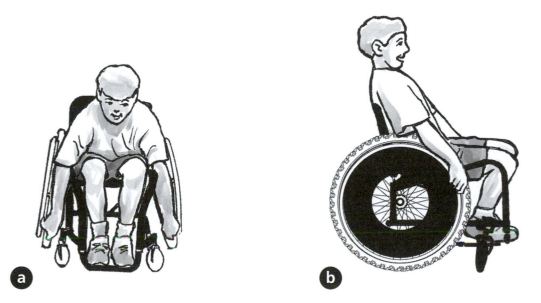

Figure 5.2 Stopping the wheelchair. *(a)* Grip both wheels for stopping. *(b)* Lean back to control the stop.

BACKWARD PROPULSION

Backward propulsion is used quite often in several wheelchair sport team games, such as wheelchair basketball and indoor wheelchair soccer. Backward propulsion allows the player to keep his body in a good position to see the court and the action taking place around him. This skill helps the player to maintain better control of his wheelchair and allows him to see dangers that could be avoided. The basic technique is a pulling type of motion.

To begin the backward propulsion maneuver, the student should be in the basic sitting position described for stopping the wheelchair. To initiate the backward propulsion, the student leans forward and reaches down on the handrims as low as possible, gripping the main tires (figure 5.3a). The student's shoulders should be directly over the hands, and all joints involved with the movement should be in alignment (i.e., wrist, elbows, and shoulders). Next, the student uses short,

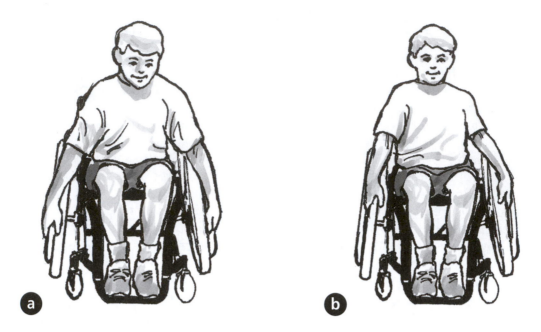

Figure 5.3 Backward propulsion. *(a)* Reach forward to begin the reverse pull. *(b)* Pull back symmetrically.

quick pulls backward on the wheels making sure to keep the pulling movement symmetrical (figure 5.3*b*). Because the front steering wheels (casters) are trailing, keeping the wheelchair under control is difficult, so the student shouldn't move too rapidly. As backward movement takes place, the student keeps his body weight forward and balanced over his knees. Make sure to instruct the student not to lean back too far as he initiates the pulling motion, because such movement could cause the wheelchair to tip over.

STATIONARY PIVOT (SPIN)

This maneuver is essential for helping a student change directions quickly during a game or activity. The stationary pivot, or spin, is performed by using a push–pull technique in coordination with proper weight shift. The direction of spin is determined by which wheel is pulled and which wheel is pushed. The spin will always move in the direction of the pulled wheel. The stationary pivot is taught from the basic forward propulsion position described earlier. The stationary pivot is the basic movement for the bounce stop and bounce spin used in wheelchair basketball (chapter 6).

To execute the stationary pivot, the student extends one arm down the handrim of the tire on the side of the intended spin (right arm for a pivot to the right; figure 5.4*a*). The opposite arm is placed at 12 o'clock on the opposite tire, or top dead center, and in a ready position to push (figure 5.4*b*). To initiate the movement, the student pulls up with the extended arm (right) and pushes with the opposite arm (left) simultaneously (figure 5.4*c*); this should spin the wheelchair. To complete the spin move, the student's pulling arm (right) should pass the top dead center of the right wheel, keeping in contact with the handrim (figure 5.4*d*). This same arm is now ready to initiate a new forward propulsion movement.

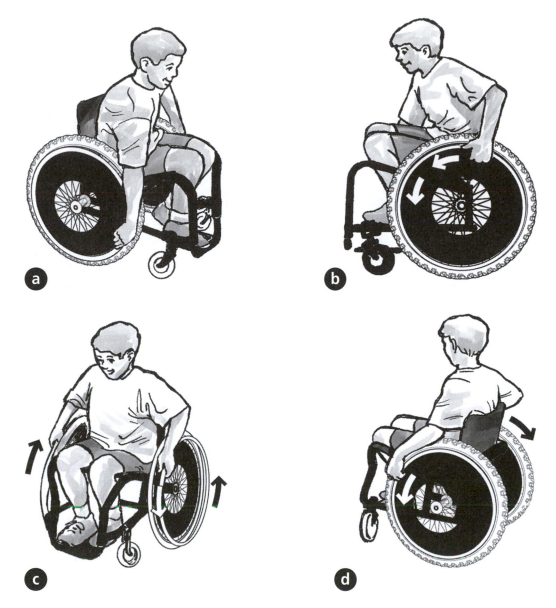

Figure 5.4 Stationary pivot. *(a)* Extend pivot arm down, ready to pull. *(b)* Position pushing arm at 12 o'clock. *(c)* Push–pull to spin the wheelchair. *(d)* Continue to push–pull through the spin.

MOVING PIVOT (SPIN)

This skill is performed in the same way as the stationary pivot, except that the student must now shift his body over to the side of the intended pivot during the pulling action. This is accomplished by leaning to one side and maintaining trunk stability so as not to fall from the wheelchair (figure 5.5*a*). To execute a right-hand moving pivot, the student shifts his body weight to the right side of the wheelchair while moving and pulls back on the right wheel, making sure his pulling hand passes top dead center, or 12 o'clock (figure 5.5*b*). As the right-hand

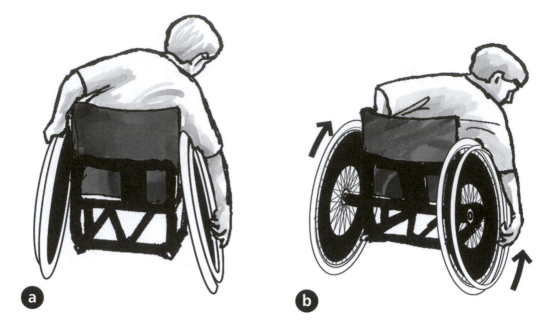

Figure 5.5 Moving pivot. *(a)* Shift body weight to the side of the pivot. *(b)* Push–pull to spin the wheelchair.

pivot is made, the student uses the pivot hand to initiate a new forward propulsion movement. Students with poor trunk stability should consider using support strapping to assist with balance. By shifting his body weight, the student places more weight over the turning side, which helps to control the moving wheelchair and executes this dynamic skill.

SOCIAL ACCEPTANCE

When integrating students with disabilities into your physical education class, you should address the issue of how the wheelchair is perceived by students without disabilities. By viewing the wheelchair as an extension of the person using it, as simply a different way to move, you encourage your students without disabilities to do the same. It is important to get your students without disabilities to see the person using the wheelchair, and not the wheelchair itself. The wheelchair helps define the person using it; it is a differentiating characteristic to be considered along with eye and hair color, height, and weight. When you as the general physical educator create a social environment in your classes that supports such an attitude, the attitude spills over to all the students.

SUMMARY

The following set of tables can be used as quick references for points discussed in this chapter. Use them to set up teaching stations or skill checklists. Remember that blank forms for assessments, IEPs, and unit and lesson plans are located on the DVD.

Teaching points	Forward wheelchair propulsion
	1. Position hands at top dead center.
	2. Rest pads of hands and thumbs on tires, fingers slightly curled under handrims.
	3. Align elbows, shoulders, and hands, ready to extend elbows forward.
	4. Flex trunk slightly, with shoulders over tires.
	5. Drive hands and elbows forward and down, using trunk flexion to reach forward.
	6. Push hands through the drive phase for at least one quarter of the wheel's circumference.

Teaching points	Wheelchair stopping technique
	1. Start from the basic position described in the forward propulsion position.
	2. Reach forward with both arms and grip the wheels as low as possible.
	3. Pull back on the wheels simultaneously by wrapping the fingers around the handrims and gripping tightly.
	4. Lean trunk backward while pulling up and back with both arms.
	5. People with weak abdominal support should consider using special strapping for support during competition. Sudden stopping could cause the person to fall from the wheelchair.

Teaching points	Backward wheelchair propulsion
	1. Start from the basic position described in the reach position of the stopping skill.
	2. Reach forward with both arms, flexing the trunk and gripping the wheel as in the forward propulsion.
	3. Shoulders should be directly over the hands on the rim, and all joints involved (wrist, elbows, shoulders) should be in alignment.
	4. Pull back using short, quick pulls.
	5. The steering wheels of the wheelchair (casters) are now trailing, thus making maneuvering difficult. Keep body weight forward and balanced over knees if possible to avoid leaning too far back and tipping the wheelchair over.

Teaching points	Stationary wheelchair pivot (spin)
	1. Extend the arm downward to the side intended to spin.
	2. Position the opposite hand at 12 o'clock on the opposite wheel.
	3. Pull the extended arm backward while pushing the opposite arm forward and down.
	4. Follow through with the spin by making sure the pulling arm passes top dead center of wheel and remains in contact with the rim as it passes the trunk.
	5. As the pulling hand and arm pass backward, keep the hand in contact with the rim. Use the same arm to initiate a push phase in the new position.

Teaching points	Moving wheelchair pivot (spin)
	1. Start from the same position as the stationary pivot.
	2. As the spin is executed, shift the weight to the intended direction of movement.
	3. Pull back on the wheel and keep the hand in contact with the rim as it passes top dead center, or 12 o'clock.
	4. As the pivot is made, use the pull hand to initiate a new push phase.
	5. People with poor trunk stability should consider using strapping to assist with balance.

Chapter 6

Wheelchair Basketball

Wheelchair basketball is considered the most widely organized and recognized of all the wheelchair sports. The National Wheelchair Basketball Association (NWBA) was founded in 1948 and has continued to grow across all levels of competition. The NWBA is organized into three divisions for men (I, II, III) and additional divisions for women, collegiate, and youth. Currently over 200 teams compete in 22 conferences across the United States. The collegiate division includes such participants as the University of Alabama, Arizona University, Edinboro University of Pennsylvania, University of Illinois, the University of Missouri, Southwest State University in Minnesota, the University of Texas at Arlington, the University of Wisconsin at Whitewater, and Wright State University. More than 25 teams compete in the youth division from several states including Arkansas, California, Minnesota, Missouri, New Jersey, Texas, Washington, and Wisconsin. Wheelchair basketball is also played at the international level as evidenced in the Paralympics and World Championships. The Paralympics are the Olympic-level competition for people with physical and sensory impairments.

DESCRIPTION OF THE SPORT

Wheelchair basketball has many similarities to traditional basketball. It is played on a traditional court using traditional backboards and rims. Players shoot from traditional free-throw and 3-point lines. There are five players per team on the floor at any one time using a traditional-size basketball. The wheelchair is considered part of the player's body. Contact with other players for the purpose of gaining an advantage, such as blocking fouls, charging fouls, and out-of-bounds touches, are considered infractions. The game is started with a jump ball at center circle, and the possession rule follows as in traditional basketball. Time limits for in-bounding the ball and crossing the ball over half court are the same as in traditional basketball. A 35-second shooting clock is used in the men's and women's divisions.

Field of Play

The game is played on a regulation court measuring 94 by 50 feet (29 by 15 m) with a 19-foot-9-inch (6 m) 3-point line. Not all basketball courts measure the same, so you may have to adjust to your facility.

Players

Any person with an irreversible lower-body impairment who cannot play traditional basketball while standing is eligible to compete in wheelchair basketball. People with spinal cord injuries, amputations, polio, and other similar conditions are all eligible to play the game. At the time of this writing the NWBA recognizes three levels of player classification based on the location of the person's impairment. Generally speaking, those with spinal cord injuries in the neck and shoulder region would be in class I. Players with injuries in the upper to lower thorax would be in class II, and those injured from the lower thorax and below would be in class III. For the most part, people in class III are the highest-functioning players, and those in class I are the lowest functioning. However, as of the 2010 NWBA National Championship, the sport is moving to adopt the functional classification system used at the international level of competition. The functional classification system includes part of the former system (location of injury) plus an assessment of the player's skill performance (pushing, stopping, turning, dribbling). Player classification is a factor when fielding a team for an official wheelchair basketball game sponsored by the NWBA. Player classifications are used to define the student functional profiles discussed later in this chapter.

Equipment

A player's wheelchair is considered part of the body. The game is played with a traditional-size basketball for men and a reduced-size basketball for women and youth.

Starting the Game

The game is started with a jump ball at the center circle. Five players are on the floor for each team.

Game Objective

Once the game has been started, the objective is to shoot the ball into the other team's basket. Shots made from the floor are scored as 2 points, as in traditional basketball. Successful free-throw shots are worth 1 point, and all bonus situations related to team fouls are the same. A shot made from beyond the 3-point line is counted as 3 points; however, it would be your decision to use such a shot in your physical education class. The 3-point shot is used in all divisions of the NWBA.

As play continues, each team moves the ball up and down the court in an attempt to either score a basket or stop the opponent. You may consider assigning player positions such as guard, center, and forward as in traditional basketball, but it is not necessary. For the purposes of this book, the recommendation is to provide students with and without disabilities the opportunity to experience the game without an overemphasis on the positions of play.

Defensive positions on the court are usually presented in either a player-to-player defense or a zone format, similar to traditional basketball. One key point related to defensive positions is *transition play*, which is movement from defense to offense, or offense to defense. Teach your students to move as quickly as possible from offense to defense once an opponent has taken a shot. Several of the passing skills mentioned in this chapter, such as the chest, hook, and bounce, will help with that.

Offensive positions on court are also similar to those in traditional basketball. Players at competitive levels try to perfect their shots from a distance of 3 to 6 feet (1 to 1.8 m) from the basket. Because shooting the basketball from more than 12 feet (3.7 m) is very difficult and often unproductive, try to emphasize close-range shooting. Several of the skills presented in this chapter, such as shooting and the bounce stop, should help with this task.

General ball movement is accomplished by dribbling or passing. The pass should be the key method of ball movement. Passing can be effective with the half-court offense or when students must transition from one end of the court to the other. Too much dribbling can be costly, so students should be encouraged to work on passing the ball from player to player. Two additional skills that should help ball movement are the bounce spin and ball retrieval. Both of these skills can be effective either to elude defensive players (bounce spin) or to assist with transition during a turnover by the other team (ball retrieval).

Game Length

The NWBA uses traditional-game length for its competition, generally two 20-minute halves for men, women, and collegiate, and four 6-minute quarters for youth. You may use whatever time allotment works for your situation.

General Rules and Penalties

As previously mentioned, most rules are similar to those of traditional basketball; however, a few are specific to wheelchair basketball.

Rules Specific to Wheelchair Basketball

If a player falls out of the wheelchair, play is continued unless the fall endangers the fallen player or other players. Players who can right themselves without assistance must be allowed to do so; no assistance from a coach is allowed on the floor. For players who cannot right themselves and return to play, play is stopped to allow a coach to assist.

Players may not rise up from the seat to gain an advantage such as attempting to reach for a ball during a rebound. Lifting of the buttocks from the seat to gain an advantage during a game results in a technical foul shot for the opponent.

A player with the ball may not push the wheelchair wheels more than twice in succession with one or both hands without bouncing the ball on the floor again. Taking more than two consecutive pushes while in possession of the ball constitutes a traveling violation. Players may dribble and push the wheelchair simultaneously just as in traditional basketball. Players who are able may execute one push and glide the length of the court while holding the basketball without dribbling, but on the next touch to their handrims, they then have to execute a dribble, pass, or shot. There is no double-dribble rule in wheelchair basketball.

The player or any part of the wheelchair besides the wheels may not come in contact with the floor while the player has possession of the ball. If this occurs, a turnover is awarded. A turnover occurs when a player in possession of the ball somehow tips forward in the wheelchair such that the footplates of the wheelchair make contact with the floor. Also, a player is considered out of bounds if any body part or part of the wheelchair touches the outside of the boundary line.

If a player is positioned in the free-throw lane for longer than four seconds during his team's offensive possession, it is considered a lane violation and the ball is awarded to the other team as a turnover. (A lane violation in traditional basketball is three seconds.)

Summary of the Sport

Table 6.1 provides a quick reference of the elements of the sport of wheelchair basketball.

Table 6.1   Overview of Wheelchair Basketball

Field of play	Basketball court: 94 by 50 ft (29 by 15 m) and no larger than 100 by 50 ft (30 by 15 m)
	Goal height: 10 ft (8.5 ft for youth) (3 m; 2.6 m for youth)
	3-point line: 19 ft 9 in. (6 m)
Players	Maximum allowed on court is five players.
Equipment	Traditional basketball for men
	Traditional basketball for women and youth
Legal start	The game is started with a center jump.
Ball movement	Players may use only their hands to move the ball.
	Players may dribble the ball with one hand.
	Players may not push or touch the handrims more than two consecutive times without dribbling, passing, or shooting the ball.
	More than two consecutive pushes or touches to the handrim without dribbling is considered traveling, which results in a turnover.
	Players may not touch the playing surface while in possession of the ball.
Free throws	All players are on each side of the free-throw lane, with team members alternated. A member of the opposing team must be allowed first position closest to the basket. All lane players can go in upon the release of the shot, but the shooter must wait until the ball touches the rim.
Blocking versus charging	Blocking is a legal move and is defined as any player positioning the wheelchair to impede another player's movement.
	The player must have established position first.
	Charging is an illegal move defined as a collision from any angle in which a player fails to gain position first or fails to control his or her own wheelchair at any time. Players are expected to maintain control of their wheelchairs at all times.
Loss of possession	The following result in the loss of possession to the victimized team:
	• Traveling: More than two consecutive touches to the handrim without a dribble or pass
	• Anytime any part of the wheelchair, other than the wheels, touches the floor
	• Offensive player considered charging another player

SKILLS TO BE TAUGHT

This section will help you establish your teaching emphasis as you read the basic skills necessary to play wheelchair basketball. Six skills could be taught in your physical education class to students with and without disabilities. Notice that the skill of passing has three variations: chest, bounce, and hook. For students with higher function, you may also use a fourth pass called the baseball pass. The baseball pass is presented in chapter 7, Indoor Wheelchair Soccer. Dribbling is also broken down into two types: stationary and continuous. There are also three skills essential to the game of wheelchair basketball that rely on general wheelchair mobility: the bounce stop, the bounce spin, and ball retrieval. It is up to you to decide which skills are within the capabilities of your students with disabilities.

Passing

Following are descriptions of three types of passes used in the game of wheelchair basketball. Teach the skills that are most appropriate given your students' abilities.

Chest Pass

The student places the hands on either side of the ball and then draws the ball into the chest by flexing the elbows. The student then extends the elbows forcefully to pass the ball, turning the thumbs inward and down upon release.

Preparation for two-handed chest pass: eyes on target; elbows flexed.

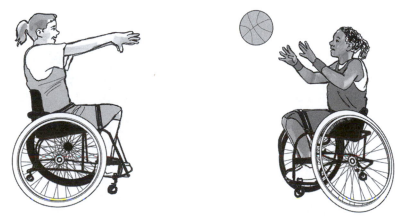

Execution of two-handed chest pass: elbows extended; thumbs point downward.

Bounce Pass

This pass uses the same mechanics as those used in the chest pass, with the following emphasis: the student passes the ball so that the bounce hits a spot on the floor halfway between the student and another student and tries to land the ball in the other student's lap.

Bouncing the ball into a partner's lap.

Hook Pass

This pass is used in a stationary situation when a defensive player is positioned between two offensive players. The offensive player holds the ball in the hand away from the defensive player by extending the arm out and away from the body. The player stabilizes the body by gripping the top of the mainwheel with the hand closest to the defensive player. Using a hooking motion, the player brings the arm with the ball up and over the head so that the elbow of the passing arm strikes the ear upon release of the ball.

Hold the ball up and away from the opponent.

Stabilize the wheelchair with the opposite hand.

Execute the hook pass.

Dribbling

The skill of dribbling is used to move the ball up the court. Two types of dribbling are addressed: stationary and continuous. You will have to decide which dribble addresses your students' levels of functional ability.

Stationary Dribble

Starting from a stationary position, the student bounces and catches the ball with two hands while leaning to one side. Next the student dribbles with one hand while bouncing the ball near the main axle of the wheelchair, controlling each bounce with the fingertips. Once dribbling in a stationary position is established, the student can move forward using an alternating sequence of pushing and dribbling. For example, the student dribbles once and then places the ball in the lap; with the ball in the lap, the student pushes the wheelchair twice and repeats the dribble. The student continues down the floor using this alternating dribble, push-push, dribble sequence, each time placing the ball in the lap.

Stationary one-handed dribble: Bounce near the mainwheel.

Fingertip control.

Control the wheelchair.

Forward dribble. Bounce the ball in front of the main axle using fingertip control.

Dribble; then place the ball in the lap.

With the ball in the lap, begin pushing the wheelchair.

Push the wheelchair. Repeat the dribble up the court.

Continuous Dribble

The student bounces the ball ahead of the wheelchair close to the front wheels or casters and quickly moves the hands to the handrims to push the wheelchair. The student continues dribbling the ball forward of the wheelchair while simultaneously pushing the wheelchair down the floor.

Continuous dribble. Bounce the ball ahead of the wheelchair.

Maintain fingertip control.

Continue dribbling while pushing the wheelchair.

Shooting

Students should master the two-handed shot before moving on to the one-handed shot. With a two-handed shot, the student faces the basket with both hands, holding the ball about chest height with elbows flexed and eyes on the target. As the student initiates the shot, emphasize full elbow extension and follow-through with the hands. The NWBA uses the acronym BEEF, which stands for *balanced* position, *elbows* flexed, *eyes* on target, and *follow* through. The BEEF acronym works for a one-handed shot also.

For a one-handed shot, the student holds the ball in the shooting hand, with the nonshooting hand acting as a support on the opposite side of the ball. Make sure to select a ball that fits the student's hand. The student raises the shooting hand, with elbow and shoulder flexion, to shoulder level and turns slightly in the wheelchair to create an angle by placing the shooting shoulder slightly closer to the basket. The student should extend the elbow fully upon release of the ball toward the basket. Use the cue *Reach into the cookie jar* as the ball is released to encourage proper wrist flexion and follow-through.

Two-handed shot. Elbows flexed; eyes on target.

Full elbow extension upon release.

One-handed shot. Balance the ball using the non-shooting hand to support.

Turn the shooting shoulder closer to the basket.

Extend the elbow upon ball release.

Flex the wrist and "reach into the cookie jar" for follow-through.

Ball Movement

Wheelchair basketball uses many kinds of ball movement similar to those in traditional basketball, including passing, dribbling, and shooting. However, wheelchair basketball has a few ball movement skills that are specific to the game. The following are some of the most important skills that players can add to their repertoires.

Bounce Stop

The bounce stop is used to help the player control the wheelchair while controlling the ball at the same time. The student bounces the ball to the side of the wheelchair in a controlled manner. Beginners should make sure the ball bounces at or above head height. As students skill develops, they may work for lower bounces. As the ball bounces up, the student grabs both handrims to stop the wheelchair. The key here is timing the release of the ball and reaching for the handrims of the wheelchair. The student then pulls back with both hands to stop the wheelchair and catches the ball as it rebounds from the floor. Students should be careful to wrap their fingers around the handrim and not into the spokes as the wheelchair stops. The student then catches the ball with one hand as the wheelchair stops. As students perfect this skill, they can begin to prepare for the bounce spin.

Bounce stop. Prepare to stop the wheelchair with the opposite hand.

Bounce the ball slightly above the head and reach for the handrims.

Stop the wheelchair and catch the ball.

Bounce Spin

The bounce spin is used to elude a defensive player when controlling the ball. The student executes this move by completing a successful bounce stop with a one-handed catch, using the hand on the opposite side of the ball to stop the wheelchair. The hand away from the ball should hold the handrim at 12 o'clock. As the ball hits the floor, the hand on the ball side pulls the handrim backward while the opposite hand pushes forward and down (this will spin the wheelchair). This should be executed as a reciprocal, or push–pull, movement. As the wheelchair spins 180 degrees, the student's feet will pass under the ball at the apex of the bounce, so the opposite arm

Bounce spin. Bounce the ball near the mainwheel axle. Extend elbow upon ball release.

Control the wheelchair with the opposite hand.

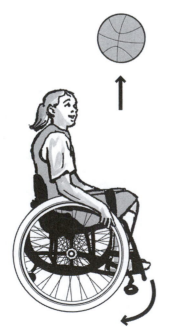

Bounce the ball above the head; pull the ball-side hand back as the ball rises.

Execute the push–pull and spin the wheelchair so that the feet pass under the ball.

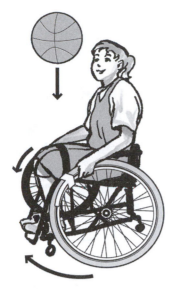

Move the wheelchair so that the opposite arm is closer to the ball.

Catch the ball with the opposite hand.

should be on the ball side ready to make the catch. Timing is key to this maneuver; students should work on staying in control and spinning while the ball is ascending.

Ball Retrieval

The ball retrieval is used to recover a loose ball on the court. While the wheelchair is moving, the student approaches a rolled ball from the side, not directly from behind or in front. Once next to the ball and having aligned the mainwheel with the ball, the student should lean over and pin the ball against the mainwheel with the hand. As the wheelchair continues to move forward, the mainwheel will roll the pinned ball up from the floor to allow the student to secure it in the lap. To help stabilize themselves during this maneuver, students should hold the opposite side of the wheelchair frame or seat-back posts.

Ball retrieval. Approach the ball from the side and align it with the mainwheel axle.

Pin the ball against the mainwheel.

Roll the ball up, keeping pressure against the mainwheel.

Pull the ball into the lap, position the hands on the rims, and push forward.

FUNCTIONAL PROFILES AND GENERAL MODIFICATIONS

Not all students with disabilities will be able to execute these skills as described. Because you cannot match activities or skills within activities to the functional levels of all your students, you will have to make certain modifications.

Student Functional Profiles

Table 6.2 suggests classifications of student profiles that might fit your teaching situation. These functional profiles are operationally defined using a variation of the classification system employed by the NWBA. You will read similar functional profiles later for indoor wheelchair soccer derived from the United States Association of Indoor Wheelchair Soccer (USA-IWS).

Table 6.2 Student Functional Profiles for Wheelchair Basketball

Functional skill level	Student profile
Low	Multiple impairments; unable to manually maneuver a wheelchair; needs assistance positioning in the wheelchair; needs assistance holding a ball; might use a power wheelchair.
Moderate	Able to maneuver a manual wheelchair independently for short distances; can hold a ball independently with two hands; has moderate active range of motion and independent sitting posture.
High	Able to maneuver a manual wheelchair independently for longer distances (30-50 ft; 10-15 m); can hold a basketball independently with one or two hands; has high active range of motion in upper body and independent sitting posture; can move continuously for 10 minutes without stopping.

General Modifications

Table 6.3 provides general modifications to the six skills necessary to play wheelchair basketball. Notice that these modifications are suggested according to the student functional profiles. You have the choice of how to apply these general modifications to your student population.

Table 6.3 General Modifications for Wheelchair Basketball

Skill level	Skill	Activity modifications
Low	Passing	Use a small ball.
	Shooting	Drop the ball in a bucket or hoop lying on the floor. Throw the ball or beanbag through a suspended hoop placed in front at eye level.
	Dribbling	Knock a ball off a table and have it bounce.
	Bounce stop, spin	Pull up next to a small Nerf ball placed on a traffic cone. Place small Nerf ball in lap and spin.
	Ball retrieval	Pull up next to a small Nerf ball placed on a traffic cone and reach to retrieve.
Moderate	Passing	Use a smaller basketball or volleyball.
	Shooting	Shoot into a garbage can. Shoot a volleyball or smaller basketball into a lower basketball goal.
	Dribbling	Use a two-handed dribble.
	Bounce stop, spin	No pressure from opponent during a game.
	Ball retrieval	Use a large playground ball instead of a basketball.
High	All skills	No modifications (used with highest-functioning students).

GAME PROGRESSIONS

The remainder of this chapter presents games you can use with your students with disabilities to teach the various skills described previously. These games are presented by class format (i.e., one on one, small group, large group). Each game description offers ideas for including both students with disabilities and students without disabilities. The one-on-one category is meant for the student with a disability to accomplish with a peer assistant or a teacher. Small group games can engage three to eight students and should include students with and without disabilities. Large group games can engage the entire class working together for a single objective. Games for students with low-functioning profiles are described first, followed by those with moderate- to high-functioning profiles. Specific assessments for skills need to be conducted using the assessment template at the end chapter 4 and on the DVD.

Use the games-by-skill-level indexes to determine which games would be appropriate for your students with disabilities, given their levels of function and skill levels, which you have determined through assessment. Keep in mind that inclusion means trying to address the three domains of learning in physical education: psychomotor, cognitive, and affective.

GAMES-BY-SKILL-LEVEL INDEX: LOW-FUNCTIONING STUDENTS

Table 6.4 is an index of skills and games for low-functioning students. To use the index, simply find the skill to be addressed and cross-reference it with the class format you desire (one on one, small group, or large group). This index is followed by game descriptions for low-functioning students. The index and game descriptions for moderate- to high-functioning students follow those for low-functioning students.

Table 6.4 Games-by-Skill-Level Index for Low-Functioning Students—Wheelchair Basketball

Skills	One on one	Small group	Large group
Passing	Hanging On	Give and Go	Triangle and Go I (Passing)
Shooting	Shot's Away	Pass and Shoot (Shooting)	Triangle and Go II (Shooting)
Dribbling	Right Back at You	Pass and Shoot (Dribbling)	Triangle and Go III (Dribbling)
Bounce stop	Gauntlet I	Gauntlet II	Gauntlet III
Bounce spin	Spinning Wheels I	Spinning Wheels II	Spinning Wheels III
Ball retrieval	Reaching Out I	Reaching Out II	Reaching Out III

GAME DESCRIPTIONS

Each game description in this section includes class format, organizational pattern, equipment, description, extensions, and inclusion suggestions. Extensions are instructional ideas that may be used to modify the activity, however slightly, by either increasing or decreasing the level of difficulty as needed (remember the interaction model from chapter 3). For games that are sequenced, such as Gauntlet I, Gauntlet II, and Gauntlet III, you can start with any game that matches the ability of your students with disabilities based on your assessment results and your teaching situation. You are not bound by the sequence; however, these games are written with the idea of moving a student from a one-on-one format to a large group format.

Skill ▶ Passing

HANGING ON

Class format: One on one

Organizational pattern: Individual with teacher or peer assistant

Equipment: Small Nerf ball, deflated playground ball, Nerf volleyball, or junior basketball

Description: Give the student with a disability the ball and have her hold it as long as possible. See how long the student can hold the ball using one hand. Help her with her grasp as needed. If necessary, the student may use two hands.

Extension: Have the student change the position of the hands and arms (e.g., in front of the body, over head).

Inclusion suggestion: The student can demonstrate to the class her ability to accomplish the task.

GIVE AND GO

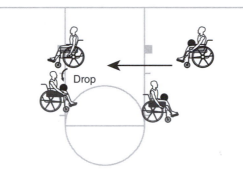

Class format: Small group

Organizational pattern: Two lines facing each other on opposite sides of the free-throw lane

Equipment: Small Nerf ball, deflated playground ball, Nerf volleyball, or junior basketball

Description: One student has a ball and, on a signal, moves across the lane to his partner. Once next to his partner, he drops the ball on the floor next to his partner. Once the ball hits the floor, another ball is placed in the partner's possession and he must move back across the lane.

Extension: Students without disabilities can alternate being partners.

Inclusion suggestions: The student with a disability can decide how many times to pass the ball and must indicate that to the class through his own form of communication. The student can also determine who should start the activity.

TRIANGLE AND GO I (PASSING)

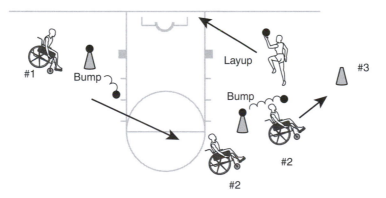

Class format: Large group

Organizational pattern: Triangle formation at least 10 feet (3 m) apart

Equipment: Tall traffic cones, Nerf balls, basketball

Description: Set up three tall traffic cones with large Nerf balls balanced on top of the first two cones. A student with a disability is at each of the first two cones, and a student without a disability is at the third cone with a basketball in hand. The object is to have the first student move forward and bump the ball off the cone to simulate a pass. Once the ball is off and rolling, the first student moves to the next cone. Once the first student arrives at the second cone, the student at that cone continues the activity by bumping off the ball and racing to the third cone, where the student without a disability then dribbles toward the basket for a layup. The activity is then repeated.

Extension: Rotate students with disabilities from cones 1 and 2 to cones 2 and 3, and have a student with a disability shoot by dropping the ball into a bucket. The student without a disability moves to the first cone.

Inclusion suggestions: The student with a disability can keep track of the number of layups made and report the team total to the class. The student can also determine the distance between cones and the distance required for the last person to dribble for the layup.

Skill ▶ Shooting

SHOT'S AWAY

Class format: One on one

Organizational pattern: Individual with peer assistant

Equipment: Small Nerf ball, deflated playground ball, Nerf volleyball, or junior basketball

Description: The student holds a ball and on command drops it into a bucket or hoop placed next to the wheelchair.

Extension: If grasp and release is an issue, physically assist with the release while verbally cueing the student that the "shot is away" as she releases.

Inclusion suggestions: The student with a disability can determine where to place the bucket or the hoop on the ground. She should attempt to move the target to at least three locations.

PASS AND SHOOT (SHOOTING)

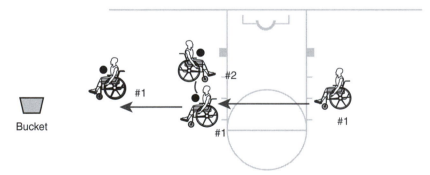

Class format: Small group

Organizational pattern: Same as Give and Go: two lines facing each other on opposite sides of the free-throw lane

Equipment: Small Nerf ball, deflated playground ball, Nerf volleyball, or junior basketball; bucket or hula hoop

Description: On the signal, a student moves across the lane to a partner, who places a ball in his lap if he has the functional ability to do so. The student then continues on to drop the ball into the bucket or hula hoop placed 10 feet (3 m) beyond his partner.

Extension: The student without the ball shouts "Pass" during the exchange. Place a second bucket beyond the partner, and have the student call out which one to shoot at (i.e., left or right).

Inclusion suggestions: The student who passes the ball can call out or somehow indicate which bucket the partner should shoot at. The student must make the call before the partner shoots.

TRIANGLE AND GO II (SHOOTING)

Class format: Large group

Organizational pattern: Refer to Triangle and Go I (Passing).

Equipment: Refer to Triangle and Go I (Passing).

Description: Refer to Triangle and Go I (Passing).

Extension: Challenge each group to complete two rotations before shooting the ball. Have each student complete one rotation clockwise; then the second, counter-clockwise.

Inclusion suggestions: The student with a disability can assign which student in the group takes the shot, track the number of shots made, or name the group after a favorite basketball team.

Skill ▶ Dribbling

RIGHT BACK AT YOU

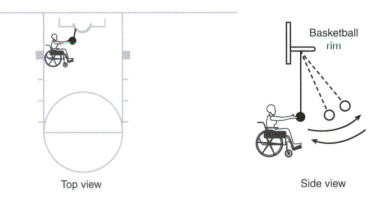

Top view

Side view

Class format: One on one

Organizational pattern: Individual with teacher or peer assistant as needed

Equipment: Elastic band or small rope, playground ball

Description: Tether a playground ball in a net bag to a basketball backboard and allow it to hang at eye level for the student with a disability. The student pushes the ball away and receives it as it returns from the push.

Extension: If grasp and release is an issue, physically assist with an emphasis on opening the hands to receive the ball.

Inclusion suggestions: The student with a disability can pick a peer assistant or select a favorite basketball team to represent during the game, or do both.

PASS AND SHOOT (DRIBBLING)

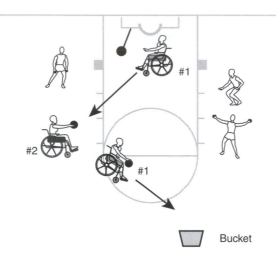

Bucket

Class format: Small group

Organizational pattern: Same as Pass and Shoot (Shooting): two lines facing each other on opposite sides of the free-throw lane. The student with a disability is positioned under the basket with the tethered ball.

Equipment: Small Nerf ball, deflated playground ball, Nerf volleyball, or junior basketball; bucket or hula hoop; rope

Description: On a signal, the student pushes the ball away to simulate a dribble; then moves down the lane to his partner. Once he reaches his partner, a ball is placed in his lap, if appropriate, and he continues on to drop it into a bucket or hoop placed 10 feet (3 m) beyond his partner. (Note: This is the same basic activity as Pass and Shoot [Shooting] with the added tethered ball push.)

Extension: If appropriate, have the student bounce the ball once on the floor after receiving it from his partner and before shooting it into the hoop or bucket.

Inclusion suggestions: The student with a disability can decide what position each student will start in and what signal to use to begin the activity (e.g., a whistle, clap, or shout).

TRIANGLE AND GO III (DRIBBLING)

Class format: Large group

Organizational pattern: Refer to Triangle and Go I and II (Passing and Shooting).

Equipment: Refer to Triangle and Go I and II (Passing and Shooting).

Description: Refer to Triangle and Go I and II (Passing and Shooting).

Extension: Challenge each group to complete two rotations before shooting the ball. Have each group complete one rotation clockwise; then the second, counterclockwise. Emphasize dribbling from spot to spot.

Inclusion suggestions: The student with a disability can assign which student in the group takes the shot, track the number of shots made, or name the group after a favorite basketball team. The student could also determine the distance between cones and the distance required for the last person to dribble in for the layup.

Skill ▶ Bounce Stop

 GAUNTLET I

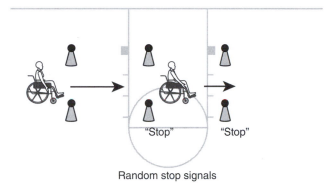

Random stop signals

Class format: One on one

Organizational pattern: Individual with teacher or peer assistant as needed. Set up two parallel rows of five or six tall traffic cones with approximately 6 feet (1.8 m) between cones. Buckets placed on top of folding chairs will also work. Place a ball or some other object that will balance on top of each of the cones (beanbags work well).

Equipment: Traffic cones, folding chairs, Nerf balls or beanbags

Description: The student is between the rows so that one row is on the student's right and one is on the left. The object is to have the student pass through the gauntlet and be able to stop next to a cone when signaled. To start, the student moves forward as fast as possible through the gauntlet. In response to a random stop signal, the student stops next to the closest cone.

Extension: Once the student has mastered a controlled stop, allow her to pass through, varying her speed and the cone to stop next to (e.g., every other cone or every third cone).

Inclusion suggestions: The student with a disability can decide the pattern of stopping and starting next to a cone. She can also pick the side of the cone to stop next to (left or right); then identify the side of the cone she is on (e.g., "I am on the right side").

GAUNTLET II

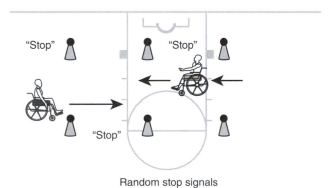

Random stop signals

Class format: Small group

Organizational pattern: Same as Gauntlet I

Equipment: Same as Gauntlet I

Description: Two students move through the activity. Students could be positioned at opposite ends of the gauntlet moving toward each other or facing the same direction in parallel formation.

Extension: If you use a student without a disability as the second student, that student can dribble a basketball while moving. If appropriate, the student with a disability can carry a ball while moving through.

Inclusion suggestions: The student with a disability can decide the sequence of stopping (e.g., every other cone or every third cone). The student can also control the starting and stopping signal as two students without disabilities move through the gauntlet.

GAUNTLET III

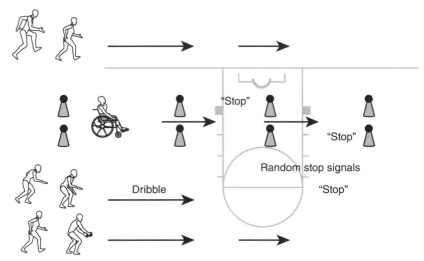

Class format: Large group

Organizational pattern: Same as Gauntlet I and II, with an increase to three lines for students without disabilities

Equipment: Same as Gauntlet I and II

Description: Students without disabilities are in three lines near the gauntlet, each with basketballs ready to dribble, while the student with a disability is positioned in the middle of the activity. At the start signal, the student with a disability moves forward through the gauntlet, and the students without disabilities move forward dribbling. Each time the stop signal is given, the student with a disability stops at the appropriate cone, and the students without disabilities stop and perform a stationary dribble. The object of the activity is to get all students moving across the floor together as a team.

Extension: The student with a disability changes sides of the gauntlet with each stop (e.g., stop on left, then on right, then on left, and so on).

Inclusion suggestions: The student with a disability can stop at the cones of his choice, and the entire class must watch him as he moves across the floor and stop in unison with him as they continue to move.

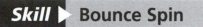

SPINNING WHEELS I

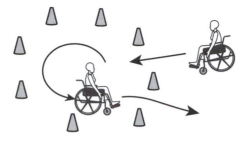

Class format: One on one

Organizational pattern: A circle of traffic cones approximately 10 feet (3 m) in diameter

Equipment: Traffic cones, basketball or Nerf ball

Description: The student with a disability is about 6 feet (1.8 m) from the circle with a ball secured in her lap. On the signal, the student moves forward into the circle and performs a 360-degree spinning motion within the boundaries of the circle. Once the spin is complete, the student moves out of the circle and returns to the starting position.

Extension: Place a single cone on the floor approximately 10 feet (3 m) from the starting position, and allow the student with a disability to move forward with a ball and complete a 360-degree spin around the cone.

Inclusion suggestions: The student with a disability can demonstrate this skill to the class. Consider replacing the circle of cones with a circle of classmates, and encourage students to reinforce performance.

SPINNING WHEELS II

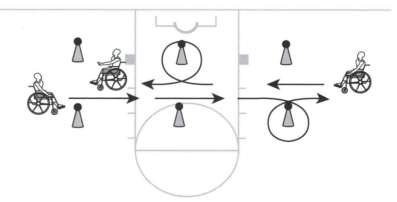

Class format: Small group

Organizational pattern: Same as Gauntlet I

Equipment: Same as Gauntlet I

Description: Using the formation from Gauntlet I, the students move through the gauntlet, stopping at the designated cone as described earlier. This time, when students stop at the cone, they must spin their wheelchairs around the cone once before continuing on to the next cone. If two students have started on opposite ends of the gauntlet, make sure to allow enough room for circling the cones.

Extension: Replace cones in the gauntlet with students from the class.

Inclusion suggestion: The student with a disability can predict (if appropriate) how much time it will take to complete the gauntlet.

SPINNING WHEELS III

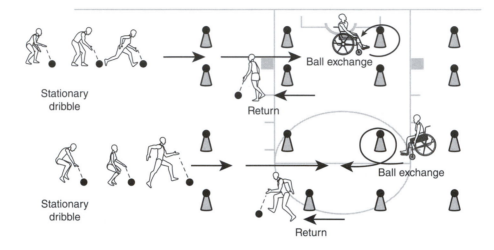

Class format: Large group

Organizational pattern: Same as Gauntlet I. Create two teams, each with students with and without disabilities ready to race each through their own gauntlets.

Equipment: Traffic cones, Nerf balls or beanbags, basketballs

Description: Equally divide the students with disabilities on each team, and place them in the gauntlet next to a designated cone. Students without disabilities form a line ready to dribble through the gauntlet. Each student waiting in line must have a ball. On the signal, the first student dribbles to the student with a disability and places the ball in his lap. Once the ball is secured, the student spins around his cone once and returns the ball to the first student. The student without a disability retrieves the ball and dribbles back to the starting line, where the next student repeats the movement. While the first student is moving through the gauntlet, the remaining students are performing a stationary dribble while waiting their turn. The activity is over when the last student passes through the gauntlet.

Extensions: Increase or decrease the distance to the first student with a disability according to the skill level of the students without disabilities. Repeat the activity, having the students without disabilities use their nondominant hands.

Inclusion suggestion: Students with disabilities can determine the order of rotation for their teams; that is, they can decide who gets to go first, second, and so on.

Skill ▶ Ball Retrieval

REACHING OUT I

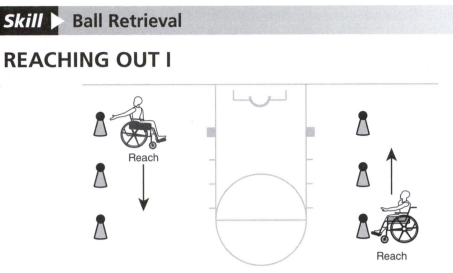

Class format: One on one

Organizational pattern: Set up a row of five or six tall traffic cones or folding chairs approximately 6 feet (1.8 m) apart. Place a ball or some other object that will balance on top of the cones or folding chairs (beanbags work well).

Equipment: Traffic cones or folding chairs, beanbags or Nerf balls

Description: The student with a disability is next to the cones or chairs and reaches to the side in an attempt to retrieve or touch the object, depending on her functional level.

Extension: Make sure to work both right- and left-side retrieval skills.

Inclusion suggestion: Replace cones with students without disabilities.

REACHING OUT II

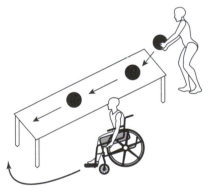

Class format: Small group

Organizational pattern: Place two long benches or tables in parallel formation wide enough to support a playground ball placed in the space created by the two benches or tables without falling through.

Equipment: Basketballs or Nerf balls, two long benches or folding tables

Description: A student without a disability is at one end of the benches ready to roll the ball forward. A student with a disability is next to the benches, ready to move forward. On a signal, the student without a disability rolls the ball forward down the benches while the student with a disability also moves forward and attempts to stop the ball before it reaches the other end.

Extension: Repeat for the right- and left-side retrieval skills.

Inclusion suggestions: The student with a disability can initiate rolling the ball to be retrieved by the student without a disability. The student with a disability can also decide how many times he must complete the activity before rotating out of the activity.

REACHING OUT III

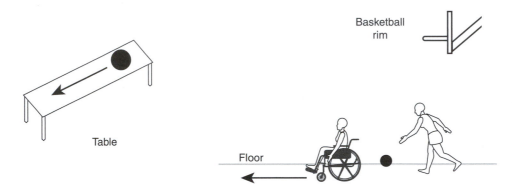

Class format: Large group

Organizational pattern: Same as Reaching Out II

Equipment: Same as Reaching Out II

Description: This time, remove the benches and roll the ball on a long folding table or on the floor. When rolling the ball on a table, make sure to allow enough room for the student with a disability to move next to the table safely. Try to use a ball that rolls with more control, such as a slightly deflated basketball, soccer ball, or playground ball.

Extension: Have a student without a disability roll the ball on the floor so the student with a disability can position next to the rolling ball to slow it down to a stop. Then reach over and touch the ball on the floor. Once this is done, have the student with a disability position the wheelchair in order to bump the ball forward on the floor to initiate a roll. As the ball begins to roll, the student without a disability runs forward, picks the ball up, and initiates a second roll for the student with a disability. This alternating progression can occur around the gymnasium floor in a continuous pattern.

Inclusion suggestions: The student with a disability can determine the distance the ball should be rolled when using the floor for retrieval. The student can also determine the number of times each team should retrieve the ball before changing positions.

GAMES-BY-SKILL-LEVEL INDEX: MODERATE- TO HIGH-FUNCTIONING STUDENTS

The index in table 6.5 addresses students with disabilities who are considered to have moderate to high functional ability. Remember that you will need to assess individual skill performance.

Table 6.5 Games-by-Skill-Level Index for Moderate- to High-Functioning Students—Wheelchair Basketball

Skills	One on one	Small group	Large group
Passing	Target Toss	Remember Me	Call It Out
Shooting	Spinning the Ball	In the Bucket	At the Hoop
Dribbling	Stationary	On the Move I	On the Move II
Bounce stop	Stop the Music I	Stop the Music II	Stop the Music III
Bounce spin	Crossover	Spin City I	Spin City II
Ball retrieval	Reach for It	Down and Back	Giddy Up

GAME DESCRIPTIONS

Eighteen games designed for moderate- to high-functioning students are described in the following section. Modify these games as needed for your teaching situation.

Skill ▶ Passing (for Chest, Bounce, Hook)

TARGET TOSS

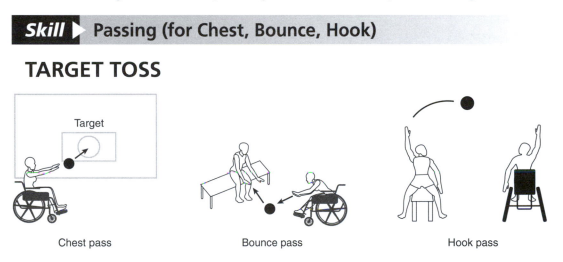

Chest pass   Bounce pass   Hook pass

Class format: One on one

Organizational pattern: Individual with teacher or peer assistant

Equipment: Basketball, targets for wall, cones for distance markers

Description: Position a student with the ball, making sure to review each of the key points for executing the chest, bounce, and hook passes. For the chest pass, place a target on the wall (e.g., a 2-foot-diameter, or 0.6-meter-diameter, circle) and have the student with a disability pass the ball into the target from a distance of 3 to 4 feet (1 to 1.2 m). For the bounce pass, position a partner about 6 to 8 feet (1.8 to 2.4 m) away facing the student with the ball. Review the cues for the bounce pass and have the partners pass back and forth. For the hook pass, use the same position as the bounce pass, except turn the partners sideways so that each player's dominant side is away from the partner before performing the pass.

Extensions: For the bounce pass, have a student without a disability sit on a bench or in a folding chair. For the hook pass, higher-skilled students can try passing with the nondominant hand.

Inclusion suggestions: The student with a disability can demonstrate to the class his ability to accomplish the activity and determine three new distances for the target. The student can also determine two additional skills to be added to this activity. Use students without disabilities as assistants for retrieving and providing appropriate feedback.

REMEMBER ME

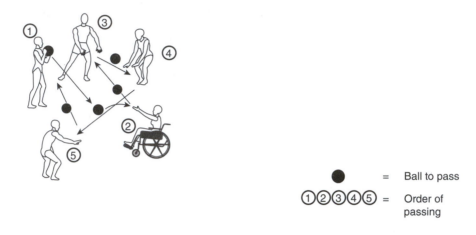

● = Ball to pass

①②③④⑤ = Order of passing

Class format: Small group

Organizational pattern: Position students with and without disabilities in a small circle with one ball per circle.

Equipment: Basketball, Nerf ball, or Nerf volleyball

Description: On a signal, the students use a chest pass to move the ball back and forth across and around the circle. The object of the activity is to pass the ball around the circle in the same sequence as the original pattern, meaning that once the ball has been passed around the circle and everyone has touched it, the second time around should follow the same pattern with students passing to the same people each time.

Extensions: Change the type of pass used. For example, for the first two trips students can use the chest pass, for the next two the bounce pass, and so on. For students who have difficulty catching a basketball, change the type of ball or change the distance needed to pass for success.

Inclusion suggestion: Students with disabilities can determine the sequence of passes (e.g., chest to bounce or bounce to hook).

CALL IT OUT

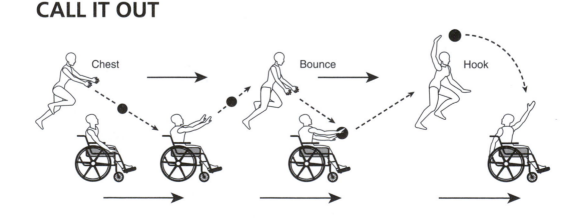

Chest   Bounce   Hook

Class format: Large group

Organizational pattern: Students are in parallel line formation opposite a partner. This is a dynamic formation with students moving forward in pairs as they pass the ball. Students with and without disabilities should be paired up.

Equipment: Basketball, playground ball, or Nerf ball

Description: Each set of partners has a ball and on the signal must move forward across the floor, passing the ball as they move. Students must stay about 15 to 20 feet (4.6 to 6 m) apart and keep the ball ahead of their partners. Change the type of pass every two or three trips down the floor by calling out a new pass (e.g., chest pass, bounce pass, hook pass). The objective is to get students to complete one trip without a miss using each of the passes presented.

Extensions: For students with varying degrees of manual wheelchair propulsion, consider changing the type of ball used to pass or the distance passed.

Inclusion suggestion: The student with a disability can call out the pass to be executed.

Skill ▶ **Shooting**

SPINNING THE BALL

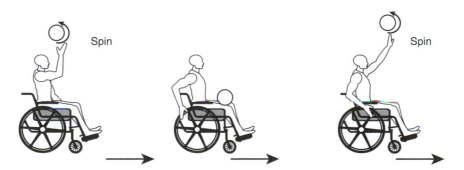

Spin   Spin

Class format: One on one

Organizational pattern: Individual with teacher or peer assistant as needed

Equipment: Basketball, playground ball, or Nerf volleyball

Description: The purpose of this activity is to allow the student with moderate functional ability to practice ball release when shooting a basketball. Using the key teaching points presented earlier, have the student balance a basketball in the shooting hand with the shooting arm up overhead. From this position, have the student flex the elbow and wrist while releasing the ball from the hand and putting a rotation, or spin, on the ball. Emphasize spinning the ball upon release with the cue *Reach into the cookie jar.*

Extension: Change the size of the ball if the student is unable to control a basketball. A Nerf volleyball and a soccer ball are good alternatives.

Inclusion suggestions: The student with a disability can demonstrate his skill level, if appropriate, or teach a small group of students without disabilities the key teaching points.

IN THE BUCKET

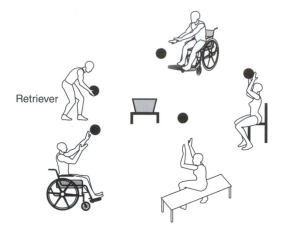

Retriever

Class format: Small group

Organizational pattern: Position students with and without disabilities in a small circle, each with a basketball. Place a plastic garbage can or large barrel on a small table in the center of the circle approximately 4 to 6 feet (1.2 to 1.8 m) from the students.

Equipment: Basketball, table, chairs or benches, bucket or garbage can

Description: On a signal, students practice their shooting skills into the garbage can or barrel. Designate one student to retrieve the balls from the bucket, and have students without disabilities shoot from a seated position on chairs or benches.

Extension: Vary the height of the garbage can or barrel by placing it either on the floor, on a small table, or on the stage or a volleyball referee's stand.

Inclusion suggestions: The student with a disability can report to you the path of the shot (e.g., short or long, left or right). The student can also select which type of ball to shoot for the group.

AT THE HOOP

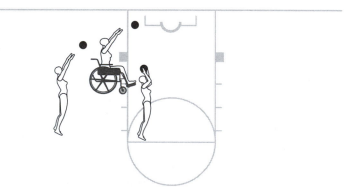

Class format: Large group

Organizational pattern: Position students with and without disabilities approximately 3 feet (1 m) from a traditional basketball backboard and rim.

Equipment: Basketball, regulation backboard and rim

Description: Students shoot at the hoop using the teaching points presented. Teamwork can be accomplished by playing several games such as HORSE or Around the World. Teamwork can also be accomplished by combining this game with Call It Out.

Extension: Students with and without disabilities could form teams that shoot at the basket, rebound the ball, and move down the court to the opposite basket while practicing passing.

Inclusion suggestion: The student with a disability can create one alternative to this activity and present it to the group.

Skill ▶ **Dribbling**

STATIONARY

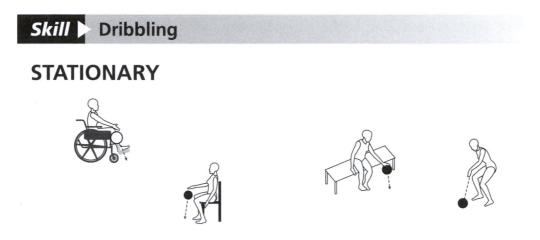

Class format: One on one

Organizational pattern: Individual with teacher or peer assistant as needed

Equipment: Basketball or 10-inch (25 cm) playground ball, folding chairs or benches

Description: The purpose of this activity is to allow the student with moderate or high functional ability to practice dribbling the ball in a stationary position.

Extensions: Students with less functional ability could start with a two-handed bounce and catch while leaning to the side of the wheelchair. Also, students who have difficulty controlling a regulation basketball could use a large playground ball. Students without disabilities could be included in this activity by placing folding chairs or benches in the same area and having them participate from a seated position.

Inclusion suggestion: The student with a disability could decide a set number of successful dribbles to accomplish before changing hands (e.g., 10 with the right hand and then 10 with the left).

ON THE MOVE I

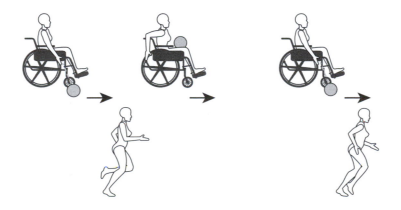

Class format: Small group

Organizational pattern: The student with a disability is partnered with a student without a disability in a side-by-side formation, facing the same direction and ready to move across the gym floor.

Equipment: Basketball or 10-inch (25 cm) playground ball, cones

Description: The student with a disability pushes forward in his wheelchair while carrying the ball in his lap. Once he is moving, he dribbles using one hand while controlling the wheelchair. He can return the ball to his lap after traveling 15 feet (4.6 m). A student without a disability walks next to the wheelchair to help with errant dribbling. Have the students continue the activity across the gymnasium floor. On the return trip, the student without a disability performs the dribble using proper techniques, and the student with a disability serves as the assistant to recover errant dribbles.

Extension: Increase the difficulty of this activity by placing traffic cones in a line about 6 to 8 feet (1.8 to 2.4 m) apart, and instruct the students to dribble in a weave pattern in and out among the cones.

Inclusion suggestions: A student without a disability performs the dribble in both directions while the student with a disability critiques her movements. At the end of both trips across the gym, the student with a disability shares which aspects look correct and which need work. The two students then reverse rolls and repeat the activity.

ON THE MOVE II

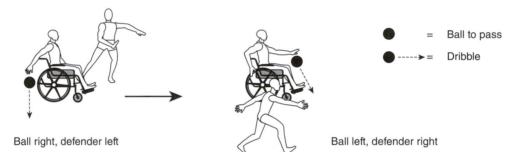

Ball right, defender left

Ball left, defender right

● = Ball to pass

● ----▶ = Dribble

Class format: Large group

Organizational pattern: Same as On the Move I

Equipment: Basketball or 10-inch (25 cm) playground ball

Description: In this activity the student without a disability challenges the dribble by representing a defender and changing positions next to the wheelchair. With each attempt at dribbling, the student with a disability must keep the ball on the opposite side of the wheelchair away from the defender. That is, as the student with a disability dribbles the ball on the right side, the defender should be on the left; and as the defender switches to the other side, so should the dribble. Once the students become efficient, you might consider some form of relay activity.

Extension: Try this activity in a stationary formation before having students move across the gym floor.

Inclusion suggestions: The student with a disability can decide who starts first with the ball. The student can also count successful switches from side to side and report the count to you.

Skill ▶ Bounce Stop

STOP THE MUSIC I

Class format: One on one

Organizational pattern: The purpose of the Stop the Music activities is to have students progress from working one on one to working in small groups and then large groups. The basic concept of Stop the Music is to allow students to move freely or in an organized pattern while dribbling the basketball with the music playing. Once the music stops, the students should perform a bounce stop using the cues provided earlier.

Equipment: Basketball or 10-inch (25 cm) playground ball, music player

Description: Students with and without disabilities each have a ball to dribble. On a signal, the student with a disability moves about the gymnasium, performing a lap or push dribble while students without disabilities walk, jog, or run dribbling a basketball. Stop the music randomly. When the music stops, all students perform the bounce stop as instructed. Students without disabilities would pick up their balls and assume a basic basketball position with a slight bend at the waist, knees bent, weight evenly distributed, and eyes forward.

Extension: Students with less functional ability could start with the two-handed bounce and catch while leaning to the side of the wheelchair.

Inclusion suggestion: The student with a disability can decide a set number of dribbles to accomplish before changing hands (e.g., 10 with the right hand, then 10 with the left).

STOP THE MUSIC II

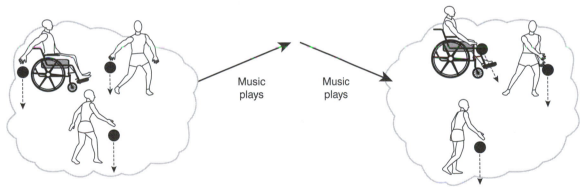

Class format: Small group

Organizational pattern: Performed as in Stop the Music I; however, this time students are in small groups around the gymnasium.

Equipment: Basketball or 10-inch (25 cm) playground ball, music player, cones

Description: The objective of the activity is to get the small group to travel together around the gymnasium while dribbling basketballs to the music. Once the music stops, the students should perform a bounce stop or assume a basic basketball-ready position.

Extension: Increase the difficulty of this activity by placing traffic cones around the gym to be avoided by the groups.

Inclusion suggestion: The student with a disability can call out or somehow indicate which hand to dribble with (e.g., "Right-hand dribble, now switch to left").

STOP THE MUSIC III

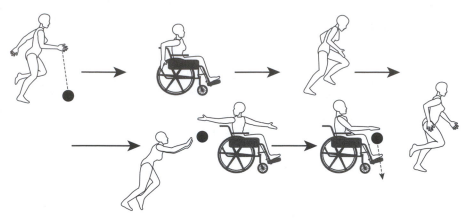

Class format: Large group

Organizational pattern: Have students form two or three lines (depending on the size of the class) trying to alternate a student with a disability and a student without a disability in each line. Spread the lines out so that students are about 10 feet (3 m) apart and all facing the same direction.

Equipment: Basketball or 10-inch (25 cm) playground ball, music player

Description: Place one basketball with the player at the back of each line. The objective of the activity is to have each student move forward dribbling the ball until they reach the student in front of them. At that point the student must perform a bounce stop under control, then pass the ball to the teammate, who continues on to the next teammate. If the music stops before a student reaches a teammate, that student must perform the bounce stop in place. As the music continues, so should the activity.

Extensions: Increase or decrease the distance between teammates. Play music with varying tempos.

Inclusion suggestion: The student with a disability can select the music.

Skill ▶ Bounce Spin

CROSSOVER

Class format: One on one

Organizational pattern: The student can work alone using a peer to help retrieve the missed played balls.

Equipment: Basketball or 10-inch (25 cm) playground ball

Description: Use all the cues suggested earlier in this chapter for the bounce spin. Allow students with less function to use two hands during the bounce-and-catch phase of the skill. Students without disabilities could be positioned next to the student with a disability to help with errant bounce spins.

Extensions: Allow students without disabilities to perform the crossover dribble maneuver used in regulation basketball. Students with less functional ability could start with the two-handed bounce and catch while leaning to the side of the wheelchair.

Inclusion suggestion: The student with a disability can decide a set number of bounce spins or crossover dribbles to be accomplished by the class.

SPIN CITY I

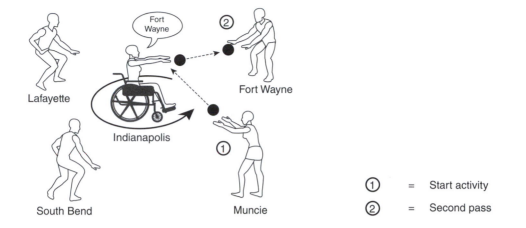

①	=	Start activity
②	=	Second pass

Class format: Small group

Organizational pattern: Students are in small circle formations around the gymnasium with one student in the middle.

Equipment: Basketball or 10-inch (25 cm) playground ball

Description: Each circle represents a state within the United States (e.g., Indiana). Each member of the circle represents a city in the state (e.g., Muncie), and the person in the middle represents the capital of the state (e.g., Indianapolis). Place a ball with any city within the state and have that person pass the ball to the capital. Once the person in the middle catches the ball, she must perform a bounce spin and pass the ball to a new city. As she passes the ball to a new city, she must call the name of the city out loud before passing it. As the new city catches the ball, she must in turn perform a bounce spin and pass it back to the capital. The activity continues until all cities have been called. Students without disabilities should perform a crossover dribble or another skill that you select.

Extension: Change the theme of the activity to use the names of universities within states or the names of automobiles within manufacturers.

Inclusion suggestion: The student with a disability can select the new category (e.g., cars, planes, boats).

SPIN CITY II

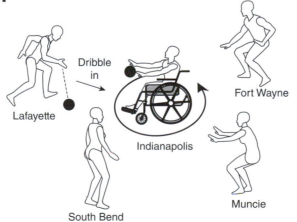

Class format: Large group

Organizational pattern: Same formation as Spin City I

Equipment: Basketball or 10-inch (25 cm) playground ball

Description: Same as Spin City I except that students get the ball to the capital by dribbling into the center instead of passing it in. The bounce spin is still performed by the person receiving the ball.

Extensions: To create more of a teamwork emphasis, increase the number of balls per state and allow any city to move forward in random order rather than sequentially around the circle. Increase or decrease the distance between teammates.

Inclusion suggestion: The student with a disability can determine which hand everyone should be dribbling with.

Skill ▶ Ball Retrieval

REACH FOR IT

Class format: One on one

Organizational pattern: Individual with teacher or peer assistant as needed

Equipment: Basketball or 10-inch (25 cm) playground ball

Description: Place a ball next to the mainwheel of the wheelchair and have the student shift his weight to the side the ball is on, support the shift with the opposite arm, and lean over to reach for the ball. Once he has the ball under control, he should initiate a small push with the opposite arm to move the wheelchair forward while pressing the ball against the mainwheel of the wheelchair. As the wheel turns forward, it should bring the ball up to the student's lap for retrieval.

Extension: The student should practice retrieving on both the left and right sides.

Inclusion suggestion: The student can demonstrate his skills to the class when appropriate.

DOWN AND BACK

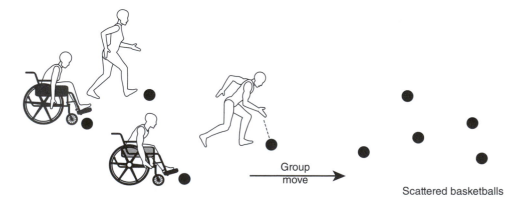

Group move

Scattered basketballs

Class format: Small group

Organization pattern: Students with and without disabilities work together in this activity. Place students in small groups scattered around the gymnasium.

Equipment: Basketballs, playground balls, or Nerf volleyballs

Description: Place as many basketballs or other balls as possible on the floor around the gymnasium. Try to have one for each student. On a signal, students move as a group to the basketballs. Once they have retrieved a ball, they move as a group to reposition the basketballs by dribbling to a new location. Emphasis is on ball retrieval. Once the group has moved to a new location, students must place the balls on the ground and be ready to repeat the activity. Groups must move at least 10 feet (3 m) to a new location.

Extensions: Change the distance between groups or between placement of the basketballs.

Inclusion suggestion: The student with a disability can determine the new location of movement.

GIDDY UP

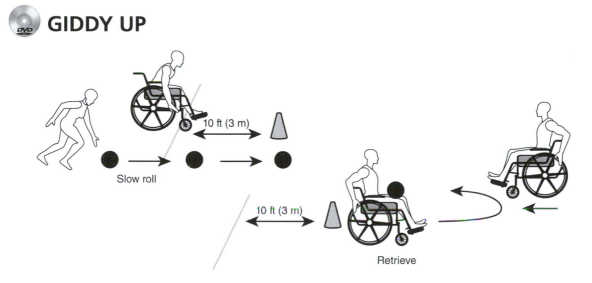

Class format: Large group

Organizational pattern: Students are in line formation. Try to alternate a student with a disability with a student without a disability in each line.

Equipment: Basketball or 10-inch (25 cm) playground ball, cones

Description: Place a basketball with the second person in line and instruct her to roll the ball forward, *slowly,* at the start signal. Place a cone about 10 feet (3 m) in front of each line to serve as a target for the person rolling the ball. The objective of the activity is to have the first person in line retrieve the ball once it has passed the cone. The retriever cannot move until the ball has passed the cone. Once the ball has been retrieved, that person returns it to her team, passing it to the second person in line. Once the second person has the ball, the activity is repeated. Continue until all students have been a roller and a retriever.

Extensions: Change the size of the ball, the weight of the ball, or the distance to the cone. Students with limited mobility might be positioned in the retrieval position and have the ball rolled to them, thus eliminating the mobility component.

Inclusion suggestion: The student with a disability can determine the order of performance for her team.

Remember that blank forms for assessments, IEPs, and unit and lesson plans are located on the DVD.

Chapter 7

Indoor Wheelchair Soccer

Indoor wheelchair soccer is a sport that is sanctioned by the United States Association of Indoor Wheelchair Soccer (USA-IWS). Each year for the past 18 years, more than 10 teams from around the United States have traveled to play in national championships. Each team carries approximately nine players, plus coaches and managers. The national championships have been hosted in Houston, Texas; San Diego, California; Atlanta, Georgia; Springfield, Massachusetts; and New London, Connecticut.

In 2003 this sport introduced a functional classification system blending all physical disabilities into five class groups: cerebral palsy and head injury, neuromuscular, bone and joint such as arthrogryposis, spinal cord injured, and amputation. The system is inclusionary bringing all disabilities together over the full range of ability, from the player in a power wheelchair, to someone with a single-leg amputation using a manual wheelchair. The system delivers parity within each class assuming all players are elite level. This parity can break down when mixing skilled players with those considered novice.

DESCRIPTION OF THE SPORT

Indoor wheelchair soccer is similar to traditional soccer because its rules were modified in 1996 after indoor soccer. The sport dates back to the early 1980s when it was played with 22 players on the floor (nine players and two goalies on each team). Although the USA-IWS has authored an extensive number of rules, only those rules considered essential to the game are presented here.

Field of Play

The game is played on a court the size of a high school basketball court, using a 10-inch (25 cm) yellow playground ball. You will be limited to the space available in your school's facility, so feel free to modify as needed. See figure 7.1 for the court diagram.

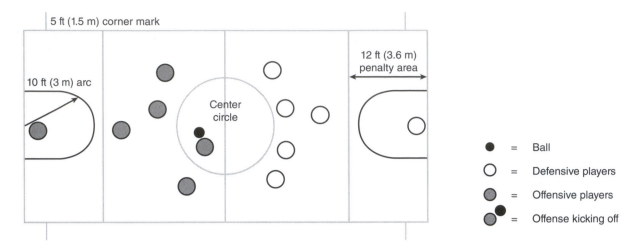

Figure 7.1 Indoor wheelchair soccer court.

Players

There are two teams of no more than six and no fewer than four players. A setup of one goalkeeper and three floor players offers an exciting game useful in teaching fundamentals. The number of players on the floor will depend on your facility and class size; use whatever works best for you.

Equipment

A 10-inch (25 cm) utility ball with a bladder is preferred. You may, however, use whatever ball works best for your situation; programs use volleyballs, beach balls, and small cage balls. For safety, use balls that are soft and cushiony on impact.

Starting the Game

The game is started with a kickoff at center court. The teams are lined up facing each other about 15 feet (4.6 m) apart until the ball has been moved by an offensive player one complete circumference (i.e., a pass to a teammate). If you do not have 15 feet available, allow enough distance for a suitable kickoff procedure.

Game Objective

Once the game has been started, the objective is to get the ball completely into the opponents' net, just as in outdoor soccer. The majority of ball movement is performed by throwing and catching; however, players who cannot throw and catch are allowed to use the lower extremities to move the ball. Therefore, a goal may be scored by throwing or kicking the ball completely into the opponents' goal. The goals in an official game are made of plastic or metal and stand 5 feet 6 inches (1.7 m) high and 5 feet (1.5 m) wide, with a 4-foot (1.2 m) depth. In your physical education class you may mark an area of compatible goal width using folding chairs or gymnastics mats.

As play continues, each team tries to maneuver up and down the court, passing the ball into position to shoot at the goal. Once a player has control of the ball, he has three seconds to pass, dribble, or shoot. A player may move the ball up the court using a continuous dribble, or he may dribble once, place the ball in his lap, and push his wheelchair forward without dribbling. If he uses this latter form of ball movement, he must dribble again or pass the ball within three seconds of the time he places the ball in his lap. The three-second infraction results in a side-out, or turnover.

The ball is always considered to be in play. It must go completely past a sideline or end line to be considered out of bounds. If a ball is ruled out of bounds, the player in-bounding the ball must use a two-handed overhead throwing motion to return the ball to play. The player has five seconds to in-bound the ball, and all defensive and offensive players must allow that player a 3-foot (1 m) area during the throw. If the ball is in-bounded and travels across the court without being touched by another player, the ball is returned to the in-bounding site and awarded as a turnover to be in-bounded by the opponent. A goal cannot be scored off a direct in-bound play without the ball touching another player.

Goals may be scored from anywhere on the court. Goals are not allowed if they are the result of a direct kick from a kickoff play or a sideline throw-in without touching another offensive or defensive player. Goals count as 1 point. The goal area directly in front of the net cannot be penetrated by either the offensive or defensive team. This area should be considered similar to the crease area in hockey, which means that the only players allowed in this area are the goalies for each team. The goal area is marked by a 10-foot-deep (3 m) arc sweeping from the center point of the end line. At 12 feet (3.7 m) from the end line and crossing from one side of the court to the other is the penalty shot line. It serves two purposes; one is to determine for the referee when a personal foul results in a penalty shot (e.g., penalties inside the line result in teams taking penalty shots). The second purpose is to serve as the shooting line for the penalty shot described in the General Results and Penalties section. See the court diagram in figure 7.1 for specific details.

Game Length

Official games are 50 minutes long, with two 25-minute halves and a 15-minute interval between halves. Obviously, the length of time will be dictated by the time available in your schedule. Each team is allowed two time-outs per half, but again, you may create any rule that fits your program needs (e.g., a running clock).

General Rules and Penalties

Penalties in the game result in a penalty shot. During the penalty shot, all players except the shooter and the defensive goalkeeper must line up at the center court line. The shooter lines up at center court in the jump ball circle. When the referee hands the player the ball, the shooter has 10 seconds to attack the goalkeeper without turning around (back facing the goalkeeper) and without touching the 12-foot (3.7 m) line. If the shooter violates the 12-foot line before any shot is attempted, a side-out or throw-in is awarded to the defense. If the shooter does not score, the defense is awarded a side-out. If the shooter scores on the penalty shot, a kickoff follows.

Several violations result in a penalty shot. Again, for the sake of easing the implementation of the game in your program, I recommend that you enforce two basic infractions. A penalty should be called if a player does not maintain control of the wheelchair, which results in ramming another player. A second infraction that should be enforced is grabbing an opponent during a shot on goal. Indoor wheelchair soccer can be an aggressive game. Because players are allowed to reach and grab for the ball as it is moved up and down the court, you will need to develop a set of safety rules specific to your situation.

Finally, indoor wheelchair soccer has a system of time penalties similar to those in soccer, using a series of colored cards indicating the severity of the infraction. Blue cards are for all personal fouls, team time penalties, and poor sporting behavior. Yellow cards are used as a warning that a player's next penalty will result in ejection, and red cards are used for ejection. Each violation results in players receiving timed penalties in the penalty box area as in soccer (e.g., player misconduct gets two minutes, poor sporting behavior gets two minutes).

Remember that in a physical education class you are trying to increase playing time and participation. Although it is important to ensure that your students are safe, an overemphasis on rules and infractions will take playing time away from your class members.

Summary of the Sport

Table 7.1 provides an overview of indoor wheelchair soccer. This quick reference will help you learn how to play the game.

Table 7.1 Overview of Indoor Wheelchair Soccer

Field of play	Basketball court: 94 by 50 ft (29 by 15 m) and no larger than 100 by 50 ft (30 by 15 m)
	Goal area: 10 ft (3 m) arc center of goal area
	Goals: 5 ft 6 in. (1.7 m) high and 5 ft (1.5 m) wide (can be made of wood, plastic, or metal)
	Penalty shot line: 12 feet (3.7 m) from the basketball end line in front of the goal
Players	Maximum allowed on court is six players.
Equipment	10 in. (25 cm) utility ball with unwound bladder inflated to 2 psi.
	All players must play in wheelchairs. Motorized scooters are not allowed in an official competition.
	Foot platform heights, at the forward point, cannot be more than 4 3/4 in. (12 cm) from the floor for safety reasons.
	All wheelchairs must have straps extending from one side of the chair to the other, behind the players legs, 6 in. (15 cm) above the platforms.
Legal start	A legal start is conducted when an offensive player takes the ball inside the center circle and moves it the distance of its own circumference in a direction parallel to or behind the center line. At least one player must touch the ball before a goal can be scored.
	If an offensive player commits a violation prior to the kicker's initial movement, the kickoff is awarded to the opposing team. If the defense commits a violation, the kickoff is repeated.
Ball in play	The ball is in play at all times—when rebounding off a goalpost or the referee, or until the referee blows the whistle.
	The ball is out of play when it completely crosses over the sideline or end line, or when it makes contact with a building structure above the area of play.
	A two-handed behind-the-head (overhead) throw is used to put the ball in play from a throw-in. Players who cannot use both hands must attempt the overhead throw using one.
	If the ball is not in-bounded within five sec, a turnover is awarded.
	The ball must travel completely over the line to be considered out of bounds. If a player is struck by a ball while out of bounds, there is no change of possession.
	Defensive players may not interfere with the in-bounding player's reentry to the court.
	In-bounding must be accomplished through the air; if the ball bounces on the line, it will be awarded to the other team at the same location.

Ball movement	A player may use hands, feet, chair, or any part of the body to move the ball.
	A player may dribble the ball with one or two hands.
	A player has three sec to pass, dribble, or shoot once in possession of the ball.
	A player may not touch the playing surface while in possession of the ball. Only those players who use their feet to propel the wheelchair are exempt.
	Goalkeepers may leave the goal area when they are in possession of the ball but are then considered as a player on the court and have three sec to pass, dribble, or shoot.
Goal area play	If the ball is in the goal area, other players may try to gain possession. They must avoid (a) touching any part of the goal area with the wheelchair or body or (b) physically interfering with the goalkeeper.
	If an offensive player violates either (a) or (b), the result is a side-out for the other team.
	If a defensive player violates either (a) or (b), the result is a penalty shot for the other team.
Goal scored	A goal is scored when the entire ball passes through the plane of the goal line.
	Goalkeepers can stop a ball halfway through the plane of the goal and hold it stationary for five sec, resulting in a throw-in for their team.
Penalty shots	All players are at center court, with offensive players on the outside and defensive players on the inside. Shooter takes the ball from the referee at midcourt and must takes the penalty shot from inside the 12 ft (3.7 m) penalty line within 10 sec of receiving the ball.
Blocking versus ramming	Blocking is a legal move and is defined by any player positioning the wheelchair to impede another player's movement. The player must have established position first.
	Ramming is an illegal move defined as a collision from any angle in which players fails to gain position first or fails to control their own wheelchairs. Players are expected to maintain control of their wheelchairs at all times.
Loss of possession	The following result in loss of possession to the victimized team:
	• Offensive player enters the goal area to gain an advantage.
	• Player touches the floor while in possession of the ball.
	• Offensive player considered ramming another player.
	• Player covers the ball with the wheelchair for more than three sec.
	• Goalkeeper gains possession of the ball in the play area and carries it back into the goal area.
Penalty shots awarded	Defensive player rams an opponent in a scoring attempt.
	Any player holds or hooks an opponent's wheelchair or body.
	Defensive player enters the goal area during an attempt to score.
	Defensive player pushes an offensive player into the goal area.

SKILLS TO BE TAUGHT

This section describes how to teach the five basic skills necessary to play indoor wheelchair soccer. These skills can be taught in your physical education class to students with and without disabilities. Notice that passing and shooting have three variations: two-handed, bounce, and baseball. You will have to decide which skills are appropriate for your students.

Passing

Indoor wheelchair soccer uses three types of passes: the two-handed pass, the bounce pass, and the baseball pass. Passing is used to move the ball up and down the court in an attempt to invade the opponent's territory. Passing is used to position players to shoot at the goal. The types of passes used in this sport are similar to the passes discussed in wheelchair basketball.

Two-Handed Pass

To perform the two-handed pass, the student places the hands on each side of the ball and draws the ball into the chest by flexing the elbows; then extends the elbows forcefully to pass the ball to a teammate. This is similar to the chest pass in wheelchair basketball.

Preparation for two-handed chest pass.

Execution of two-handed chest pass.

Bounce Pass

The bounce pass uses the same mechanics as that of the two-handed pass with the following emphasis: the student tries to land the ball in the receiver's lap by bouncing it on the floor between them.

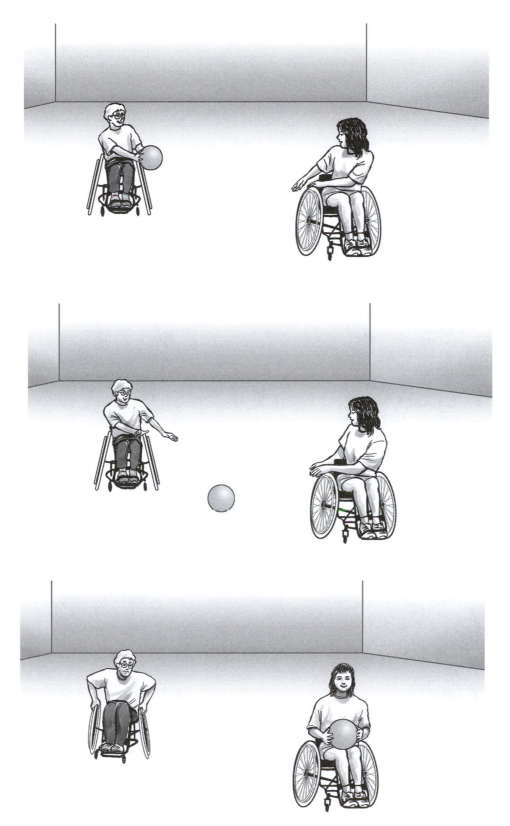

Bounce ball into partner's lap.

Baseball Pass

The baseball pass is used to move the ball up the floor in a hurry or to shoot a goal. The student stabilizes and balances the trunk in the wheelchair while bringing the ball back and up to a baseball throwing position. Then the student raises the ball under control, moves it up and forward, maintains balance upon release, and follows through.

Position ball in baseball throwing position.

Move ball forward.

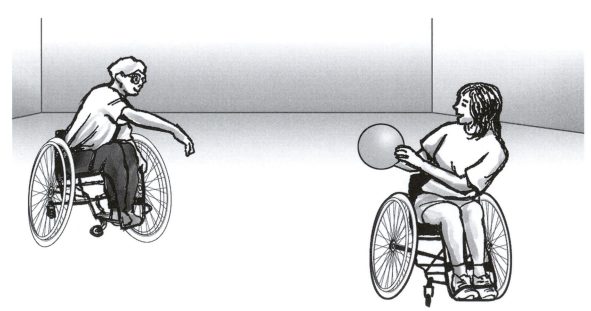

Release and follow through.

Dribbling

The skill of dribbling is used to move the ball up the court. Only the push dribble is discussed for soccer because the lap dribble from basketball might encourage a violation of the three-second rule discussed earlier.

The student bounces the ball ahead of the wheelchair closer to the front wheels, or casters. As the ball moves ahead, the student moves the hands quickly to the handrims and wheels to push the wheelchair. The student then continues dribbling the ball forward of the wheelchair while simultaneously pushing the wheelchair down the floor.

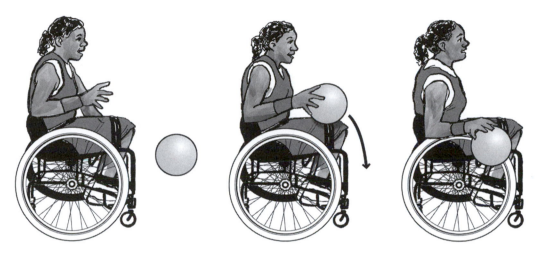

Bounce the ball ahead of the wheelchair.

Continue dribbling up the floor.

Throw-In

The throw-in is used to place the ball in play after a turnover or an out-of-bounds call by the referee. The throw-in must be performed with a two-handed overhead motion if possible.

While maintaining a balanced sitting position and facing the court, the student grips the ball with two hands as in the two-handed chest pass. Maintaining balance, the student raises the ball up with both hands over and behind the head. Once the ball is completely behind the head, the student pulls both hands forward to release the ball. The student should be sure to extend the elbow upon release of the ball toward the court with full range of motion and follow through upon release.

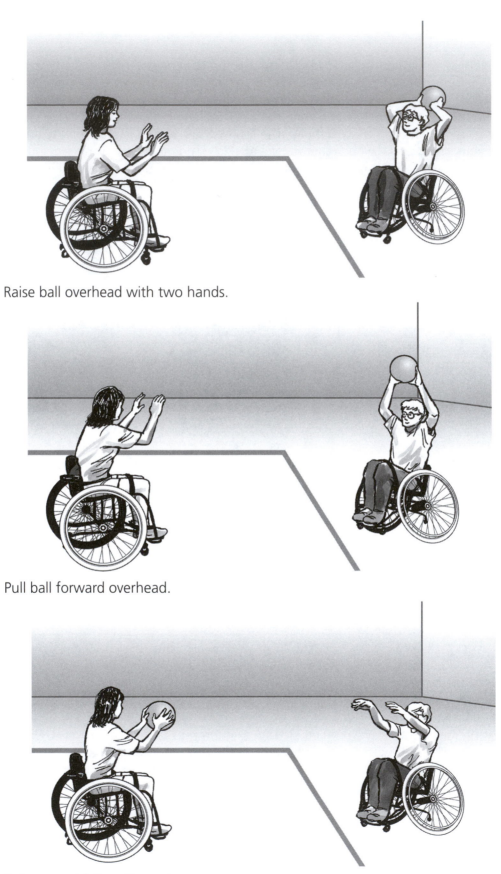

Raise ball overhead with two hands.

Pull ball forward overhead.

Release and follow through.

Blocking

Blocking is a key position for the defense. Students without disabilities can play this position in an inclusive setting by blocking with their nondominant hands or arms. The block described here is the goalkeeper block.

Positioned in front of the attacker, the student's hands are on the rims ready to move the wheelchair as needed to reduce the angle of the shot (forward, backward, left, or right). The goalie should maintain a balanced position, sitting as tall as possible. As the shot is taken, the student extends the arms upward and minimizes the space between the arms to help protect the face and head. The

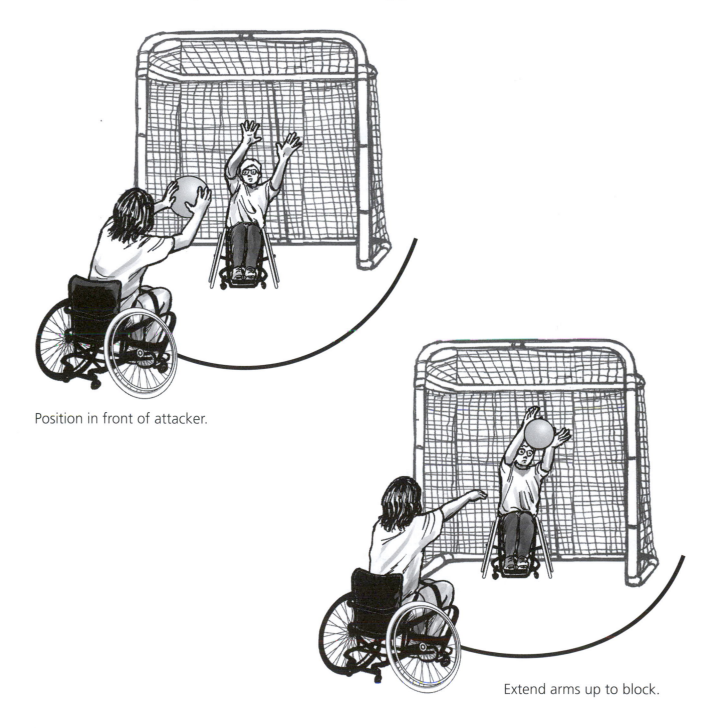

Position in front of attacker.

Extend arms up to block.

student should try to block the shot as far in front of the goal as possible and, if blocked, attempt to control the ball and execute either of three options (i.e., hold the ball for a count of 5 seconds and force a throw-in, pass the ball long down the court on a fast break to teammates, or carry the ball into play on the court and pass to a teammate).

FUNCTIONAL PROFILES AND GENERAL MODIFICATIONS

As in wheelchair basketball, not all students will be able to execute the skills described for this sport. The athlete classification systems employed by the sporting organizations that govern indoor wheelchair soccer use a more functional description of the athletes allowed to play.

Student Functional Profiles

Table 7.2 is a modification of the suggested classifications for students with disabilities designated to play. Read the table to see if you have students that might fit these profiles. A student with multiple disabilities, such as quadriplegic athetoid cerebral palsy and visual impairment, might fit the low functional skill level.

General Modifications for Indoor Wheelchair Soccer

Table 7.3 shows how you might apply general modifications to the five skills necessary to play indoor wheelchair soccer. Notice that these modifications are suggested according to the student functional profiles. Again, it is up to you to decide which skills and modifications are appropriate for your situation (see chapter 3).

Table 7.2 Student Functional Profiles for Indoor Wheelchair Soccer

Functional skill level	Student profile
Low	Severe disabilities in all four extremities; uses an electric or power wheelchair.
Low to moderate	Severe to moderate disabilities in three of the four extremities; can use a manual wheelchair for short distances.
Moderate	Minimal paraplegic (two lower) or hemiplegic (one side) disabilities; uses a manual wheelchair and can push the wheelchair at a moderate to high level.
High	No neurological or physical disability in the upper extremity or trunk; has some severe disability in at least one lower extremity.

Table 7.3   General Modifications for Indoor Wheelchair Soccer

Skill level	Skill	Activity modifications
Low	Passing	Use a smaller ball.
	Shooting	Strike the ball into the goal area or push it into the goal with the wheelchair. Throw a ball or beanbag into a wider goal area.
	Dribbling	Push a ball larger than 10 in. (25 cm). Attach a cardboard bumper to the front of the wheelchair.
	Throw-in	Knock a ball off a table or traffic cone into the court. Push the ball into the court with the wheelchair.
	Blocking	Block a rolled ball.
Low to moderate	Passing	Shoot from a designated area to minimize wheelchair pushing.
	Shooting	Keep a 3-foot (1 m) space between defensive players at all times.
	Dribbling	Use a two-handed dribble and allow five sec instead of three sec to control the ball.
	Throw-in	Allow more time to throw in. Classmate assists—e.g., stabilizes the ball in position before a throw-in.
	Blocking	Practice blocking each swing of a ball tethered from a basketball goal.
Moderate to high	All skills	No modifications: Used with highest-functioning students.

GAME PROGRESSIONS

The games listed in the remainder of this chapter are presented in the class formats of one on one, small group, and large group. Students may begin in a one-on-one format with an individual focus and then move on to the small group or large group format as they improve. Keep in mind that inclusion means trying to address the three domains of physical education: psychomotor, cognitive, and affective.

GAMES-BY-SKILL-LEVEL INDEX: LOW-FUNCTIONING STUDENTS

The skill-level index in table 7.4 presents the games according to the functional level of your students. This index is for low-functioning students and is followed by game descriptions for this population. The index for higher-functioning students and game descriptions for that population follow the game description section for the

Table 7.4 Games-by-Skill-Level Index for Low-Functioning Students—Indoor Wheelchair Soccer

Skills	One on one	Small group	Large group
Passing	Pass It On I	Pass It On II	Capture It
Shooting	Charge!	Rebound	Score It
Dribbling	Bump and Go I	Bump and Go II	Bump and Go III
Throw-in	Knock It Off I	Knock It Off II	Knock It Off III
Blocking	Keep It Out I	Keep It Out II	Keep It Out III

lower-functioning population. Find the skill you want to address and cross-reference it with the class format you desire (one on one, small group, or large group).

GAME DESCRIPTIONS

Each game description in this section includes class format, organizational pattern, equipment, description, extension, and inclusion suggestions. You will notice again that some games are presented in sequence, such as Knock It Off I, Knock It Off II, and Knock It Off III. You are not bound by the sequence.

Skill ▶ Passing

PASS IT ON I

Class format: One on one

Organizational pattern: Individual with teacher or peer assistant as needed

Equipment: Beanbag, small ball, Wiffle ball, or Nerf ball

Description: The student attempts to hold a beanbag or small ball in her lap as long as possible in a stationary position.

Extension: Once the student can control the object, she can move across the gym carrying the object to a teammate.

Inclusion suggestion: The student can demonstrate to the class her ability to accomplish the task.

PASS IT ON II

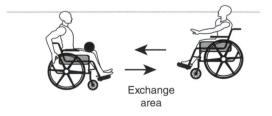

Exchange
area

Class format: Small group

Organizational pattern: A continuation of Pass It On I, in which students on opposite sides of the free-throw lane face each other

Equipment: Beanbags, small balls, Wiffle balls, Nerf balls, or beach balls

Description: One student has an object to control, such as a beanbag or beach ball. On a signal he moves across the lane to his partner, where the two exchange the object.

Extensions: Vary the activity by increasing the distance, size, and weight of the object or by placing a time limit on the performance.

Inclusion suggestions: Students with and without disabilities can participate. The student with a disability can call out his partner's name as he passes the object. The student with a disability may also suggest one modification for how the object should be carried.

CAPTURE IT

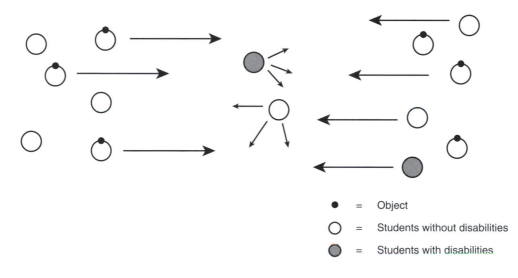

• = Object

○ = Students without disabilities

⬤ = Students with disabilities

Class format: Large group

Organizational pattern: The class is in two teams, half at one end of the gym and half at the other.

Equipment: 10-inch (25 cm) playground balls, beanbags, small balls, Wiffle balls, Nerf balls, or beach balls

Description: Three students from each team have an object to pass, such as a small ball, a beanbag, or a 10-inch (25 cm) playground ball. Two students, one with a disability and one without a disability, are in the middle of the gym. On a signal, both teams try to exchange places to the opposite end of the gym while passing the objects. As the teams exchange places, the students in the middle try to capture the balls or objects away from either team. If an object is captured, the student last in control exchanges places with the student in the middle who captured it for the next exchange.

Extension: The student with a disability can play the middle position only two consecutive times.

Inclusion suggestion: The student with a disability can verbalize or in some way suggest one modification of how the groups should be allowed to move (e.g., forward, backward, two pushes, stop and go).

Skill ▶ Shooting

CHARGE!

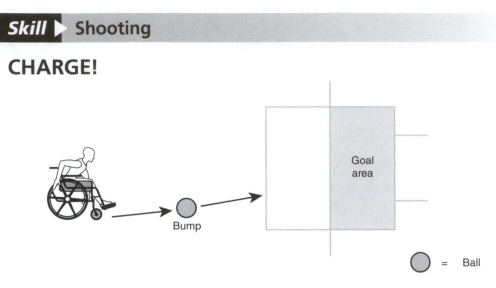

Class format: One on One

Organizational pattern: Individual with the teacher or peer assistant as needed

Equipment: 10-inch (25 cm) playground ball, beach ball, or basketball

Description: A larger ball is on the floor in front of the power wheelchair approximately 6 feet (1.8 m) in front of the goal. The student with a disability takes a moving start at the ball and bumps or pushes it into the goal area.

Extension: Vary the distance and angle of the shot on goal.

Inclusion suggestion: The student can demonstrate to the class his ability to accomplish the task.

REBOUND

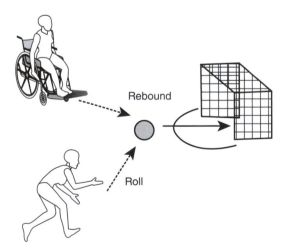

Class format: Small group

Organizational pattern: Two students, one with and one without a disability, in a triangle position, using the goal area as the third point of the triangle

Equipment: 10-inch (25 cm) playground balls, beach balls, or basketballs

Description: The student without a disability rolls a ball on the floor in front of the goal area so that the student using the wheelchair can attack the ball and rebound it into the goal.

Extension: Change the angle, position, or speed of the roll.

Inclusion suggestion: The student with a disability can decide where to reposition the student rolling the ball.

SCORE IT

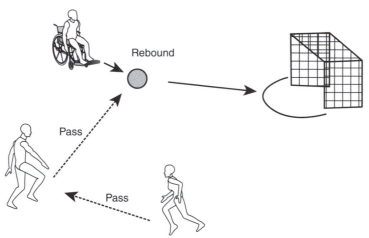

Class format: Large group

Organizational pattern: Use the same starting positions as in the game Rebound, with the following change: have two students pass the ball before the student with a disability attempts to shoot it into the goal.

Equipment: 10-inch (25 cm) playground ball, beach ball, or basketball

Description: Two passes must occur before the team can score, and the passes can come from any student. However, all three students must be involved with the play before scoring.

Extension: Increase the difficulty of this game by placing a defender in the group. As the teamwork gets better, rotate the defender with the player who scores the goal and restart the game.

Inclusion suggestions: The student with a disability can decide who will initiate the first pass or communicate two additional skills to add to this game.

Skill ▶ Dribbling

BUMP AND GO I

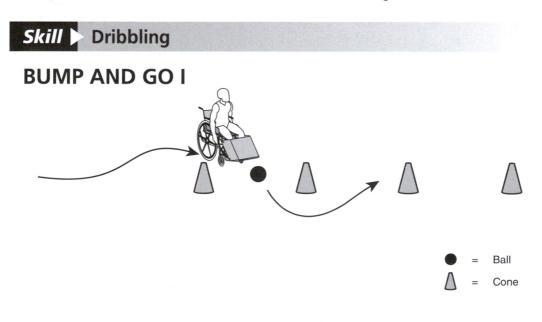

● = Ball

⬛ = Cone

Class format: One on one

Organizational pattern: A series of traffic cones in a line and 6 feet (1.8 m) apart. A ball larger than 10 inches (25 cm) in diameter is in front of the power wheelchair.

Equipment: 10-inch (25 cm) or larger playground ball, traffic cones, sheet of cardboard, bands for attaching cardboard to wheelchair

Description: The student maneuvers through the traffic cones while controlling the ball. A large piece of cardboard attached to the front of the wheelchair with bungee cords can help the student control the ball.

Extension: Vary the distance between the cones.

Inclusion suggestion: The student with a disability is in charge of creating a new pattern for moving through the cones (e.g., every other cone).

BUMP AND GO II

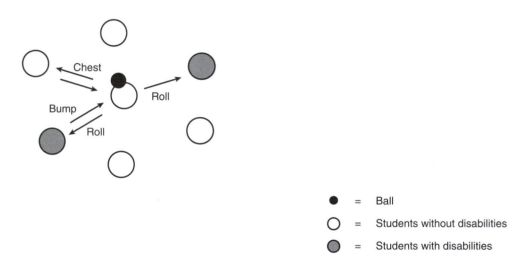

● = Ball

○ = Students without disabilities

◐ = Students with disabilities

Class format: Small group

Organizational pattern: Students with and without disabilities in a circle formation with a student without a disability in the center holding a 10-inch (25 cm) playground ball

Equipment: 10-inch (25 cm) playground balls, beach balls, or Nerf volleyballs

Description: On a signal, the student in the center passes the ball around the circle using either a chest pass to students without disabilities or a rolled pass to those with disabilities. Students without disabilities catch the ball, perform three left-handed, then three right-handed dribbles, and pass it back to the center. The student with a disability tries to bump the ball back to the center of the circle using the front of her wheelchair.

Extensions: Increase the size of the circle and the number of dribbles students must complete. Try completing the activity with two balls moving around at one time.

Inclusion suggestion: The student with a disability can be in charge of creating a new pattern for moving the ball around the circle (e.g., to every other person).

BUMP AND GO III

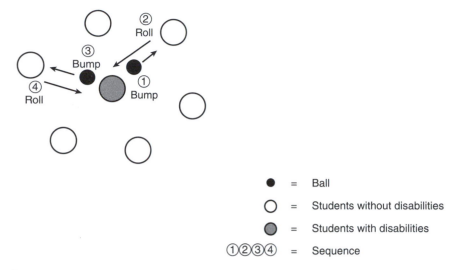

● = Ball

○ = Students without disabilities

◐ = Students with disabilities

①②③④ = Sequence

Class format: Large group

Organizational pattern: Use the same formation as Bump and Go II, only this time a student with a disability is in the center of the circle.

Equipment: 10-inch (25 cm) playground ball, beach ball, Nerf volleyball

Description: The ball starts in the center, and the student bumps the ball out to the other students. The other students must pick up the ball and roll it back to the middle, where the student using the wheelchair bumps or dribbles the ball back out to the next student. The objective is to continue this ball movement around the circle.

Extension: Create several circles, and have each group attempt to move the ball around in the shortest amount of time.

Inclusion suggestion: The student with a disability can be in charge of choosing the next center player.

Skill ▶ **Throw-In**

KNOCK IT OFF I

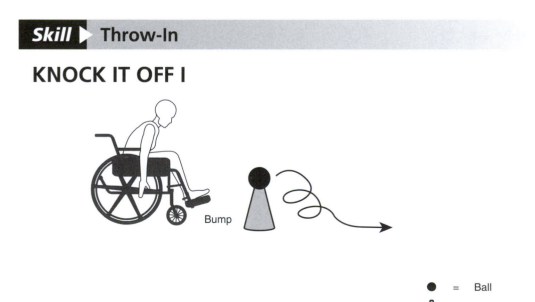

● = Ball

◭ = Cone

Class format: One on one

Organizational pattern: A large ball balanced on top of a tall traffic cone or table

Equipment: 10-inch (25 cm) or larger playground ball, tall traffic cone (or folding table or bench), plastic floor hockey stick

Description: The student in a wheelchair approaches the ball rapidly. The student may use any part of the wheelchair or body to knock the ball off the cone or table, making sure to avoid contact with the cone or table. The objective is to put the ball into play.

Extension: The student may use an object to strike the ball from the cone or tabletop.

Inclusion suggestion: The student should practice this activity with wheelchair control in mind and be able to demonstrate to classmates the successful completion of this task. The student should be able to judge the amount of wheelchair speed needed to knock the ball off the cone and safely put the ball into play.

KNOCK IT OFF II

Bump

Class format: Small group

Organizational pattern: Same starting formation as in Knock It Off I

Equipment: 10-inch (25 cm) or larger playground balls, tall traffic cones (or folding tables or benches), plastic floor hockey sticks

Description: This time the student placing the ball into play (throwing in) must anticipate his approach so that he knocks the ball into play as a teammate is passing in front of the cone. Students without disabilities are positioned in the court area and, on the signal, move to the throw-in as if to receive the ball. The student throwing the ball into play must do so as his teammate is in position to receive the ball.

Extension: The student may use an object to strike the ball from the cone or tabletop.

Inclusion suggestion: The student with a disability can give the starting signal for his teammate to move into position to accept the throw-in.

KNOCK IT OFF III

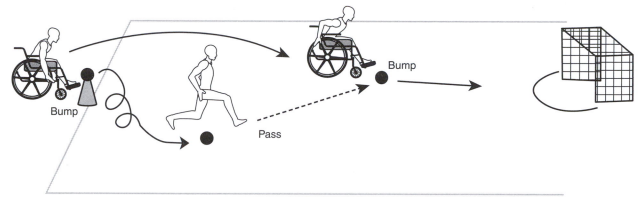

Class format: Large group

Organizational pattern: Same starting formation as in Knock It Off I

Equipment: 10-inch (25 cm) or larger playground ball, tall traffic cone (or folding table or bench)

Description: In this game, the students are closer to the goal. The student with a disability can throw the ball in (see Knock It Off I), and a student without a disability should receive the ball in the court area (see Knock It Off II). As the student in the court area receives the ball, the student with a disability moves on court and takes a pass from a teammate. She then attempts to bump the ball into the goal (see Bump and Go II).

Extension: Place a defender in the court to attempt a steal of the throw-in.

Inclusion suggestion: The student with a disability can decide how the players should rotate positions for each throw-in by communicating verbally, visually (i.e., pointing), or by demonstration.

Skill ▶ Blocking

KEEP IT OUT I

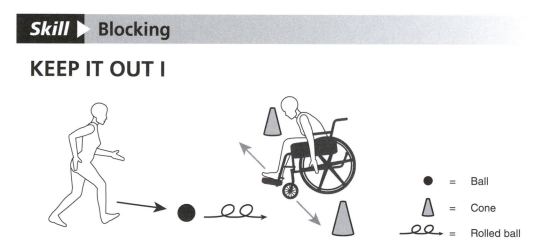

● = Ball

▲ = Cone

꩜→ = Rolled ball

Class format: One on one

Organizational pattern: A student with a disability is between two traffic cones approximately 15 feet (4.6 m) apart.

Equipment: 10-inch (25 cm) or larger playground ball, two traffic cones

Description: A student without a disability rolls a ball at the student with a disability, attempting to roll the ball between the cones. The objective of the game is for the student with a disability to position the wheelchair to block the ball from passing between the cones.

Extensions: Vary the distance rolled, the tempo of the roll, and the angle of the roll to help improve the defensive blocking.

Inclusion suggestion: The student with a disability can determine the distance between the cones to either increase or decrease the difficulty of the activity.

KEEP IT OUT II

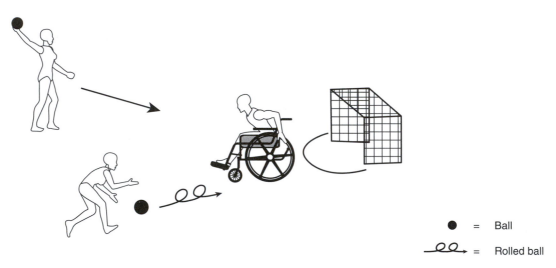

● = Ball

◯◯➛ = Rolled ball

Class format: Small group

Organizational pattern: The student with a disability is in the position of goalkeeper in front of the goal or net.

Equipment: 10-inch (25 cm) or larger playground balls, traffic cones or gym mats for goals

Description: Two students without disabilities roll or bounce a ball toward the goal. The student with a disability attempts to block the ball from entering the goal or net.

Extensions: Vary the distance rolled, the tempo of the roll, and the angle of the roll to help improve the defensive blocking. Start with one ball at a time; then progress to two balls thrown alternately toward the net at a faster pace.

Inclusion suggestions: The student with a disability can determine the distance of the throw at the goal or net, or the rotation of players during the activity.

KEEP IT OUT III

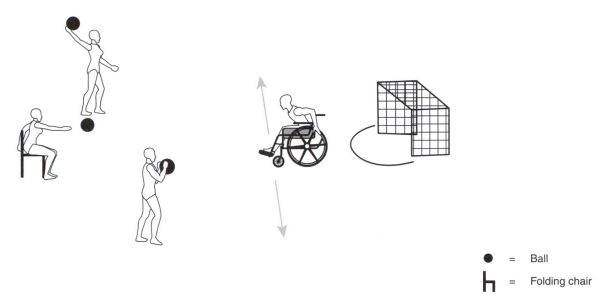

● = Ball

⌐ = Folding chair

Class format: Large group

Organizational pattern: One student with a disability as goalkeeper and three or four students without disabilities 15 feet (4.6 m) in front of the net, each with a ball

Equipment: 10-inch (25 cm) or larger playground ball, traffic cones, folding chair, gym mats as goals to replace nets if not available

Description: Using a random order, the students without disabilities attempt shots on the goal by rolling or bouncing the ball into the goal. They may not throw the ball into the net. The objective is for the student with a disability to position or reposition herself after each shot to block the goal attempt. You should control the tempo of the shots on goal but allow the students to shoot in any order. Once each student has taken a turn, all students can rotate positions. The student with a disability can bump the ball into the net as her shot attempt from a pass by her teammate.

Extension: Students without disabilities may be positioned on their knees in the goalkeeper position and can block using only their nondominant arms.

Inclusion suggestions: The student with a disability can determine the rotation of shots by players during the activity. The student can also report shots blocked versus goals scored.

GAMES-BY-SKILL-LEVEL INDEX: MODERATE-TO HIGH-FUNCTIONING STUDENTS

Table 7.5 addresses students with moderate to high function. The class formats remain the same: one on one, small group, and large group.

Table 7.5 Games-by-Skill-Level Index for Moderate- to High-Functioning Students—Indoor Wheelchair Soccer

Skills	One on one	Small group	Large group
Passing	Target Toss	Partner Pass	Call It Out
Shooting	Feed Me	Feed and Go (Shooting)	Feed and Go Plus 1 (Shooting)
Dribbling	Stationary	On the Move I	On the Move II
Throw-in	Reach Back	Pick a Spot	Pick a Spot With D
Blocking	Pin Block	Feed and Go (Blocking)	Feed and Go Plus 1 (Blocking)

GAME DESCRIPTIONS

The 15 games in this next section will help you teach moderate- to high-functioning students with disabilities in your classes. Modify any or all of these games to meet your needs. Keep in mind the approach to inclusion mentioned throughout this book and the fact that you will need to assess skill performance prior to playing games.

Skill ▶ Passing (Two-Handed, Bounce, and Baseball Pass)

TARGET TOSS

Class format: One on one

Organizational pattern: Individual with teacher or peer assistant as needed

Equipment: 10-inch (25 cm) playground ball, targets for wall, cones for distance markers

Description: After reviewing each of the key points for executing the two-handed and baseball passes, the student with a disability passes the ball into a target (e.g., a 2-foot-diameter, or 0.6 m, circle) from a distance of 6 to 8 feet (1.8 to 2.4 m).

Extensions: Higher-skilled students can pass with the nondominant hand. Students without disabilities can assist by retrieving and providing appropriate feedback.

Inclusion suggestions: The student can demonstrate to the class his ability to accomplish the task and determine three new distances for the target. The student can also determine two additional skills to be added to this activity.

PARTNER PASS

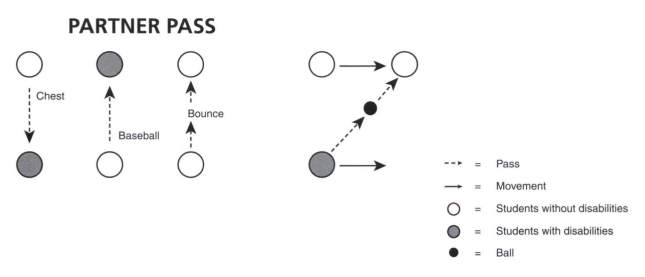

--→ = Pass

—→ = Movement

○ = Students without disabilities

⬤ = Students with disabilities

● = Ball

Class format: Small group

Organizational pattern: Students with and without disabilities are in two parallel lines facing each other about 15 feet (4.6 m) apart.

Equipment: 10-inch (25 cm) playground balls

Description: Using the two-handed pass or baseball pass, students try to pass to their partners from a stationary position. Score 1 point for passes that are complete, and subtract 2 points for each errant pass, or set up any type of scoring activity that works for you.

Extension: Once they are successful with stationary passing, the partners move across the gym floor using either of the two passes.

Inclusion suggestions: The student with a disability can be in charge of determining the type of pass to be used for each trip across the gym and reporting the score at the end of each trip.

CALL IT OUT

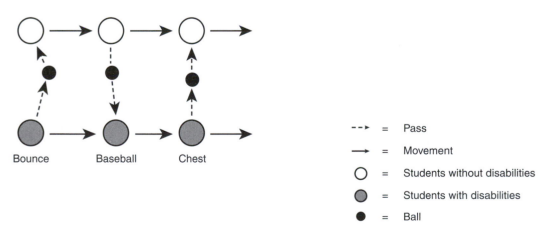

--→ = Pass

—→ = Movement

○ = Students without disabilities

⬤ = Students with disabilities

● = Ball

Class format: Large group

Organizational pattern: Students are in parallel line formation opposite their partners. This is a dynamic formation with students moving forward in pairs as they pass the ball. Students with and without disabilities should be paired up.

Equipment: 10-inch (25 cm) playground balls

Description: Each set of partners has a 10-inch (25 cm) playground ball and, on the signal, must move forward across the floor, passing the ball as they move. Partners must stay about 15 to 20 feet (4.6 to 6 m) apart and emphasize keeping the ball ahead of their partners. Change the type of pass every two or three trips down the floor by calling out a new pass (i.e., two-handed pass, bounce pass, baseball pass). The objective is to complete one trip without a miss using each of the passes.

Extension: For students with varying degrees of manual propulsion, change the type of ball used to pass or the distance passed.

Inclusion suggestion: The student with a disability can call out the pass to be executed.

Skill ▶ Shooting

FEED ME

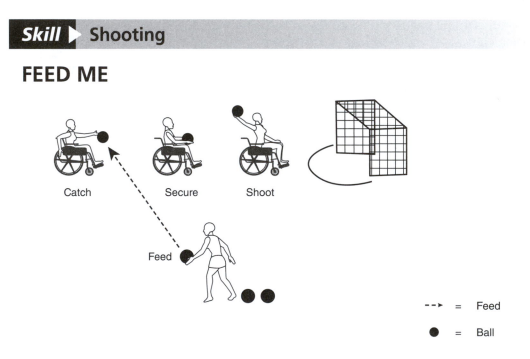

Catch   Secure   Shoot

Feed

- - → = Feed

● = Ball

Class format: One on one

Organizational pattern: One student without a disability is at the corner of the goal net with three 10-inch (25 cm) playground balls. The student with a disability is positioned about 13 to 15 feet (4 to 4.6 m) in front of the net.

Equipment: 10-inch (25 cm) playground balls, goal or gym mats to simulate a goal

Description: The purpose of this activity is for the student with moderate to high functional ability to practice catching, securing, and shooting the ball into the goal area. On a signal, the student using the wheelchair moves forward toward the goal as the student with the playground balls "feeds" the student in the wheelchair with a pass. The student using the wheelchair must catch, secure, and shoot the ball into the net using the same movements as taught for passing (i.e., either a two-handed push shot or a baseball throw). As soon as the shot is taken, the student in the wheelchair recovers and repositions at the starting point, and the activity continues.

Extension: Vary the distance and angle of the shot on goal.

Inclusion suggestion: The student with a disability may suggest one new skill to the activity.

FEED AND GO (SHOOTING)

Class format: Small group

Organizational pattern: Use the same formation as Feed Me; however, now start the activity at the center circle area.

Equipment: 10-inch (25 cm) playground ball, goal or gym mats to simulate a goal

Description: The student using the wheelchair catches the ball (feed) and secures it for a count of three seconds while moving toward the net (go). As he moves closer to the net, he shoots using either a two-handed or baseball pass.

Extension: Rotate the student with a disability to the feeder position.

Inclusion suggestion: The student with a disability can report to you where the shot on goal went (e.g., high and in the corner or low and in the middle).

FEED AND GO PLUS 1 (SHOOTING)

Catch

Secure

Shoot

Block

Feed

→ = Movement

--► = Feed

● = Ball

Class format: Large group

Organizational pattern: Same formation as Feed and Go (Shooting), except a third person is added to the activity (plus 1) as a defender

Equipment: 10-inch (25 cm) playground ball, goal or gym mats to simulate a goal

Description: The defender is positioned as the goalkeeper and attempts to block the shot taken.

Extensions: Rotate the students through each of the positions (e.g., the student feeding moves to the shooter position, the shooter moves to goalkeeper, and the goalkeeper moves to feeder). Students with and without disabilities can be placed at any of the positions. Adjust the distance of the shot, speed of the movement, and tempo of the pass according to students' abilities.

Inclusion suggestions: The student with a disability can determine the order of rotation or establish one new version of the activity (e.g., adding a second defender).

Skill ▶ Dribbling (Push Dribble Only)

STATIONARY

Class format: One on one

Organizational pattern: This is the same activity described for wheelchair basketball (see chapter 6) using a 10-inch (25 cm) playground ball. The purpose of this activity is to allow the student with moderate or high functional ability to practice dribbling the ball in a stationary position.

Equipment: 10-inch (25 cm) playground ball, folding chairs or benches

Description: Students with less functional ability could start with a two-handed bounce and catch while leaning to the side of the wheelchair.

Extensions: Students having difficulty controlling a regulation 10-inch (25 cm) playground ball might try one slightly deflated (less than 2 psi). Students without disabilities could be included in this activity by participating from folding chairs or benches.

Inclusion suggestion: The student with a disability can decide a set number of dribbles to accomplish before changing hands (e.g., 10 with the right hand, then 10 with the left).

ON THE MOVE I

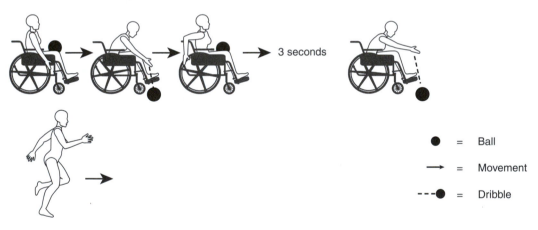

3 seconds

● = Ball

→ = Movement

---● = Dribble

Class format: Small group

Organizational pattern: The student with a disability is partnered with a student without a disability in a side-by-side formation facing the same direction and ready to move across the gym floor.

Equipment: 10-inch (25 cm) playground balls

Description: The student with a disability pushes forward in her wheelchair while carrying the ball in her lap. Once she is moving, she must dribble using one hand while controlling her wheelchair. She may return the ball to her lap after traveling 15 feet (4.6 m) but must return to dribbling within the three-second time limit. The student without a disability walks next to the wheelchair to help with errant dribbling. The student with a disability continues the activity across the gymnasium floor. On the return trip, the student without a disability performs the dribble using proper techniques, and the student with a disability serves as the assistant recovering errant dribbles.

Extension: Increase the difficulty of this activity by placing traffic cones in a line about 6 to 8 feet (1.8 to 2.4 m) apart, and instruct the students to dribble in a weave pattern in and out among the cones.

Inclusion suggestion: The student without a disability performs the dribble in both directions while the student with a disability critiques her movement. At the end of both trips across the gym, the student with a disability shares which aspects look correct and which need work. The two students then reverse roles and repeat the activity.

ON THE MOVE II

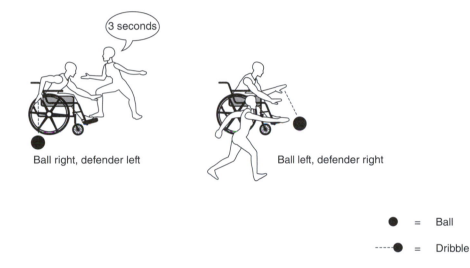

Ball right, defender left   Ball left, defender right

● = Ball

----● = Dribble

Class format: Large group

Organizational pattern: Same as On the Move I

Equipment: 10-inch (25 cm) playground ball

Description: In this activity the student without a disability challenges the dribble by representing a defender and changing positions next to the wheelchair. With each attempt at dribbling, the student with a disability must keep the ball on the opposite side of the wheelchair away from the defender; that is, as the student with a disability dribbles the ball on the right side, the defender should be on the left; and as the defender switches to the other side, so should the dribbler. The student without a disability counts out loud for three seconds each time the student using the wheelchair places the ball in his lap as he changes positions.

Extension: Have students try this activity in a stationary formation before moving across the gym floor.

Inclusion suggestions: The student with a disability can decide who starts first with the ball. The same student can count successful switches from side to side and report the count to you.

Skill ▶ Throw-In

REACH BACK

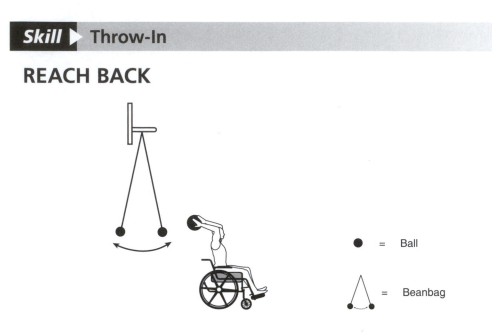

● = Ball

△ = Beanbag

Class format: One on one

Organizational pattern: The student with a disability is under a basketball goal holding a 10-inch (25 cm) playground ball in both hands. A beanbag is suspended from the basketball goal so that it hangs about 8 inches (20 cm) above and behind the student's head.

Equipment: 10-inch (cm) playground ball, basketball goal and backboard, rope, beanbag

Description: The student raises the ball into the throw-in position, using both arms if possible, and tries to strike the beanbag with the ball while bringing it behind his head to perform the throw-in facing the court. The student must reach back as much as possible to ensure a legal throw-in.

Extension: Adjust the length of the rope to increase or decrease the student's reach.

Inclusion suggestion: The student with a disability can tell you how much to increase or decrease the length of the rope.

PICK A SPOT

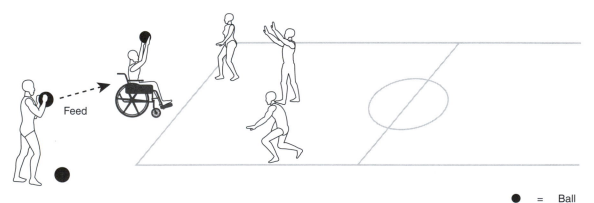

Feed

● = Ball

Class format: Small group

Organizational pattern: A student with a disability is in the throw-in position on the sideline of the court facing the playing area, and a student without a disability is next to her serving as a feeder for this activity. Three or four students with or without disabilities in a semicircular formation are about 15 to 20 feet (4.6 to 6 m) away in the playing area facing the throw-in.

Equipment: 10-inch (25 cm) playground balls

Description: On a signal, the student with a disability in-bounds the ball using the throw-in skill to any of the players in the court. As soon as one ball is thrown in, another one is ready for the student to repeat the throw-in. This activity continues until all students in the playing area have received a ball.

Extension: Adjust the distance of the receiving players from the student on the court, either increasing or decreasing the distance for the throw-in.

Inclusion suggestion: The student with a disability can call out the receiving student's name before throwing in the ball. Nonverbal students can use another form of communication, such as pointing or nodding in the direction of the throw-in.

PICK A SPOT WITH D

Feed

● = Ball

👤 = D

Class format: Large group

Organizational pattern: Same position as Pick a Spot, except that the distance of the throw-in is increased and a defender (D) is added

Equipment: 10-inch (25 cm) playground ball

Description: A student with or without disabilities is between the player performing the throw-in and the players trying to receive the throw-in. The objective is for the student to complete as many throw-ins as possible without the D intercepting the ball. Students rotate positions after one minute.

Extension: The student without a disability acting as a defender may use a scooter board.

Inclusion suggestions: The student with a disability can call out the receiving student's name before throwing in the ball. Nonverbal students may use another form of communication, such as pointing or nodding in the direction of the throw-in. The student can also report the number of successful throw-ins during the activity.

Skill ▶ Blocking

PIN BLOCK

Class format: One on one

Organizational pattern: Three or four plastic bowling pins (or other like objects) arranged on a bench or table to be used as targets. A student with a disability is in front of the pins to serve as a defender.

Equipment: 10-inch (cm) playground ball, plastic bowling pins, bench

Description: A student with or without disabilities throws the playground ball at the pins attempting to knock them off one by one. The student defending must position to block the shot attempt and not allow the pins to fall. The student shooting must allow the defender to reposition after each shot. Shooting distance must be greater than 19 feet (5.8 m).

Extensions: Change the shooting distance, size of the ball, or texture of the ball (Nerf ball). Students without disabilities can throw with their nondominant hands or play the defender position from their knees or sitting on gym scooters.

Inclusion suggestion: The student with a disability can choose the first defender.

FEED AND GO (BLOCKING)

Class format: Small group

Organizational pattern: Same as described for Feed and Go (Shooting), except that the emphasis is on blocking rather than shooting

Equipment: 10-inch (25 cm) playground balls, goal or gym mats to simulate a goal

Description: The student using the wheelchair catches the ball (feed) and secures the ball for a count of three seconds while moving toward the net (go). As she moves closer to the net, she shoots using either a two-handed or baseball pass.

Extension: Rotate the student with a disability to the feeder position.

Inclusion suggestion: The student with a disability can report to you how many shots were blocked.

FEED AND GO PLUS 1 (BLOCKING)

Class format: Large group

Organizational pattern: Same formation as in Feed and Go, except a third person is added to the activity (plus 1) as a defender and the emphasis is on blocking

Equipment: 10-inch (25 cm) playground ball, goal or gym mats to simulate a goal

Description: The defender is positioned as the goalkeeper and attempts to block the shot.

Extensions: You can rotate the students through each of the positions. For example, the student feeding can move to the shooter position, the shooter can move to the goalkeeper position, and the goalkeeper can move to the feeder position. Students with and without disabilities can be placed at any of the positions. Adjust the distance of the shot, the speed of the movement, and the tempo of the pass according to your students' functional skill levels.

Inclusion suggestions: The student with a disability can determine the order of rotation. The student may also establish one new version of the activity (e.g., add a second defender).

Remember that blank forms for assessments, IEPs, and unit and lesson plans are located on the DVD.

Chapter 8

Sitting Volleyball

Sitting volleyball was established in the Netherlands in the mid-1950s by the Dutch Sports Committee. The sport was created by combining traditional volleyball with a German game called sitzball. Since its introduction, sitting volleyball, which includes people with and without disabilities, has grown to be one of the Netherlands' largest competitive sports.

The International Sports Organization for the Disabled (ISOD), which is a Paralympic organization, adopted sitting volleyball in the late 1970s. Sitting volleyball has been in every Paralympic competition since 1980. Seven teams participated in the first year of Paralympic competition, although the United States did not compete until 1984. The inclusion of sitting volleyball has spread to other international competitions, including the World and European Championships for athletes with disabilities.

In the 1996 Atlanta Paralympics, 12 countries were entered in the sitting volleyball competition for men only. The Islamic Republic of Iran won the gold medal that year. A strong showing from the European countries was very evident, as second through sixth places were won by Norway, Finland, the Netherlands, Germany, and Hungary, respectively. The United States' showing in Atlanta and then in Sydney indicated a stronger need to develop this sport in our country, as we finished 11th and 12th. The 2004 Paralympics in Athens marked the first competition for women in sitting volleyball. The U.S. women won the bronze in Athens and followed up with a silver medal in the 2008 Paralympics in China. In Europe sitting volleyball is the fastest-growing sport for inclusion of people with and without disabilities. Try integrating this sport in your physical education curriculum and help further its development and growth in this country.

DESCRIPTION OF THE SPORT

The sport of sitting volleyball has many similarities to traditional volleyball. In fact, the four skills mentioned in this chapter are the same as those used in traditional volleyball: pass (overhead and forearm, to include the set), attack-hit, block, and serve. The objective of the game is to send the ball over the net so that it is not returned by the opponent—in other words, to ground the ball on the opponents' court.

The ball is put into play with a serve, and each team is allowed three hits to return it to the opponents' court. A block of a hit ball is not counted as one of the three hits. Once the ball has been put into play after the serve, each team attempts to return the ball to the opponents' court, or "rally the ball," by using passing skills.

Rally scoring is used to score in sitting volleyball. Rally scoring means that points can be awarded to the offense or defense on a ball not returned to the opponents' court. When the nonserving team wins a rally, it is awarded a point and the right to serve. Former rules for scoring allowed only the serving team to score points by winning a rally. Each time the receiving team wins a rally and a serve, it must rotate player positions one place in a clockwise direction.

Field of Play

The game is played on a court measuring 32 by 20 feet (10 by 6 m). A regulation court for standing volleyball is 60 by 30 feet (18 by 9 m). The attack line in sitting volleyball is shorter, measuring 6 feet 6 inches (2 m) back and perpendicular to the center line, rather than 23 feet (7 m) as in standing volleyball. See figure 8.1.

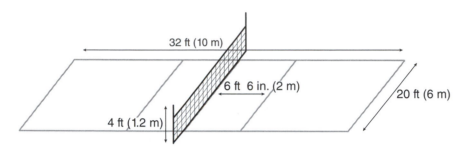

Figure 8.1   Sitting volleyball court.

Players

Any person with a permanent lower-body impairment is eligible to play; however, all players must play from a seated position on the floor. People with amputations, *les autres* conditions, cerebral palsy, or spinal cord injuries, and who are considered paraplegic, are eligible to play. *Les autres* ("the other") conditions include polio, muscular dystrophy, and multiple sclerosis. In official competition, athletes must be classified using a sport classification system, and all athletes must meet a "minimal disability" criterion. *Minimal disability* means that the athlete must have a disability severe enough to prevent her from playing in a traditional volleyball game for people without disabilities.

Equipment

The height of the net is 4 feet (1.2 m) for men and 3 feet 6 inches (1 m) for women. The ball is usually a lighter color (white) or multicolor (blue and yellow) and approximately 65 to 67 centimeters in circumference. The ball should be inflated to the proper pressure as suggested by the manufacturer. Players in an official sitting volleyball match may wear long pants, and they must sit directly on the floor. Players are not allowed to sit on thick padding while on the court of play. You can, of course, modify this rule in your physical education class, as you may want your students to sit on a wrestling mat for comfort. You can use a lighter ball and a lower net for students with more severe disabilities. As always, make any modifications necessary for your teaching situation.

Starting the Game

The game is started by first deciding which team will serve, which is accomplished by a coin toss. The team winning the toss chooses either to serve first or to defend a preferred court. Sets are played to 25 points using rally scoring. Remember that with rally scoring the receiving team can score points despite not having served. An official team consists of 12 players, but only 6 are on the court at one time. All player positions are determined by the position of the buttocks on the floor and not the position of legs or arms. For example, it is possible for a player who does not have use of his legs to be seated in the court area but have his legs positioned outside the court.

Game Objective

The objective of the game is the same as in traditional, or standing, volleyball, and that is to rally the ball in such a manner as to ground it on the opponents' court. Grounding the ball on the opponents' court may come from a serve, a well-placed pass, or an attack-hit. Teams are allowed three touches to rally the ball to the opponents' court in an attempt to ground the ball.

Team formations are similar to those in standing volleyball. The two rows of three players are considered front-row and back-row players. Blocking the serve by front-row players is allowed when the ball is in the front area of the court and positioned higher than the top of the net. A back-row player in sitting volleyball may carry out an attack-hit from any ball height, provided that the player's buttocks do not touch or cross over the front attack line.

Offensively, teams should work on passing the ball as setups for attack-hits. As players develop their skills, they need to consider passing the ball with appropriate height and speed to a teammate. A high pass is characterized by a high, arching, slower-paced pass to a teammate, either from the back to the front row or from side to side. A moderate pass is more deliberate and direct, with less arch and more speed. The quickest pass is flat and fast-paced and is used in quick setting for attack-hits. All three of these passes are subject to your students' ability levels and should be considered only if you feel they are appropriate.

Players move on the court from a seated position by using their hands and arms to momentarily lift the buttocks from the floor and slide to a new position. They may stand and run to get an errant ball if able, but they must be seated or have one butt cheek in contact with the floor when playing the ball. Players must have the ability to move in all directions. Generally, players travel 3 to 6 feet (1 to 1.8 m) to rally a ball with teammates. Once in position to rally a ball, players should have adequate trunk stability and balance to hold themselves in position for the play. Players may use their nonstriking arms as support for balance during an attack-hit or while serving a ball.

Defensively, players attempting to block a ball at the net should have substantial sitting balance and trunk stability. A block is performed by extending both arms straight up, palms facing the net and shoulder-width apart, and leaning slightly forward with the intent of sending the ball directly back to the opponents' court. One-arm blocks are possible; however, players must be able to brace themselves with one arm to the floor, reach up as high as possible, and block the ball without losing balance. Generally speaking, one-arm blocks are not as effective at the net but can be successful farther back on the court.

Remember, you can change the rules, equipment, player organizational patterns, or court size and can conduct the game according to your needs. Try to get your students to perform this sequence of skills in an attempt to ground the ball in the opponents' court: pass, set, and attack-hit. These three basic skills will help them conduct successful rallies in sitting volleyball.

Game Length

The World Organization of Volleyball for the Disabled (WOVD) determined for the 2000 Paralympic Games that the sitting volleyball competition would use rally scoring with sets to 25 points. Teams had to win by at least 2 points. All matches included five sets, with the winner of three sets declared the overall winner. Tie-breaker sets had to be played to 15 points, and teams had to win by 2 points.

General Rules and Penalties

As previously mentioned, many of the rules for sitting volleyball are similar to those for traditional volleyball. Following are the rules that are specific to sitting volleyball.

Rules Specific to Sitting Volleyball

The court size is smaller (32 by 20 feet, or 10 by 6 m); attack lines are closer to the net (6 feet, 6 inches, or 2 m); and the net height, length, and width are all reduced for the sport of sitting volleyball. Player positions are determined by where the player is seated, not by the position of arms or legs. This rule allows the player's impaired limbs to touch out-of-bound lines without penalty. Players are allowed to wear long pants during play; however, special padded material is not allowed underneath the player.

All players in an official sitting volleyball contest must be considered disabled, but two players on the roster are allowed to be evaluated as "minimally disabled." Only one player classified as minimally disabled is allowed on the court during an actual game. An example of minimally disabled would be a person who has a lower-body impairment but ambulates unassisted (such as a person with a below-knee amputation). People with single-leg amputations are eligible to play both sitting and standing volleyball.

Player positions are determined by the contact point of the players' buttocks and the floor. Player positions in standing volleyball are determined by the contact point of the players' feet. During a serve, the player's buttocks must remain in the service area and cannot make contact with the court area. Again, a player's feet or legs may touch the opponents' court during play as long as there is no interference with play. If a player's feet or legs touch the opponents' court during play, the player must return them to his own court as soon as possible.

A special rule for front-row players concerning blocking service is different from the rules of standing volleyball. When defending a serve, front-row players in sitting volleyball are allowed to block the service of the opponent. Also, at the 2000 Paralympics it was ruled that balls touching the net during a serve be allowed for play and not considered an infraction, forcing a side-out.

During a rally, players are not allowed to stand up or take steps to reposition themselves on the court. Players must remain in contact with the court with any part of their body between their shoulders and hips or buttocks. A momentary lifting of the buttocks is allowed during play.

Summary of the Sport

Table 8.1 is an overview of sitting volleyball. Use this table as a quick reference to the game.

Table 8.1 Overview of Sitting Volleyball

Field of play	The court is 32 by 20 ft (10 by 6 m). Attack lines are drawn 6 ft 6 in. (2 m) from the center line.
Players	Maximum allowed on court is six players. Only one can be classified as minimally disabled.
Equipment	The net is 21 ft (6.4 m) long and 2 ft 6 in. (30 cm) wide and is 4 ft (1.2 m) high for men and 3 ft 6 in. (1 m) high for women. The ball is a traditional volleyball usually 65-67 cm in circumference.
Legal start and scoring	The game is started with a serve. The player must be in the service area and in contact with the floor. Balls touching the net on a serve are legal. Rally scoring is used to score games to 25 points. In traditional matches, the winning team must win three of five games.
Ball movement	The ball is moved by either a pass (to include set), attack-hit, or serve. Only three touches are allowed on one team to move the ball across the net to the opponents' court during a rally.
Player positions	There are two rows with three players in each row. All player positions are established by the contact of the player's buttocks and the court. There are two front-row attackers, one setter, and three back-row players.
Player movement during play	Touching feet or legs to the opponents' court is permitted at any time during the play, provided that the player does not interfere with an opposing player. Touching the opponents' court with a hand is permitted; again, the player should avoid interference during the game. Defenders may attempt to block the serve.

SKILLS TO BE TAUGHT

Four skills can be taught in your physical education class for sitting volleyball: the pass, the attack-hit, the block, and the serve. Notice that the skill of passing has two variations: overhead and forearm. Most teachers refer to these two passes as set and bump, which is what they will be called in this chapter.

Players must have the ability to move about the court independently. Their methods of movement are specific to their disabilities and will not be discussed in this chapter. However, you should encourage them to learn to move quickly and anticipate the position of the ball during a rally. If your students are not capable of moving quickly while seated on the floor, you can slow the flight of the ball by changing the type of ball used in the game. You might consider using a beach ball or Volley-Lite volleyball, which is a ball the size of a volleyball but made of lightweight rubberized material similar to a Nerf ball.

Whether your students play on a padded surface or not, there are benefits for the student with a disability to playing volleyball on the floor. The greatest benefit is that the student can get out of the wheelchair and experience independent movement. Another advantage is that everyone can play on the floor, students with and without disabilities together, which helps to create an environment of inclusion. It is up to you to decide where and how to have your students play sitting volleyball. The following skills are taken from the competitive sport but can be modified for your teaching situation.

Passing

The two types of passes used in the game of sitting volleyball are the overhead pass and the forearm pass. Feel free to teach these skills according to your students' abilities.

Overhead Pass and Set

Positioned under the ball facing the net, the student holds the hands at or near the forehead with thumbs together. As the ball approaches, the student spreads the fingers and flexes the wrists; the thumbs and forefingers should form a triangle, or window, through which to see the ball. The student makes contact with the ball cleanly with the pads of fingers and thumbs while extending the elbows forcefully up and through the ball. As the ball departs from the hands, there should be minimal to no rotation or spin. The same mechanics are used for the set; however, the location of the pass is different.

When using the overhead pass to set a volleyball, the student should direct the ball using one of the three passes mentioned earlier: high, moderate, or quick. Placement of the set is critical to the execution of an attack-hit. The student should

Contact the ball with the pads of the fingers for an overhead pass.

Extend the elbows forcefully, minimizing ball rotation.

attempt to set the ball high and close enough to the net to allow an attack player to execute the hit. Sets are generally 6 to 18 inches (15 to 46 cm) from the net. The height of the set is determined by the tempo used.

Forearm Pass

This pass is used to pass a ball received at or below waist height. This is a two-handed pass and should be executed by having the ball strike the wrists, the lower arms, or the tops of the thumbs. The student clasps hands by holding the thumb of the right hand with the fingers of the left hand, palms turned slightly upward. Arms are extended, with a slight flexion at the elbows; shoulders are internally rotated. At contact with the ball, the student attempts to pass the ball up with gentle force, trying to absorb the ball's impact as much as possible.

Preparation for the forearm pass.

Position under the ball, hands clasped and elbows extended.

Absorbing the force of the ball's impact.

In traditional volleyball, players are told to bend their knees and lift as the ball is passed. Because such a maneuver is not possible for students with disabilities, they must develop a touch for absorbing the force of the ball at contact. This pass is often used to move a ball from the back row to the front row in preparation to set and attack-hit.

Attack-Hit

The attack-hit has also been referred to as the kill shot in volleyball and sitting volleyball. The attack-hit is a downward, forceful strike at the ball designed to ground the ball immediately on the opponents' court. To execute the attack-hit, the student should be in position underneath a descending ball and slightly behind its drop path, while facing the net. As the ball descends, the student rotates the striking shoulder away from the net and positions the striking arm back and away from the body, with wrist cocked. Contact with the ball is made by rotating the striking arm and shoulder forward and striking the ball with a slightly open hand at or near the top of the ball. The emphasis at contact is to strike the ball with a strong force resulting in a downward trajectory of the ball into the opponents'

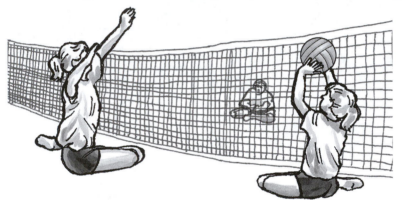

Position the body under the ball with the arm and wrist ready.

Rotate the striking shoulder away from the net and position the striking arm back.

Contact the ball with a slightly open hand in a downward direction.

court. Contact should be made at the highest point possible above the net. The contact point will vary according to the student's functional ability and skill level.

Block

The block is a skill that can be executed individually or with a teammate. It is performed by positioning as close to the net as possible, being careful not to interfere with the opponents' play. Remember, a student's limbs are allowed to pass under the net and lie in the opponents' court provided there is no interference. However, the student is responsible for keeping control of these limbs during play.

Individual Block

Using a stable, balanced sitting position, the student reaches up with both arms, elbows fully extended and about shoulder-width apart, and with palms facing toward the net. The block is performed by deflecting the ball directly back to the opponents' court in a downward pattern. Timing is the key component of this skill. The student must be able to time the blocking move appropriately to make it an effective defensive maneuver.

Position close to the net ready for a block.

Reach up with both arms; keep hands together for a block.

Two-Person Block

To execute a two-person block at the net, students should practice moving into correct court positions prior to attempting the block. A two-person block is performed the same as an individual block; however, both teammates must make every effort to align shoulders and arms parallel to the net. Blocking can occur away from the net but is often executed with one arm extended upward in an attempt to deflect the ball to a teammate for a possible set and attack-hit combination.

Two-person block.

Serve

The serve is used to put the ball into play at the beginning of a game. The serve described here is the overhand serve. Although you may want to start your students with an underhand serve, competitive serves are usually made with the overhand technique.

To execute the overhand serve (right-handed), have the student sit facing the net with a slight rotation of the striking shoulder away from the net. The student should hold the ball in the left hand slightly higher than eye level, with the elbow extended. The right arm is drawn back as the elbow is flexed and the wrist cocked in position to strike the ball (see passing skill). To serve the ball, the student raises the left arm slightly above the forehead while bringing the right arm forward to strike the ball. Emphasize striking the ball from the support hand (left) with minimal vertical toss. Contact should be made with the heel of the hand and cupped fingers at a point just above the head. It is important to emphasize follow-through on contact, because this will help direct the ball to the opponents' court. The motion is similar to the overhand throw in baseball.

Hold the ball higher than eye level with the striking arm drawn back.

Raise the ball above the head and make contact with the heel of the hand and the fingers slightly open.

FUNCTIONAL PROFILES AND GENERAL MODIFICATIONS

Table 8.2 presents student profiles that might fit your teaching situation. Read the table to determine the functional level of your student(s); then consider the activity modifications listed in table 8.3.

Table 8.2 Student Functional Profiles for Sitting Volleyball

Functional skill level	Student profile
Low	Multiple impairments; unable to sit independently without trunk support; unable to move independently on the floor; might use an electric or power wheelchair.
Moderate	Able to sit independently for short durations; can sit independently by bracing with one arm to the floor; has moderate strength in upper body and can momentarily lift buttocks from floor while seated using two arms; able to move 3 ft (1 m) independently on the floor.
High	Able to sustain a seated position on the floor without support; can lift buttocks from the floor and move 3-6 ft (1-1.8 m) independently; is able to hold both arms overhead and maintain balance while in seated position without support; is able to lean backward to reach or strike a volleyball without losing balance when seated on the floor.

Student Functional Profiles

Student functional profiles are operationally defined as low, moderate, and high. To play sitting volleyball, players must have a fair degree of trunk stability and independent sitting balance; that is, they must be moderate to high functioning. Students considered low functioning are those who would not be able to hold a balanced seated position out of the wheelchair without some form of assistance. *All activities written for low-functioning students should be implemented with the student in the wheelchair* unless some form of assisted seating is provided (e.g., support from a teacher or teacher's assistant). However, official sitting volleyball rules do not allow players to use wheelchairs on the court.

General Modifications

Table 8.3 shows how to apply general modifications for students with disabilities to the skills of sitting volleyball. These modifications are based on the student functional profiles in table 8.2. You can decide how best to apply these general modifications to your unique student population.

GAME PROGRESSIONS

The games listed in the remainder of this chapter are presented in the class formats of one on one, small group, and large group. Higher-functioning students can begin with small or large group activities as appropriate. These games are intended to help you include your students with disabilities in a volleyball unit. Keep in mind that students considered low functioning will have to perform these games from their wheelchairs. Also, remember that the inclusion suggestions are meant to help you place students with disabilities in more decision-making roles.

Table 8.3 General Modifications for Sitting Volleyball

Skill level	Skill	Activity modifications
Low	Passing	Roll a ball back and forth across the length of a table to a partner.
	Attack-hit	Strike a swinging lightweight ball to simulate an attack-hit.
	Block	From 2 ft (0.6 m) in front of a tabletop, move the wheelchair to block a ball before it rolls off the table's edge. Balls come from any direction.
	Serve	Seated in front of a table with a ball tethered overhead, swing the ball forward over the table to the opposite end to simulate a serve.
Moderate	Passing	Seated on the floor, roll or toss a ball to another student.
	Attack-hit	Seated on the floor beside a tall traffic cone, balance a volleyball on the cone and strike the ball from the cone.
	Block	Seated on the floor beneath a ball tethered to a basketball rim, block the ball with two arms as it swings forward.
	Serve	Throw the ball from a serving position on the floor.
High	All skills	No modifications: Used with highest-functioning students.

GAMES-BY-SKILL-LEVEL INDEX: LOW-FUNCTIONING STUDENTS

The index in table 8.4 will help you choose games for low-functioning students according to their needs. Find the skill you want to address and make sure to assess this skill using the assessment templates provided in chapter 4 and on the DVD. The index is followed by activities specifically for students who are lower functioning. An index for moderate- to high-functioning students follows the game descriptions for low-functioning students.

Table 8.4 Games-by-Skill-Level Index for Low-Functioning Students—Sitting Volleyball

Skills	One on one	Small group	Large group
Passing	Table Target Pass I	Table Target Pass II	Table Target Pass III
Attack-hit	Tarzan Attack I	Tarzan Attack II	Tarzan Attack III
Block	Right Back at You	Roll and Block	Keep It In
Serve	Serving Cone	Serving Line	Over It Goes

GAME DESCRIPTIONS

Each game description in this section includes class format, organizational pattern, equipment, description, extensions, and inclusion suggestions. These games are written with the idea of moving a student from a one-on-one situation to a large group environment.

Skill ▶ Passing

TABLE TARGET PASS I

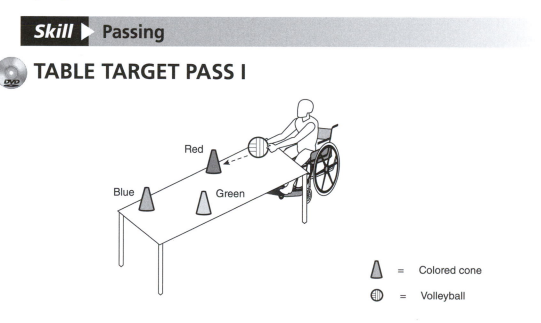

Red

Blue   Green

⬛ = Colored cone

⬤ = Volleyball

Class format: One on one

Organizational pattern: The student is at one end of the table, and colored targets are at each of the three remaining sides of the table.

Equipment: Volleyball, small Nerf ball, or deflated playground ball; long folding table; colored targets (e.g., red cone, blue beanbag)

Description: Students who have grip reach for a ball on the tabletop, lift the ball with two hands, return it to the tabletop, and roll it to a designated colored target (e.g., a red cone or a blue beanbag).

Extension: Have the student use one hand to simulate the bump pass.

Inclusion suggestions: The student can demonstrate to the class her ability to accomplish the task. The student can also select the order of passing, such as red target, then blue, then green.

 # TABLE TARGET PASS II

Class format: Small group

Organizational pattern: The student with a disability is at one end of the table, and classmates (without disabilities) are at each of the three remaining sides.

Equipment: Small Nerf ball or deflated playground ball, long folding table

Description: Same concept as Table Target Pass I, except that the student passes the ball to classmates. The passes should rotate from student to student around the table.

Extension: Have students without disabilities alternate at the table with others from the class.

Inclusion suggestions: The student with a disability can decide how many times to pass the ball and must indicate that to those at the table. The student can also determine a change in the order of passing and decide who should pass the ball first.

TABLE TARGET PASS III

🏐 = Volleyball

↑ = Set

Class format: Large group

Organizational pattern: Students without disabilities are in small circles around the gym, and the student with a disability is at a double-wide table (two tables side by side) with four or five students without disabilities at the table.

Equipment: Small Nerf ball or deflated playground balls, two long folding tables

Description: The game for the class is to use overhead passing and forearm passing to move the ball around the circle so that each person passes the ball using the two passes. The students at the table must do the same, except that they roll the ball to initiate the pass to their teammates. Once the ball reaches a teammate at the table, that student must pick the ball up from the table and complete one overhead pass to herself, return the ball to the table, and pass it to another student who repeats the overhead self-pass. Once everyone has passed the ball twice, the game is over.

Extensions: Have students without disabilities alternate overhead and forearm passes. Rotate a new team of students without disabilities at the table for each round.

Inclusion suggestions: The student with a disability can decide which pass the team should perform first. The student can also determine who should start the game with the first pass.

Skill ▶ Attack-Hit

TARZAN ATTACK I

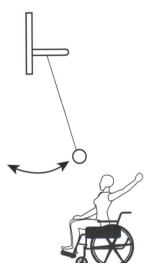

O = Tethered ball

Class format: One on one

Organizational pattern: The student is seated in a wheelchair under a ball that is tethered from a basketball rim so that it swings slightly above the student's head.

Equipment: Nerf volleyball, small Nerf ball, or deflated playground ball; rope for tethering; small net bag to hold the tethered ball

Description: On a signal, the ball is released so that it swings toward the student in a wheelchair. As the ball nears the student's overhead position, the student strikes or attack-hits the ball. The student may require physical assistance.

Extensions: Shorten the distance of the swing, use a larger ball, or use a beach ball.

Inclusion suggestions: Students without disabilities can release the ball. The student with a disability can determine the distance to swing prior to the release of the tethered ball.

TARZAN ATTACK II

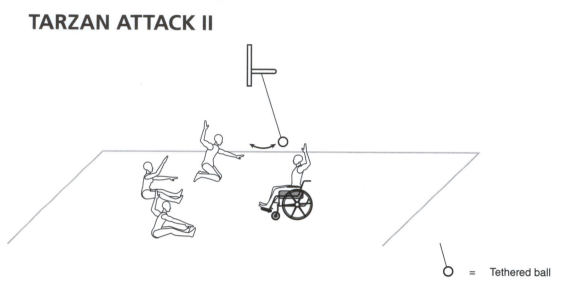

= Tethered ball

Class format: Small group

Organizational pattern: Two or three students in a semicircle formation in front of the tethered ball from the basketball rim (see Tarzan Attack I)

Equipment: Nerf volleyball, small Nerf ball, or deflated playground ball; rope for tethering; small net bag to hold the tethered ball

Description: Students without disabilities are seated on the floor along with the student using a wheelchair; they are in a semicircle formation facing the tethered ball. On a signal, the ball is released so that it swings toward the students. As the ball nears a student's overhead position, that student performs an attack-hit on the ball. Make sure to provide enough distance between students in the semicircle. The student with a disability may require physical assistance.

Extensions: Extend the number of hits to be made on the ball, use a larger ball, or use a beach ball.

Inclusion suggestion: The student with a disability can release the ball on the initial swing.

TARZAN ATTACK III

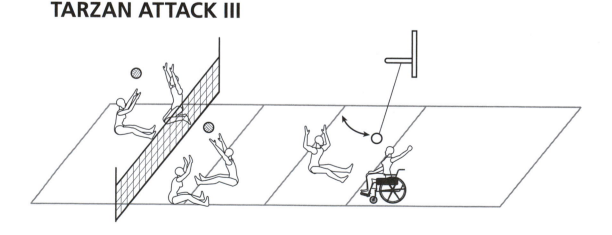

Class format: Large group

Organizational pattern: Divide the class into teams with equal numbers. Set up your volleyball court near a basketball goal so you can use the rim to tether the volleyball. Place one team at each court; all students should be seated. The student using a wheelchair should be positioned by the tethered ball under the basketball rim near his team's court. If this is not possible, other means of tethering the ball must be used.

Equipment: Traditional volleyball, Nerf volleyball, small Nerf ball, or deflated playground ball; rope for tethering; small net bag to hold the tethered ball

Description: The objective of the game is for each team to attack-hit a ball over the net. The objective for the student using a wheelchair is to attack-hit the swinging ball cleanly on each of two attempts. Minimal assistance should be provided for the student with a disability during the hit. The student without a disability should swing the ball forward for the teammate. Each team gets two rounds before switching; the number of attack-hits that are grounded in the opponents' court are totaled. For the students without disabilities, the attack-hit should be set up by a high toss from a teammate.

Extension: Move the student with a disability to the court and attempt a toss and attack-hit combination using a slower-moving ball, such as a beach ball.

Inclusion suggestion: The student with a disability can decide the number of successful attack-hits each team must complete.

Skill ▶ Block

RIGHT BACK AT YOU

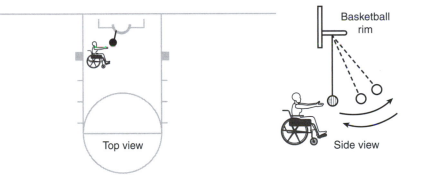

(from chapter 6, Wheelchair Basketball, page 61)

Class format: One on one

Organizational pattern: Individual with teacher or peer assistant as needed

Equipment: Nerf volleyball, small Nerf ball, or deflated playground ball; rope for tethering; small net bag to hold the tethered ball

Description: A ball tethered to a basketball rim hangs at eye level for the student with a disability. The student pushes the ball away and blocks it as it returns from the push. Use student assistants throughout the class session.

Extension: If grasp and release is an issue, physically assist, with emphasis on opening the hands to receive the ball.

Inclusion suggestion: The student with a disability can pick a partner to work with prior to moving to any small group activity.

ROLL AND BLOCK

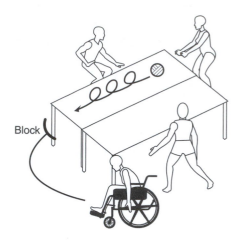

⊘ ‒ℓℓ→ = Rolled ball

Class format: Small group

Organizational pattern: Students without disabilities on each of three sides of two folding tables placed side by side and a student with a disability on the fourth side

Equipment: Nerf volleyball, small Nerf ball, or deflated playground ball; two folding tables placed side by side

Description: Allow the student with a wheelchair enough room to move her motorized wheelchair back and forth freely on her own table side. On a cue, the students without disabilities release the ball across the table. The objective is to have the student using the wheelchair move quickly to block the ball from dropping off the table's edge. Students should roll the ball slowly enough to challenge the student using a wheelchair. The student with a disability should return to a neutral position at the table after each blocking attempt.

Extensions: Change the type of ball used; rotate new students to the table.

Inclusion suggestion: The student with a disability can point to or indicate in some manner which student should roll the ball, rather than going in random order.

KEEP IT IN

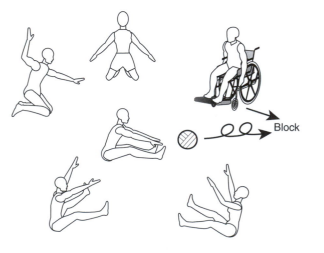

───→ = Turn to block

⊘ ‒ℓℓ→ = Rolled ball

Class format: Large group

Organizational pattern: Divide the class into small groups and have the groups sit in circles around the gymnasium. Place one student without a disability in the center of the circle. The student using a wheelchair should be included in one of the circles.

Equipment: Traditional volleyballs, Nerf volleyballs, small Nerf balls, deflated playground balls, or large beach balls

Description: The student in the center of the circle, while seated, must attempt to pass the ball out of the circle using quick tosses. The objective is to have the students block the ball from exiting the circle. The tosses cannot be higher than arm's reach overhead, and blockers are allowed to use one or two arms to block. The student in the center makes five attempts. After five attempts, a new student takes the center position. When attempting to toss the ball out of the circle against the student using the wheelchair, students must roll the ball. The student using a wheelchair must position the wheelchair quickly to block the ball from exiting the circle.

Extension: When the student using the wheelchair plays the center position, all students in the circle formation must sit with their backs to the middle. The student using a wheelchair must release a ball, with assistance as needed, and the students attempting to block the ball must listen carefully to the sound of the bouncing ball as it rolls toward them. They must block the ball without turning to watch where it has been rolled.

Inclusion suggestion: The student with a disability can decide the distance of the circle's diameter when it is his turn to play the middle position.

Skill ▶ Serve

💿 SERVING CONE

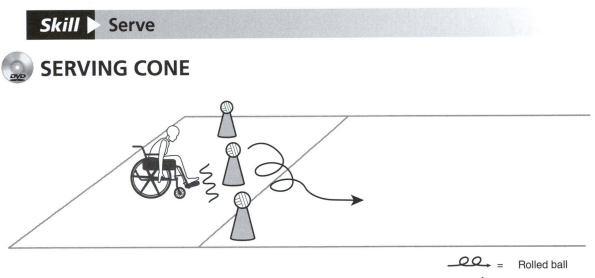

⌒ℓℓ→ = Rolled ball

ⵘ = Ball bumped from cone

Class format: One on one

Organizational pattern: Three tall traffic cones with volleyballs balanced on each and a student with a disability approximately 3 or 4 feet (1 to 1.2 m) behind one of the cones

Equipment: Three tall traffic cones; traditional volleyballs, Nerf volleyballs, small Nerf balls, deflated playground balls, or large beach balls

Description: On a signal, the student using the wheelchair approaches the traffic cone and attempts to bump the cone so as to knock the ball from it. The serve is complete when the ball is displaced from the cone. The student repeats the movement for each of the remaining two traffic cones.

Extensions: If the student has the functional ability, allow her to strike the ball with her hand or arm. Establish a distance the ball must travel after leaving the cone for the serve to be considered successful (e.g., 10 feet or 3 m).

Inclusion suggestion: The student with a disability can decide the distance the ball must travel to be considered a successful serve.

SERVING LINE

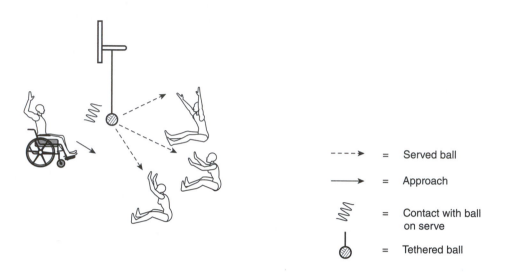

- - - - → = Served ball

———→ = Approach

〰 = Contact with ball on serve

⬤ = Tethered ball

Class format: Small group

Organizational pattern: Students without disabilities in a semicircle formation facing a student with a disability, who is positioned ready to serve a tethered ball

Equipment: Line or rope to tether the ball; traditional volleyball, Nerf volleyball, small Nerf ball, deflated playground ball, or large beach ball

Description: The student with a disability is in front of the tethered ball, which should be stationary as it hangs from the basketball rim approximately 4 to 5 inches (10 to 13 cm) above the student's head. Two or three students without disabilities receive the serve in semicircle formation facing the server. On the signal, the student with a disability moves to strike the ball using an overhead serve motion with his arm. The student serves to all members of the group; then rotates out.

Extension: Students without disabilities can participate in this game from a seated position on the floor. Lower the tethered ball so that it hangs about 4 to 5 inches (10 to 13 cm) above the serving student's head and have him serve to the group using an overhead serve motion. Make sure to allow enough distance between the server and the group when the students without disabilities serve. Rotate students without disabilities through this game.

Inclusion suggestion: The student with a disability can decide the order of servers.

 OVER IT GOES

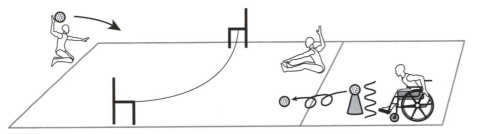

⚬⚬ ⊛ = Rolled ball

〜 = Ball bumped from cone

Class format: Large group

Organizational pattern: Teams on the court, practicing serving from a seated position

Equipment: Regulation volleyball, Nerf volleyball, small Nerf ball, or large beach ball; volleyball net

Description: The class is divided into teams with each team situated on a separate court in a seated position. Place a net at regulation height, or use other material to create a net (e.g., a rope strung across two folding chairs). Students without disabilities should practice overhead serving as described. The student with a disability should use the traffic cone from the Serving Cone game. Have the cone placed on the court with a volleyball balanced on top. A successful serve for the student with a disability occurs when the ball has been struck from the cone and rolls a predetermined distance, such as 5 feet (1.5 m). Each team should count successful serves within three minutes. All teams should rotate to new courts every three minutes.

Extensions: Move the student with a disability closer to the net and have her attempt to serve the ball up and over the net. You might consider using a beach ball to help increase ball trajectory.

Inclusion suggestions: The student with a disability can determine the distance the ball should roll to be considered a successful serve. The student can also determine the number of times each team should serve before changing courts.

GAMES-BY-SKILL-LEVEL INDEX: MODERATE-TO HIGH-FUNCTIONING STUDENTS

The index in table 8.5 addresses those students with disabilities who are considered to have moderate to high function. The class formats remain the same (one on one, small group, large group). Moderate to high functioning students should be able to work on the floor with minimal support. Descriptions of games for this population follow.

Table 8.5 Games-by-Skill-Level Index for Moderate- to High-Functioning Students—Sitting Volleyball

Skills	One on one	Small group	Large group
Passing	Pass It Up	Up and Over I	Up and Over II
Attack-hit	Throw It Over I (Attack-Hit)	Throw It Over II (Attack-Hit)	Rip It
Block	Put 'Em Up	The Wall	Just the Three of Us
Serve	Throw It Over I (Serve)	Clean the Kitchen	Serving Math

GAME DESCRIPTIONS

The 12 games described in this section are specifically designed for students with moderate to high ability. As always, feel free to choose games appropriate to your unique physical education situation and population, as well as to modify any games as needed.

Skill ▶ Passing (Overhead and Forearm)

PASS IT UP

Class format: One on one

Organizational pattern: Individual with peer assistant

Equipment: Traditional volleyball, Nerf volleyball, small Nerf ball, or large beach ball; rope for tethering; small net bag to hold the tethered ball

Description: The student with a disability and a partner are seated on the floor under a ball tethered to a basketball rim. The ball should hang between 6 and 8 inches (15 and 20 cm) overhead. The student practices executing a correct overhead pass to his partner. After completing a predetermined number of overhead passes, the student with a disability practices forearm passes (bumps) to his partner. The tether will have to be lowered during the forearm passing activity.

Extension: Have the student alternate on each pass with an overhead pass and then a forearm pass, and repeat for a predetermined number of passes.

Inclusion suggestions: The student with a disability can demonstrate to the class his ability to accomplish the task and decide how many passes to make before switching.

UP AND OVER I

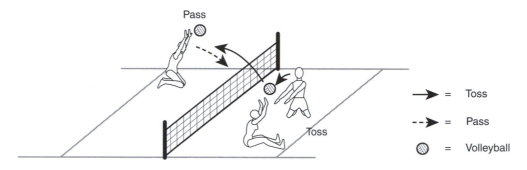

Class format: Small group

Organizational pattern: Students get together in groups of three, two seated on the same side of the net facing the third partner. The third partner is positioned on the opposite side of the net and will serve as the tosser to begin the activity.

Equipment: Traditional volleyballs, Nerf volleyballs, or small Nerf balls; net

Description: All students should be seated facing their partners across the net. Students work to pass the ball up and over the net to their partners. One student begins the activity with a toss of the ball to the student using an overhead pass. The toss must be high enough so that the passer can position underneath the ball as it descends. As the pass is made over the net, the receiving student attempts to pass it back using the same overhead passing technique. Groups attempt to make as many successful passes as possible in a given time.

Extensions: Increase the distance of the tosser from the passer. Rotate positions so that each student experiences tossing and passing.

Inclusion suggestion: The student with a disability can determine which students should toss and pass for each rotation.

UP AND OVER II

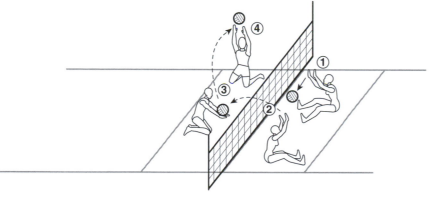

① = Toss

② = Overhead pass

③ = Bump

④ = Overhead pass

Class format: Large group

Organizational pattern: Students in teams of two seated on each side of the net facing one another

Equipment: Traditional volleyballs, Nerf volleyballs, or small Nerf balls; net (Use a rope strung between two folding chairs if you don't have a net.)

Description: All students, those with and without disabilities, should be seated on both sides of the net facing the net. The game begins with a toss to the passer, who uses an overhead pass to move the ball to the opposite court. The receiving student uses a forearm pass (bump) to pass the ball to her teammate, who in turn sends the ball back over the net using an overhead pass. The sequence should be toss, overhead pass, forearm pass, overhead pass, ending with a catch by the original tosser. The objective of the game is to perform as many complete cycles of this sequence as possible in the time provided. The student with a disability is on the floor with other students and must perform all skills (toss, overhead pass, and forearm pass).

Extensions: Attempt the game without the net first; then add the net when students are successful. If students are successful, change to a traditional volleyball.

Inclusion suggestion: The student with a disability can determine which students should toss and pass for each rotation.

Skill ▶ Attack-Hit

THROW IT OVER I (ATTACK-HIT)

Class format: One on one

Organizational pattern: Individual with peer partner

Equipment: Traditional volleyball, Nerf volleyball, or small Nerf ball; net (Use a rope strung between two folding chairs if you don't have a net.)

Description: The student with a disability is seated on the floor facing the net. This is a simple game of throwing; the objective is to throw the ball over the net. Concentrate on teaching the student proper arm mechanics, because these are the same as those used to execute the attack-hit. The student should be positioned at a distance from the net that facilitates a successful performance.

Extensions: Change the distance to the net as the student becomes more successful with the task. A student without a disability can help to retrieve the balls thrown.

Inclusion suggestions: The student with a disability can demonstrate his skill level if appropriate. The student can also teach a small group of students without disabilities the key points.

THROW IT OVER II (ATTACK-HIT)

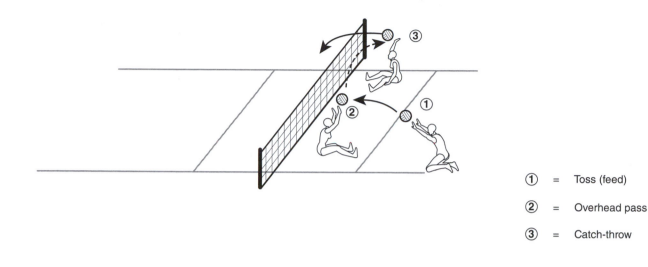

① = Toss (feed)

② = Overhead pass

③ = Catch-throw

Class format: Small group

Organizational pattern: Small groups of three students seated on the floor in triangle formation

Equipment: Traditional volleyballs, Nerf volleyballs, or small Nerf balls; net (Use a rope strung between two folding chairs if you don't have a net.)

Description: Students with and without disabilities participate in this activity. One student starts the activity with a toss, or feed, to the second student. The second student passes the ball (overhead or set) up and close to the net for the third student, who catches the ball and throws it down to the opponents' court with force. The sequence should be toss, pass, catch-throw. The objective is to make sure the passes are above and close to the net so that the catch-and-throw-down movement can be made forcefully. As skill levels improve, the students can begin to attack-hit the ball instead of catching and throwing, using the skill mechanics mentioned earlier in this chapter for the attack-hit.

Extensions: Have students rotate positions during the activity. Change the type of ball for the student with a disability if that student is not successful with the traditional volleyball.

Inclusion suggestion: The student with a disability can decide the new positions and rotation for the group.

RIP IT

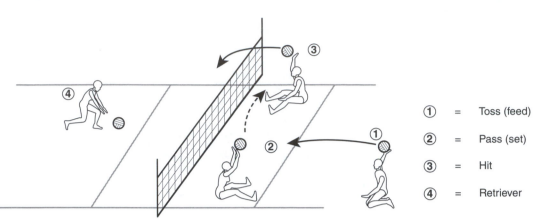

①	=	Toss (feed)
②	=	Pass (set)
③	=	Hit
④	=	Retriever

Class format: Large group

Organizational pattern: Students with and without disabilities are in triangle formation on the floor in teams of three or four. One student retrieves the ball as needed.

Equipment: Traditional volleyballs, Nerf volleyballs, or small Nerf balls; net (Use a rope strung between two folding chairs if you don't have a net.)

Description: The activity is very similar to Throw It Over, with the exception that students are required to attack-hit the ball at the net. One student starts the activity with a toss, or feed, to the second student. The second student passes the ball (overhead or set) up and close to the net for the third student, who attack-hits the ball to the opponents' court. There should be no attempt to block the attack-hit. The sequence is toss, pass (set), hit. Each student should attempt to attack-hit at least once during three rotations.

Extensions: Have students rotate positions in the activity. Change the type of ball for the student with a disability if that student is not successful with the traditional volleyball.

Inclusion suggestion: The student with a disability can decide one new combination or sequence to this activity—for example toss, pass (forearm), pass (set), hit.

Skill ▶ Block

PUT 'EM UP

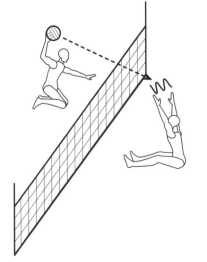

- - ➤	=	Tossed ball
⌇	=	Blocked ball

Class format: One on one

Organizational pattern: Two students on either side of the net facing each other

Equipment: Traditional volleyball, Nerf volleyball, or small Nerf ball; net (Use a rope strung between two folding chairs if you don't have a net.)

Description: The student with a disability is seated in front of the volleyball net. A partner tosses a ball at the top of the net from the opposite side, and the student with a disability attempts to put her arms and hands up to block the toss. The toss should be forceful and directed at the top of the net to simulate an attack-hit from an opponent.

Extension: Change the type of ball used if the student with a disability cannot move into position quickly enough to block or if the ball is too heavy and the student is at risk for injury.

Inclusion suggestion: The student can demonstrate her skill level to the class after several sessions playing this game.

THE WALL

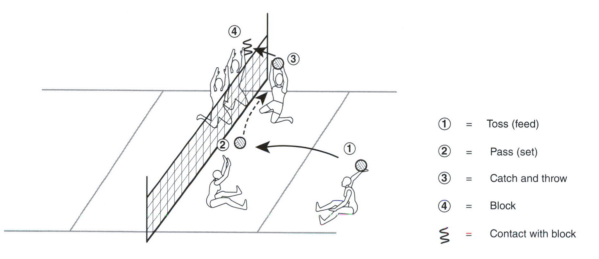

①	=	Toss (feed)
②	=	Pass (set)
③	=	Catch and throw
④	=	Block
⧤	=	Contact with block

Class format: Small group

Organizational pattern: Pairs of students seated side-by-side on the floor

Equipment: Traditional volleyballs, Nerf volleyballs, or small Nerf balls; net (Use a rope strung between two folding chairs if you don't have a net.)

Description: This is an extension of Throw It Over II and should be played by students with and without disabilities. The objective of this game is to have two students side by side form a wall and attempt to block the throw-over. As the throw-over is made after a toss and pass from students on one side of the net, two students on the opposite side of the net block the throw by positioning themselves in a blocking stance as described earlier in this chapter. The emphasis here is on the position of both students, who should be side by side with arms extended overhead and hands held together. Timing is the key to this game, because the students must learn to move into the blocking position as the ball is being readied for the throw-over.

Extension: Change the type of ball to block for the student with a disability if the ball being used presents a risk of injury.

Inclusion suggestion: The student with a disability can decide how many blocks are made before all students rotate positions.

JUST THE THREE OF US

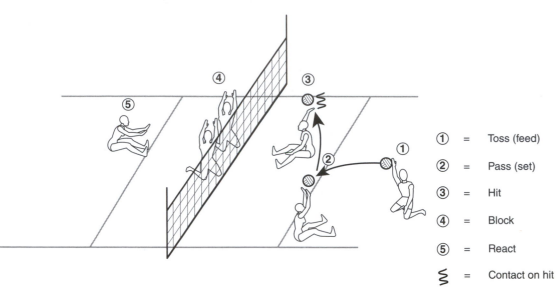

①	=	Toss (feed)
②	=	Pass (set)
③	=	Hit
④	=	Block
⑤	=	React
⟨	=	Contact on hit

Class format: Large group

Organizational pattern: Small groups of three students seated on the floor in a triangle formation

Equipment: Traditional volleyballs, Nerf volleyballs, or small Nerf balls; net (Use a rope strung between two folding chairs if you don't have a net.)

Description: This is an extension of Rip It and should be played by students with and without disabilities. In the game Rip It, students practice the sequence of pass, set, and attack-hit. In this game, a set of blockers is added on the opposite side of the net. The block is made by two of the three students positioned at the net in a blocking position. The third student is positioned behind and to the side of the blockers, ready to react to the rebound of the block. If the ball is blocked and it rebounds to the same side of the court, the third student must react in an attempt to pass the ball up for his teammates. If the ball is blocked back to the opponents' court, the third student changes places with one of the blockers for the next attack-hit. The activity continues until all students have played each of the three positions.

Extension: Change the type of ball to block for the student with a disability if the ball being used presents a risk of injury.

Inclusion suggestion: The student with a disability can decide who starts at the net for blocking and who is positioned as the third student on the team.

Skill ▶ Serve

THROW IT OVER I (SERVE)

Class format: One on one

Organizational pattern: Individual with teacher or peer partner

Equipment: Traditional volleyball, Nerf volleyball, or small Nerf ball; net (Use a rope strung between two folding chairs if you don't have a net.)

Description: The student with a disability is seated on the floor facing the net. This is a simple throwing game; the objective is to throw the ball over the net. The student should concentrate on proper arm mechanics, because these mechanics are the same as those used in the serve. The student should be positioned at a successful distance from the net.

Extensions: Change the distance to the net as the student becomes more successful with the game. A student without a disability can retrieve the balls thrown.

Inclusion suggestion: The student with a disability can demonstrate her skill level if appropriate.

CLEAN THE KITCHEN

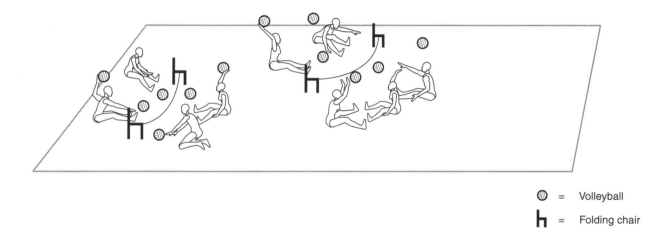

⚽ = Volleyball

h = Folding chair

Class format: Small group

Organizational pattern: Small groups positioned on each side of several nets. If you set up three nets, you will have six groups (one group on each side). At least one student per court can retrieve and then rotate into the game. Students with and without disabilities participate in this activity.

Equipment: Traditional volleyballs, Nerf volleyballs, or small Nerf balls; nets (Use ropes strung between two folding chairs if you don't have a net.)

Description: Start the activity with an equal number of balls on each side of the nets. On the signal, the students attempt to serve the ball over the net to their opponents' court and "keep their kitchen clean." As the ball is received into the court, that team must return it as soon as possible in the same attempt to keep their kitchen clean. The objective is to have the least number of balls in your court (kitchen) when the whistle blows. The only method of ball movement is serving; students are not allowed to throw or pass the ball over to the opposite court (kitchen). One student on each court retrieves errant balls, because everyone participating is seated. The student retriever is rotated as each new game begins.

Extension: Eliminate the net until students' skill levels improve.

Inclusion suggestion: The student with a disability can suggest one variation to this activity (e.g., changing the number of balls on each court).

SERVING MATH

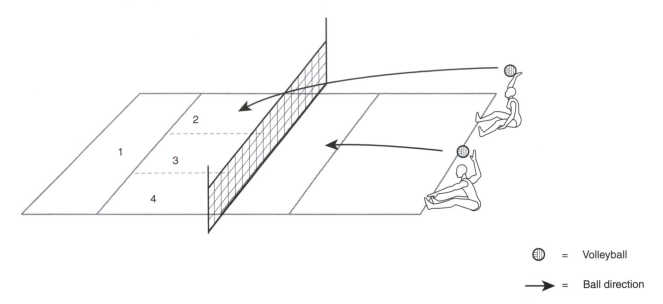

= Volleyball

= Ball direction

Class format: Large group

Organizational pattern: Teams of three to five students with and without disabilities, seated on the floor

Equipment: Traditional volleyballs, Nerf volleyballs, or small Nerf balls; net (Use a rope strung between two folding chairs if you don't have a net.)

Description: Divide the court into four sections and give each section a number (any numbers you choose). Position the teams at the serving lines of their respective courts. The objective of the game is to reach a predetermined number (i.e., 22) by serving the ball into the correct numerical sections of the opponents' court. Each member must attempt to reach the designated value by serving. You may present the problem as an addition, subtraction, multiplication, or division problem. For example, you might say, "Divide the number 100 by 10 and serve into the correct sections until your team gets the correct answer." The students would then try to serve into their opponents' court until they reach the number 10. If the problem cannot be answered by using the skill of serving, have the students come as close as possible without going over the value.

Extensions: Change the sections to a series of colors and tell the class to serve the ball in a particular sequence (e.g., blue-red-green or red-green-blue). Or, make each section of the court a state and present geography problems (e.g., Which state is closest to the Atlantic Ocean?).

Inclusion suggestion: The student with a disability can suggest a topic for the court sections (e.g., favorite basketball teams, famous musicians).

Remember that blank forms for assessments, IEPs, and unit and lesson plans are located on the DVD.

Chapter 9

Wheelchair Tennis

The history of wheelchair tennis in the United States can be traced to three people: Brad Parks, Randy Snow, and Dr. Bal Moore. Each has contributed to the sport at the local, national, collegiate, and international levels of competition.

Brad Parks had been an athlete prior to his spinal cord injury in the mid-1970s. During a family vacation, he began to experiment with wheelchair tennis and soon found success with the sport. Parks is credited with developing the two-bounce rule and, along with his therapist, David Saltz, establishing the National Foundation of Wheelchair Tennis in 1979.

Randy Snow and Dr. Bal Moore teamed up to become perhaps the greatest player–coach combination ever to grace the wheelchair tennis world. Snow was injured in a farming accident at the age of 16, and Moore redirected his basketball coaching career to make himself one of the leading tennis instruction professionals in the world. Snow and Moore met in 1989 at the Lakeshore Rehabilitation Hospital in Birmingham, Alabama. Snow was conducting a wheelchair tennis camp at Lakeshore when he caught Moore's eye. Moore, then head tennis coach at Jefferson State Community College, noted Snow's athleticism and invited him to practice with the college team. Intrigued with wheelchair tennis, Moore began to apply his kinesiology and biomechanics education to the sport. As the friendship between the two men grew, so did their professional relationship, and in the early 1990s they established the World Wheelchair Tennis Academy, which is now part of Camp Deerhorn in Rhinelander, Wisconsin (http://deerhorn.com). They teamed up to win wheelchair tennis titles at the 1990 World Games for the Disabled and at the 1992 and 1996 Paralympics.

Wheelchair tennis in the United State grew from its humble beginnings in the 1970s to over 55 sanctioned tournaments and more than 2,000 competitors by 1986. In 1992, wheelchair tennis was officially recognized as a medal sport at the Barcelona Paralympics. According to the 2009 International Tennis Foundation (ITF), over 100 athletes competed in wheelchair tennis for the 2008 Paralympics averaging over 9,000 spectators during gold medal matches (www.itftennis.com).

This chapter is dedicated to my friend Randy Snow, who passed away this year while conducting a tennis clinic. Randy was instrumental in helping me write this chapter for the first edition of this text, and was in the process of editing the current chapter at the time of his death. Randy was a friend, professional colleague, and someone who always had time for me. You will be missed, Randy.

DESCRIPTION OF THE SPORT

Wheelchair tennis is very similar to tennis played by people without disabilities. The game is played on the same traditional court, using the same boundary lines and markings. There are competition categories for men and women in singles and doubles, plus a mixed category. The game is started with a serve that must bounce within the opponent's court. The most noticeable difference between wheelchair tennis and traditional tennis is that two bounces are allowed before the player must return the ball during a rally.

Field of Play

The game is played on a traditional court measuring 78 feet (24 m) long and 36 feet (11 m) wide for doubles and 27 feet (8.2 m) wide for singles. The net is 3 feet (1 m) high, and the doubles alleys are 4 feet 6 inches (1.4 m) wide. The singles serving court is 13 feet 6 inches (4 m) wide and 26 feet (7.9 m) long.

Players

Any person medically diagnosed as having a mobility-related disability is eligible to play wheelchair tennis. Those who play the sport might have one of the following limitations: spinal cord injury (paraplegic or quadriplegic), polio, spina bifida, or cerebral palsy. This list of conditions is not meant to be all inclusive; those with other mobility limitations may be eligible to play wheelchair tennis.

Equipment

A player's wheelchair is considered part of the player's body. The game is played with a regulation-size racket and official USTA tennis balls.

Starting the Game

The game is started with a serve. The server must have all wheels of the wheelchair behind the baseline during the serve. The server must remain stationary during the serve and is not allowed to roll into the serve or adjust the wheelchair position to gain an advantage. The small wheels (casters) are not allowed to be over the baseline in the court area during the serve.

Game Objective

The objective of the game is to serve the ball in such a manner as to not allow the opponent to have a successful return. If the service return is successful and a rally ensues, players continue to rally the ball until one player fails to return the ball successfully. Unsuccessful returns in wheelchair tennis are those returned after more than two bounces, returns sent out of bounds, or returns not sent over the net.

In doubles competition, the same objective exists. Each player on a team serves a game during his turn. The right to serve remains with a team until a ball is not returned legally by the serving team; at that time the serve is given to the other team. When the serve is awarded back to the original team, the second member of the team has the opportunity to serve. This rotation continues throughout the game.

Success in wheelchair tennis depends on players' functional abilities and wheelchair mobility skills. The majority of play for the beginner happens deep in the court area, behind the baseline. Players taught to play deeper in the court have much more success. Remember, in wheelchair tennis the ball is allowed to bounce twice, and only one of the bounces must be within the boundaries of the court area. The second bounce can occur outside the boundary lines and is still considered eligible for play.

The area of the court that has the second most frequent rallies is between the baseline and the service line. This is usually the area where the ball bounces once, thus forcing the player to make a decision about hitting a quick return for a "winner." Rally play in this area requires very good wheelchair skills (reverse mobility) and an above-average command of several tennis strokes (e.g., the topspin forehand and the backhand slice).

The third area of the court is between the net and the service line; it is the forwardmost area on the court. This area should be addressed by more advanced players. Rally points played from this area usually end with the player attempting to end the point. The player must have excellent wheelchair and racket control to rally a ball from this area.

The skills mentioned in this chapter and the games suggested are for beginners and not advanced players. Students with disabilities, and those without, who are learning wheelchair tennis for the first time should practice their play from behind the baseline. As they develop in skill and wheelchair mobility, they can play closer to the net.

Game Length

Wheelchair tennis follows USTA rules regarding game, set, and match lengths. Scoring is the same for a game (love, 15, 30, 40, deuce, advantage, and game), and it takes six games to win a set. If two players have each won five games, then the set is continued until a player has won by two games. A player must win three sets in official men's competition and two sets in women's competition to be declared the match winner.

General Rules and Penalties

As mentioned, all the rules in traditional tennis apply to wheelchair tennis, with the exception of a few that are specific to the game.

Rules Specific to Wheelchair Tennis

The most visible rule change specific to wheelchair tennis is the two-bounce rule. The players are allowed two bounces to return a ball to the opponent's court. Keep in mind that only the first bounce has to be inside the court's boundary lines.

When serving the ball, all wheels must remain behind the baseline. The player serving the ball may not change positions throughout the serve by rolling or spinning his wheels. If a player uses any part of his body to stabilize or stop the wheelchair during service delivery, the serve is considered a fault. A player is allowed to use unconventional methods to initiate the serve as a result of physical limitations (e.g., a second person may drop the ball to the server).

The wheelchair is considered part of the player's body along with anything that is carried on the wheelchair. If a ball touches the wheelchair or anything carried on the wheelchair (besides the player's racket) during a rally, it is considered a loss of point. Likewise, in doubles competition if a player hits her partner during the serve or a rally, it is considered a fault and results in the loss of a point.

During a rally, if a player uses her feet to stop, change directions, or turn the wheelchair, it is considered a fault and the player loses a point. Also, the player must maintain contact with the seat of the wheelchair with at least one buttock during a rally. A player is allowed to fall from the wheelchair, get back in unassisted, and complete a rally without penalty.

Tournament directors may enforce rules to protect the court from damage by wheelchairs. Players may be asked to pad footplates and secure antitip devices behind their wheelchairs.

Summary of the Sport

Table 9.1 is a summary of wheelchair tennis. Use it as a quick reference to the sport.

Table 9.1   Overview of Wheelchair Tennis

Field of play	Tennis court: 78 by 36 ft (24 by 11 m) for doubles; 78 by 27 ft (24 by 8.2 m) for singles
Players	Singles and doubles competition
Equipment	Traditional tennis court and net Traditional tennis racket and tennis balls
Legal start	The game is started with a serve.
Ball movement	Players rally the ball using rackets. Players are allowed two bounces before the ball must be returned during a rally. The first of the two bounces must be within the boundaries of the tennis court. A player may not touch the playing surface while in possession of the ball. A player may receive assistance during a serve if physical limitations restrict the movement (e.g., someone may drop the ball in front of the player in preparation to serve).
Rally play	Serving must take place behind the baseline with all wheels off the court markings. Rally play becomes more difficult and requires greater skill level the closer the student plays to the net. The objective is to move the opponent out of position so as not to allow a safe rally return.
Faults	Points are lost if any of the following occurs: • The ball strikes the player or any part of the wheelchair during a serve or rally play. • The ball strikes anything carried on the wheelchair, except the racket, during rally play. • In doubles, the ball strikes the partner during a serve or rally play. • A player uses the feet to stop, change directions, or turn the wheelchair during play.

SKILLS TO BE TAUGHT

Two areas of skill development should be addressed in wheelchair tennis: wheelchair mobility and tennis skills. Wheelchair mobility skills are at the core of success for a competitive wheelchair tennis player. So as not to overlook these important skills, please review the information presented in chapter 5, Wheelchair Basics, regarding propelling, stopping, and turning a wheelchair. All of these skills are crucial in wheelchair tennis.

This chapter focuses on the three tennis skills associated with striking the ball: the forehand, the backhand, and the serve. Because these are likely the same skills you teach to students without disabilities during your tennis unit, wheelchair tennis is a logical game to help you with inclusion.

Because tennis is an individual sport rather than a team sport, it is somewhat easier to include students with and without disabilities in the same unit, which should help you with curriculum delivery and class format selection. Unlike wheelchair basketball, in which you might need several wheelchairs to play, with wheelchair tennis you need only one additional wheelchair to create a game or activity.

As you have read in previous chapters, you must be able to assess your students' skills and functional ability to play wheelchair tennis. Remember, you can modify several aspects of the game, such as racket and ball size, net height, and court dimensions, to make this sport appropriate for your students with disabilities.

Grip

In traditional tennis, the type of grip used is not directly related to the player's ability to move about the court. In wheelchair tennis, however, the interface between racket grip and wheelchair mobility is extremely important.

Because in wheelchair tennis the player must hold the racket while pushing the wheelchair, the correct racket grip is paramount to the player's performance. The player must choose a grip that combines racket control with wheelchair mobility.

The grip considered the most versatile is the eastern grip. The eastern grip is described as shaking hands with the racket. In this chapter it is assumed that the player is using the eastern grip.

Eastern grip for wheelchair mobility.

Forehand

To execute a forehand from the baseline on a ball hit directly at the player, the player must pull back on the dominant wheel first in preparation for the stroke. As the ball nears, the player pulls back on the nondominant wheel and positions the racket back in preparation to strike the ball. The racket should be held with an extended arm, and the dominant shoulder should be rotated away from the net. At contact, the player swings forward and pulls harder on the nondominant wheel. This combination of striking the forehand and pulling on the nondominant wheel helps turn the player into the shot. Turning into the shot adds additional power to the forehand stroke.

Pull back with the nondominant hand and prepare to hit forehand.

Turn into the shot during ball contact.

Backhand

To execute a backhand shot on a ball hit directly at the player, the player may want to turn into the ball as the stroke is made. To turn into a backhand shot, the player must execute a cross-hand turn prior to striking the ball. To do so, the player reaches across the wheelchair with the nondominant arm and grabs the dominate wheel. The player needs to stabilize the body by pressing the forearm of the nondominant arm against the thigh on the dominant side. While holding the nondominant arm in this position, the player should start to turn the wheelchair into the oncoming ball to be in position to strike with a backhand stroke. Once in position to strike the ball, the player executes the backhand with the same back-to-forward motion taught in traditional tennis. The racket should be drawn back to a point close to the opposite hip, and the elbow should be slightly flexed. The player turns into the shot and makes contact with the ball, remembering to keep the wrist firm during the follow-through.

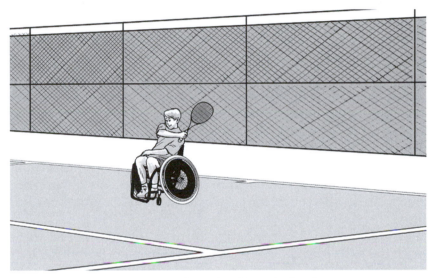

Use the cross-hand turn to prepare for a backhand; the forearm presses on the thigh and the striking arm is drawn back.

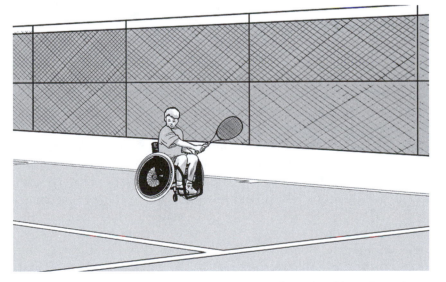

Use the nondominant arm to turn into position for a backhand stroke.

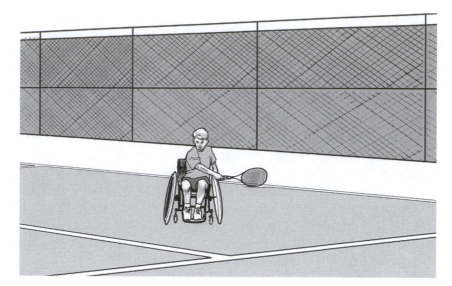

Move forward and strike with a firm wrist.

Serve

The types of serves used in wheelchair tennis are the topspin, slice, modified slice, reverse cut, and kick serve. However, because this chapter is written with the beginning wheelchair tennis player in mind, only the topspin serve is discussed.

The key to all serves is coordinating turning the wheelchair with making contact with the ball. To do so, the player should position the wheelchair behind the baseline and turn it at a 45-degree angle to the net. Positioning the wheelchair slightly behind the baseline allows the player to turn into the serve and not allow the front casters to cross the baseline during the serve. Turned 45 degrees away from the net, the player starts the serving motion with both arms straight and slightly down.

To initiate the service movement, both arms rise simultaneously until the player is ready to toss the ball. The player should toss the ball as the hand reaches head height or slightly higher. The racket continues to rise and be pulled back behind the head in preparation to strike the ball. As the ball is tossed, the nondominant hand must return immediately to the front wheel as the striking arm continues backward in preparation to be moved forward. As the tossed ball reaches its apex and begins to descend, the nondominant hand must pull back on the front wheel, generating a turn or rotational movement. This turning movement is analogous to the hip and shoulder rotation seen during the tennis serve in people without disabilities. The ball is struck with an extended arm and pronated forearm above the front casters of the wheelchair. As the serve is made, the nondominant hand continues to pull backward helping to increase the power applied to the serve. Once contact is made, the dominant arm continues down and across the body for follow-through, and in preparation to move the wheelchair in anticipation of the opponent's service return.

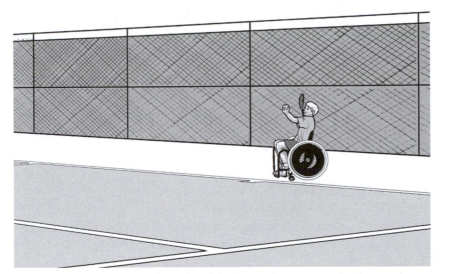

Position at the baseline: turn the wheelchair 45 degrees and release the toss at head height.

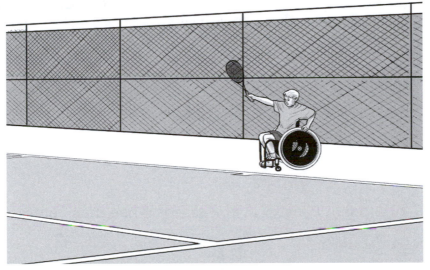

Return the nondominant hand to the front wheel after the toss.

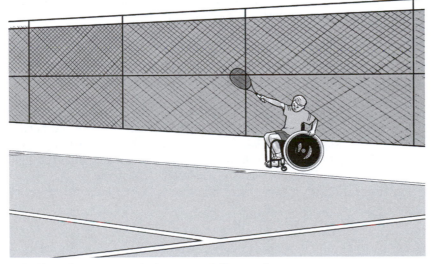

Serve the ball with an extended arm and firm wrist.

FUNCTIONAL PROFILES AND GENERAL MODIFICATIONS

Table 9.2 suggests student profiles that might fit your teaching situation. Remember, this book is about helping you to make sound pedagogical decisions while using your personal creativity. Read the table to see if you have students that might fit these profiles. Then consider the activity modifications listed in table 9.3.

Student Functional Profiles

Much of a student's success in wheelchair tennis depends on the ability to hold the racket and manually move the wheelchair. Functional profiles for this sport focus on the levels of assistance needed to help the student grip the tennis racket. While it is recognized that wheelchair tennis does not use an athlete classification system, functional profiles for players are provided using operationally defined classification systems employed by several disability sport organizations, including the National Wheelchair Basketball Association, Disabled Sports USA, and Wheelchair & Ambulatory Sports, USA (formerly Wheelchair Sports USA). For the purposes of this book, it is not important that you precisely classify your students with disabilities. Rather, these profiles are merely suggestions to help you begin more appropriate physical education programming. Again, you must assess your students' skills for tennis and use the functional profile to help select activities.

Table 9.2   Student Functional Profiles for Wheelchair Tennis

Functional skill level	Student profile
Low	Multiple impairments; unable to manually maneuver a wheelchair; needs assistance positioning in a wheelchair; needs assistance holding a racket; might use a power wheelchair.
Moderate	Able to maneuver a manual wheelchair independently for short distances; can hold a racket independently with one hand; has moderate active range of motion and independent sitting posture.
High	Able to maneuver a manual wheelchair independently for longer distances (30-50 ft, or 9-15 m); can hold a racket independently with one hand and maneuver the wheelchair simultaneously; has high active range of motion in upper body and independent sitting posture; can move continuously for 10 min without stopping.

Table 9.3 General Modifications for Wheelchair Tennis

Skill level	Skill	Activity modifications
Low	Forehand/backhand	Use a modified or lightweight racket (e.g., badminton) to strike a suspended ball for all three skills. Use an elastic bandage to wrap the racket to the hand. Use a lightweight butterfly net to catch tossed Nerf balls.
	Serve	Attach a lightweight racket to the armrest of the wheelchair and strike a suspended ball while turning the entire wheelchair.
Moderate	Forehand/backhand	Use a semi-lightweight racket (e.g., racquetball) to strike a suspended ball for all three skills. Use larger balls for striking (e.g., a 4 in., or 10 cm, playground ball).
	Serve	Reduce the distance to be served.
High	All skills	No modifications: Used with highest-functioning students.

General Modifications

Table 9.3 offers suggestions for general modifications that you might use when teaching wheelchair tennis to your students with disabilities. These modifications are meant as general overviews and are not specific to a student's functional profile. You can decide how to apply these modifications to your unique student population.

GAME PROGRESSIONS

As you use the activities and games presented in the following section, keep in mind that you are trying to address all three learning domains (psychomotor, cognitive, and affective).

GAMES-BY-SKILL-LEVEL INDEX: LOW-FUNCTIONING STUDENTS

Table 9.4 presents an index of activities for low-functioning students that are cross-referenced to the skills you may want to address in your physical education class. For low-functioning students, it is probably helpful to start with individual, or one-on-one, activities before moving on to small and large group situations. Refer back to table 9.2 and your skill assessments to help you decide whether to use the activities in this section or those in the section for moderate- to high-functioning students that follows.

Table 9.4   Games-by-Skill-Level Index for Low-Functioning Students—Wheelchair Tennis

Skills	One on one	Small group	Large group
Forehand	Strike It Rich I (Forehand)	Tabletop Tennis	Tarzan Tennis
Backhand	Strike It Rich II (Backhand)	Balloon Backhand	Zigzag Tennis
Serve	Strike It Rich III (Serve)	Delivery Service	Guest Server

GAME DESCRIPTIONS

From the games that follow, feel free to select any game that you believe matches the ability level of your students with mobility impairments. As mentioned, these games are written with the idea of moving a student from a one-on-one situation to a large group setting.

Skill ▶ Forehand

STRIKE IT RICH I (FOREHAND)

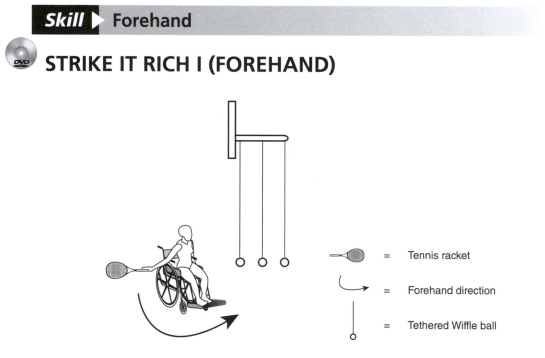

= Tennis racket

= Forehand direction

= Tethered Wiffle ball

Class format: One on one

Organizational pattern: Individual with teacher or a peer assistant as needed

Equipment: Wiffle balls, ropes or cords for tether, modified racket

Description: Tether several Wiffle balls with thin rope or cord from a basketball rim or some overhead support so they hang approximately at sitting height. Space the suspended balls about 3 feet (1 m) apart. The student with a disability is at an angle that allows him to turn the wheelchair into the suspended ball as he performs a forehand shot. For example, if the student is right-handed, the ball would hang closer to the left side of the wheelchair. To perform the forehand stroke, the student turns the wheelchair sharply to the left (counterclockwise) bringing the racket around to strike the ball.

Extensions: Set up three or four forehand striking stations around the gymnasium and have the student move from one to the other. The student can start the activity using only his hand to strike.

Inclusion suggestion: The student can decide how and when to rotate stations.

TABLETOP TENNIS

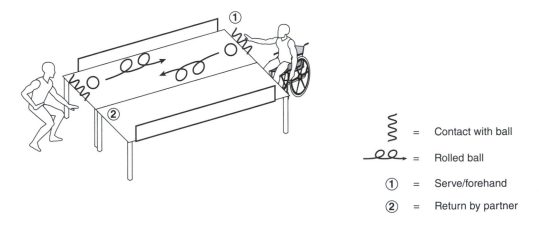

$\lessgtr$ = Contact with ball

$\ell\ell$ = Rolled ball

① = Serve/forehand

② = Return by partner

Class format: Small group

Organizational pattern: The student is at one end of a double-wide tabletop, and a partner is at the opposite end. A third student should retrieve errant forehand strokes.

Equipment: Beach ball, beanbag, two folding tables, modified rackets (badminton), cardboard panels

Description: The student with a disability is at one end of the table in the ready position to execute a forehand stroke. A beach ball is on the end of the table closest to the student, balanced on the beanbag to help keep the ball stationary. A student without a disability is at the opposite end of the table ready to return the ball. Using a forearm motion, the student with a disability strikes the ball toward the opposite end of the table; then prepares for the return stroke. The student acting as a retriever should help reposition the ball after it has been hit. The objective is to have the beach ball roll down the table to the opponent. Cardboard panels set up on each side of the table can help keep the ball from rolling off the side edge.

Extensions: Use a heavier ball (playground, Nerf, deflated volleyball) if the beach ball does not work. A racquetball racquet can also be used in place of the badminton racket. Rotate the student retrieving with the student returning the forehand stroke, and make sure to rotate all classmates through this activity during class time. The student may strike using only his hand.

Inclusion suggestions: The student with a disability can change ends of the table when he is ready. The student may also be allowed to choose the size and type of ball to use.

TARZAN TENNIS

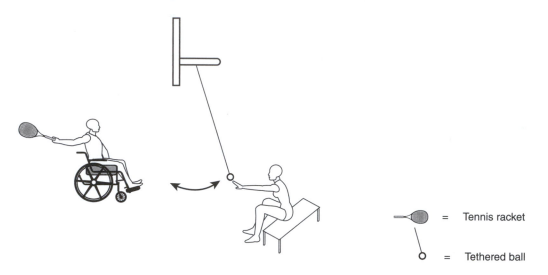

= Tennis racket

= Tethered ball

Class format: Large group

Organizational pattern: The student with a disability is in front of a suspended ball as in the game Strike It Rich I (Forehand). A classmate is opposite this student seated in a folding chair or on a bench ready to return the ball. The student should be far enough away to allow a safe swing with the racket. There are pairs of students working around the gym so you should rotate students without disabilities into this activity station during the class session.

Equipment: Wiffle ball, rope or cord for tether, modified racket, folding chair or bench

Description: Tether a Wiffle ball with thin rope or cord from a basketball rim or some overhead support so that it hangs at sitting height. The student without a disability should hold the ball far enough away to create a pendulum swing of the ball toward the student with a disability. The student with a disability should be at an angle that allows her to turn the wheelchair into the swinging ball to perform the forehand shot (counterclockwise turn for right-handers). As the ball approaches, the student with a disability must time the swing of the ball and use a forehand stroke to send the ball back in the direction of her opponent. The objective of the game is to complete a designated number of successive forehand strokes without missing (e.g., five forehands).

Extension: Change the size, weight, or height of the suspended ball as needed.

Inclusion suggestion: The student with a disability can decide how many forehands she must hit before the game ends.

Skill ▶ Backhand

⬭ STRIKE IT RICH II (BACKHAND)

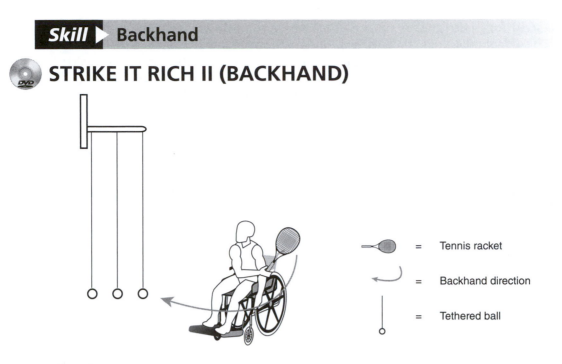

= Tennis racket

= Backhand direction

= Tethered ball

Class format: One on one

Organizational pattern: Same formation as Strike It Rich I (Forehand) using a peer assistant

Equipment: Wiffle balls, ropes or cords for tether, modified racket

Description: Tether several Wiffle balls with thin rope or cord from a basketball rim or some overhead support so they hang approximately at sitting height. Space the suspended balls about 3 feet (1 m) apart. The student with a disability should be at an angle that allows him to turn the wheelchair into the suspended ball as he performs a backhand shot. For example, if the student is right-handed, the ball would hang closer to the right side of the wheelchair. To perform the backhand stroke, the student turns the wheelchair sharply to the right (clockwise) bringing the racket around to strike the ball.

Extension: Set up three or four backhand striking stations around the gymnasium and have the student move from one to the other.

Inclusion suggestion: The student can decide how and when to rotate stations.

BALLOON BACKHAND

Class format: Small group

Organizational pattern: The student with a disability is in the middle of a circle formation.

Equipment: Balloons, modified rackets (badminton)

Description: Each student has a balloon. As the student with a disability turns to face each student, that student tosses the balloon in the air to free float toward the student in the middle. The objective is to have the student with a disability position the wheelchair to execute a backhand stroke and send the balloon out of the circle. The student with a disability moves around the circle to address each student with a balloon. The game is over when all balloons have been tossed.

Extensions: Make the circle wider and use medium-sized Nerf balls instead of balloons. Have students bounce the balls into the center of the circle and have the student with a disability backhand the ball after two bounces.

Inclusion suggestions: The student with a disability can decide the size of the circle and the object to be tossed or bounced into the middle. The student can also decide who moves to the center next.

ZIGZAG TENNIS

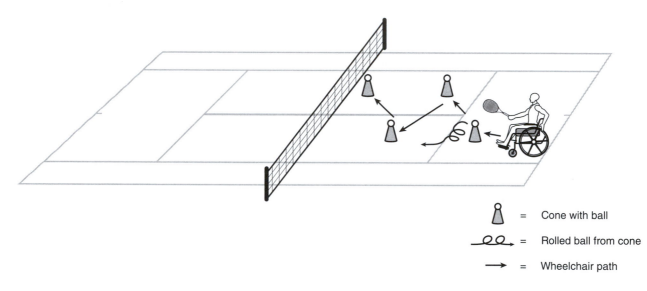

🔔 = Cone with ball

〇〇➝ = Rolled ball from cone

➝ = Wheelchair path

Class format: Large group

Organizational pattern: Three- or four-person teams

Equipment: Tall traffic cones, tennis balls, modified rackets, tennis court (indoor or outdoor)

Description: The students without disabilities are divided into three-person teams. The objective of the game is to have one teammate bounce the ball to a second teammate, who sends it over the net using a backhand stroke to a third teammate, who catches it. Once the third teammate has caught four tennis balls, she must run to exchange positions with her teammates. The retriever becomes the feeder, the feeder becomes the backhand striker, and the backhand striker becomes the retriever.

To include the student with a disability in this game, assist the student with gripping the racket as needed or secure the racket to the wheelchair if appropriate. Place four tall traffic cones on the tennis court in a zigzag pattern. Balance a tennis ball on each traffic cone. On the signal, start the student with a disability from the centerline/baseline intersect. The objective is to have the student move to each cone and strike the ball from the cone using a backhand stroke. The student should move from one side of the court to the opposite side as she moves to strike the tennis balls. The feeder and the retriever place the balls on the traffic cones.

Extensions: Increase the distance between the traffic cones; attempt to bounce-feed the student with a disability for a backhand stroke.

Inclusion suggestion: The student can decide where to place the traffic cones or how many traffic cones to use.

Skill ▶ Serve

STRIKE IT RICH III (SERVE)

Class format: One on one

Organizational pattern: Individual with teacher or a peer assistant as needed

Equipment: Wiffle balls, ropes or cords for tether, modified racket

Description: Tether several Wiffle balls with thin rope or cord from a basketball rim or some overhead support so they hang approximately at sitting height. Space the suspended balls about 3 feet (1 m) apart. The student with a disability should be at an angle that allows him to turn the wheelchair into the suspended ball as he performs a serve. For example, if the student is right-handed, the ball would hang closer to the left side of the wheelchair. To perform the serve, the student turns the wheelchair sharply to the left (counterclockwise) bringing the racket around to strike the ball.

Extension: Set up three or four serving stations around the gymnasium and have the student move from one to the other.

Inclusion suggestion: The student can decide how and when to rotate stations.

DELIVERY SERVICE

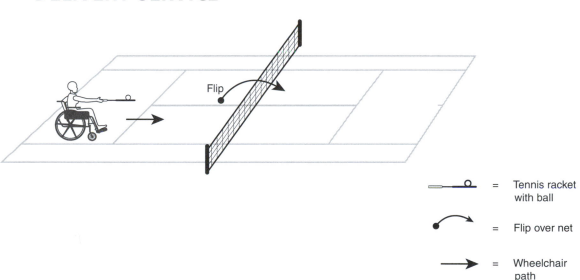

Class format: Small group

Organizational pattern: Students are in groups of two or three at the baseline.

Equipment: Modified rackets; tennis rackets; beanbags, small Nerf balls, or tennis balls

Description: Students without disabilities are at the baseline and practicing serving the ball using the teachings cues from your lesson. For the student with a disability, assist with racket grip as needed. (You can secure the racket with Velcro straps or elastic wraps to either the hand or wheelchair armrest). Position the racket face up, level, and parallel with the court surface. Balance a beanbag on the racket face and instruct the student to deliver the beanbag to the net by moving the wheelchair forward. Once at the net, instruct the student to flip the racket and serve the beanbag to the opponent's court. Repeat the activity as needed for the time allotted.

Extensions: Change the object carried on the racket; for example, use a Nerf ball or a tennis ball. Increase the distance from the net to the delivery, and have the student serve the object from farther away.

Inclusion suggestions: Challenge each group to get as many serves into the opponent's court as possible in the time available, and rotate the student with a disability through each group. The student with a disability can be responsible for reporting the number of serves for each group.

GUEST SERVER

Class format: Large group

Organizational pattern: The class is divided into doubles teams and positioned at the courts.

Equipment: Modified rackets; tennis rackets; beanbags, small Nerf balls, or tennis balls

Description: The class plays doubles tennis, and the student with a disability is the guest server for at least one game on every court. The student with a disability is the guest long enough to bring the ball to the net to simulate a serve. The objective is to have the student with a disability move from court to court and serve the ball as described in the game Delivery Service. To serve, the student with a disability balances the ball on the racket and travels to the net to flip the ball over the net to serve. If the serve is successful, play is stopped momentarily while the ball is retrieved. During that time the student with a disability exits the court, and the team who received the serve continues play with a forehand groundstroke. As play continues on the first court, the student with a disability travels to the next court and waits for a service break before becoming the guest server. This rotational guest serving continues until all courts have been visited.

Extensions: Change the object carried on the racket; for example, use a Nerf ball or a tennis ball. Increase the distance from the net to the delivery, and have the student serve the object from farther away.

Inclusion suggestion: Create two guest servers by positioning a student without a disability on a scooter and having that student perform in the same manner as the student with a disability.

GAMES-BY-SKILL-LEVEL INDEX: MODERATE-TO HIGH-FUNCTIONING STUDENTS

The index in table 9.5 addresses students with disabilities who are considered to have moderate to high function. The progression for game activity is the same, but a combination of skills is necessary to address skill development. You will notice in this section that several of the activities are used for the same strokes

Table 9.5 Games-by-Skill-Level Index for Moderate- to High-Functioning Students—Wheelchair Tennis

Skills	One on one	Small group	Large group
Forehand	Wall to Net	Reverse and Go	Mixed Doubles Plus I
Backhand	Wall to Net	Reverse and Go	Mixed Doubles Plus I
Serve	Wall to Net	Serving the Reverse and Go	The Serving Chair

(forehand, backhand, and serve). These strokes are combined in the activity to help develop wheelchair mobility skills simultaneously with tennis striking skills.

GAME DESCRIPTIONS

There are five activities in this section. Several of the activities are repeated for different skills. Use these activities in any combination of skill progression that meets your needs, based on your skill assessments.

Skill ▶ Forehand, Backhand, Serve

WALL TO NET

Class format: One on one

Organizational pattern: Individual with teacher or peer assistant as needed

Equipment: Wall, tennis court, tennis rackets, tennis balls, folding chairs

Description: In this activity, students with and without disabilities practice individually on the forehand, backhand, and serve by rebounding the ball off a gymnasium wall or outside wall. Students should work for control and successive contacts before moving to another stroke (e.g., 10 forehands, then 10 backhands, and so on). Once they have success with rebounding off the wall, they may move to the court and practice hitting over a net. Students can return these strokes based on their individual skill levels. Students may have more success if those on one court practice while those on the receiving court catch and gather the balls instead of trying to return. Once one set of students has practiced, that set rotates and the other set of students on the opposite side of the net hit.

Extension: For the student with a disability, make sure to adjust the type of ball to be used and the distance to the net as needed.

Inclusion suggestions: Make sure to rotate the peer assistant throughout the class time. Students without disabilities can perform the skills from folding chairs next to the student with a disability.

Skill ▶ Forehand and Backhand

REVERSE AND GO

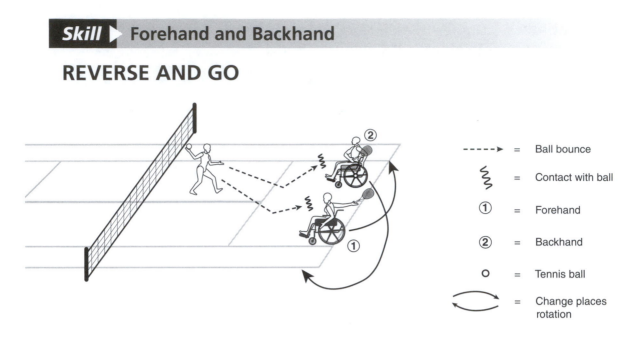

- - - - ▶ = Ball bounce

〜 = Contact with ball

① = Forehand

② = Backhand

O = Tennis ball

⌣ = Change places rotation

Class format: Small group

Organizational pattern: Small groups of three or four students in triangle formations

Equipment: Tennis court, tennis rackets, tennis balls, two folding chairs

Description: This activity can be repeated for both the forehand and the backhand. Divide the class into small groups and position them on the tennis court or any open space. Students should be in a triangle formation, with one student acting as the feeder and the remaining students positioned to hit a forehand or backhand stroke from 6 feet (1.8 m) in front of the baseline. The feeder stands about 5 feet (1.5 m) from the net facing his classmates and bounces a ball to them to be struck. The student in the forehand position should use a forehand stroke, and the student in the backhand position should use a backhand stroke. The bounce must be controlled and at a tempo that allows the student striking the ball to move into position to complete the stroke. Once the student using the forehand has completed his turn, he should reverse his position and travel to the backhand position. The same is true for the student who has used a backhand stroke. Once each student has completed five strokes of each type, a new student feeder is established and the activity continued.

This is not meant to be a fast-paced activity. The students should have ample time to reposition on the court to complete each new stroke. This is an excellent activity for working on wheelchair mobility skills, because it requires the student using a wheelchair to strike the ball from the side of the court, push the wheelchair to the other side, and get ready to perform a new stroke. Students should aim to strike the ball over the net.

Extension: The student with a disability should be able to perform this activity with minimal modifications. Allow the student using the wheelchair to adjust the distance for striking the ball, and don't forget to allow two bounces from the feeder.

Inclusion suggestion: Set up one court that has one folding chair each at the forehand and backhand positions. Students without disabilities can sit in the folding chairs to strike the tennis ball while the student with a disability acts as the feeder.

Skill ▶ Serve

SERVING THE REVERSE AND GO

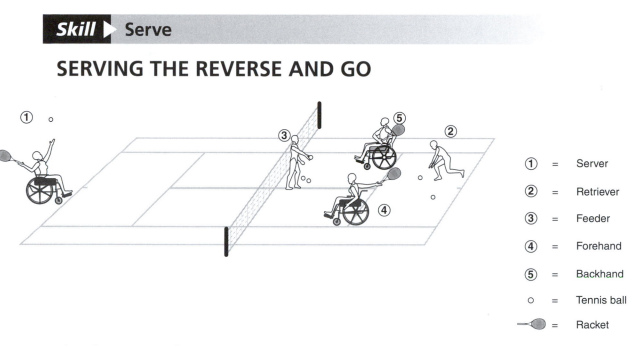

①	=	Server
②	=	Retriever
③	=	Feeder
④	=	Forehand
⑤	=	Backhand
o	=	Tennis ball
◖●━	=	Racket

Class format: Small group

Organizational pattern: Small groups of three or four students

Equipment: Tennis court, tennis rackets, tennis balls, folding chair

Description: This is the same activity as described in the game Reverse and Go, except that the activity is initiated with a serve from the opposite court. From behind the baseline on the opposite court, a student with or without a disability serves the ball to a student retriever. Once the student retriever has the ball, she must toss it to the student feeder, and the activity continues as described earlier. Make sure to rotate students through all positions.

Extension: The student with a disability should be able to perform this activity with minimal modifications. The student using the wheelchair can adjust the distance for striking the ball.

Inclusion suggestions: Students without disabilities can sit in folding chairs to serve the tennis ball. The student with a disability can decide which positions her teammates should take to start the activity.

Skill ▶ Forehand and Backhand

MIXED DOUBLES PLUS 1

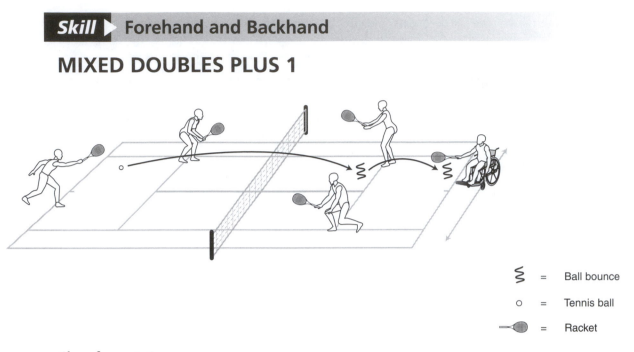

```
⸉  =  Ball bounce

o  =  Tennis ball

◖—  =  Racket
```

Class format: Large group

Organizational pattern: Normal doubles formation for a tennis match, with an additional player (student with a disability) added to one team (three players on one side and two on the other)

Equipment: Tennis court, tennis rackets, tennis balls or slightly deflated 4-inch (10 cm) playground balls

Description: The activity is played the same as any doubles play, except that a student with a disability is positioned at or near the baseline for one team and responsible for all balls hit deep on the court. The student with a disability is allowed two bounces to return a ball and must attempt to use either the forehand or backhand stroke during the game. The remaining two teammates should play forward in the regular doubles position and must return a ball before it strikes the ground. The student using the wheelchair needs to cover the court from sideline to sideline during each rally. (This will be a very challenging game and should be reserved for your most talented students.)

Extensions: Increase the number of allowed bounces as needed for your student with a disability. Change the distance or coverage area as needed for the student using the wheelchair. Rotate the student with a disability to other teams throughout the tennis unit. Change the type of ball used in this game; a slightly deflated 4-inch (10 cm) playground ball works well.

Inclusion suggestion: The student with a disability can announce the score prior to any service, dependent on communication methods, such as a word board, hand gestures, or flip cards.

Skill ▶ Serve

THE SERVING CHAIR

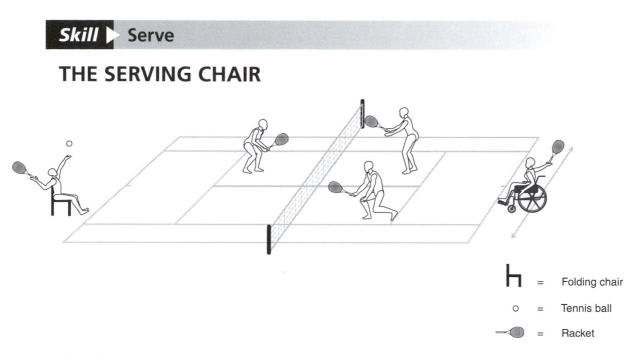

⊢	=	Folding chair
○	=	Tennis ball
⬭	=	Racket

Class format: Large group

Organizational pattern: Normal doubles formation for a tennis match, except that an additional player (student with a disability) is added to one team (three players on one side and two on the other)

Equipment: Folding chair, tennis court, tennis rackets, tennis balls or slightly deflated 4-inch (10 cm) playground ball

Description: This is the same activity as described in Mixed Doubles Plus 1, with the following exception: the team without a student with a disability must start the game serving from a seated position in a folding chair. Once the serve has been made, the folding chair is removed, and play continues as described earlier.

Extensions: Place a folding chair on each court, and require all students to serve from a seated position. Change the size and weight of the ball; a slightly deflated 4-inch (10 cm) playground ball often works well.

Inclusion suggestion: The student with a disability can assign classmates to teams.

Remember that blank forms for assessments, IEPs, and unit and lesson plans are located on the DVD.

Chapter 10

Goalball

Goalball is a sport played by people who are blind or visually impaired. The game is played indoors on a court the size of a volleyball court. The sport of goalball is governed by the United States Association of Blind Athletes (USABA), which adopted the rules of goalball from its international counterpart, the International Blind Sports Association (IBSA). The USABA was founded in 1976 and has more than 3,000 athletes participating in sports that include alpine and nordic skiing, judo, powerlifting, swimming, tandem cycling, track and field, and wrestling.

DESCRIPTION OF THE SPORT

In goalball two teams, consisting of three members each, oppose each other at opposite ends of the court. All players wear eye shades. The game is played by trying to roll (referred to as a throw) the goalball past the opposition's goal line, which is the end line of the court. The goalball emits an auditory cue, made by bells within the ball, to help the players track the path of the thrown ball. Players have specific areas to cover according to their positions as they try to stop the rolled ball. Players must attempt to stop the rolled ball and, if successful, quickly return it toward the opposition in hopes of throwing it past them for a score. Players hold a stationary position during play, moving only to slide and block the ball while diving to the floor.

Field of Play

The goalball court is 60 feet long and 30 feet wide (18 by 9 m) and is divided into three areas that extend the width of the court (see figure 10.1). The middle of the court is called the neutral area and is 20 feet (6 m) long. The remaining two areas are called the throwing area and the team area; they are marked for each team and are 10 feet long (3 m).

To help the players recognize their areas of play, a narrow rope or clothesline is placed on the floor and covered by floor tape to create a tactile border around each section of the court. Lines marking team areas are parallel to and 10 feet (3 m) from the back, or goal, lines. High ball lines, which start the neutral area and are explained later, are marked parallel to and 20 feet (6 m) from the back, or goal, lines. The center line is marked parallel to and midway between the two goal lines. In addition, small pieces of rope are covered with tape to help mark the player positions of center, left wing, and right wing.

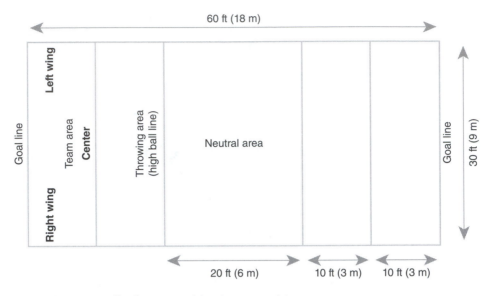

Figure 10.1 Goalball court with player positions.

Players

People who are blind or have a visual impairment can play goalball. The degree of vision is not an issue with goalball because all players must wear eye shades. Official USABA players must adhere to the following sport classifications of visual impairment:

- People classified as B1 have vision ranges from no light perception in either eye up to and including the ability to perceive light. There is no visual ability to recognize objects in any direction or at any distance.
- People classified as B2 can see at 2 meters what people with normal vision see at 60 meters (i.e., below 2/60 vision), have a field of vision less than 5 degrees, or both.
- People classified as B3 can recognize objects between 2 and 60 meters away. They can see at 2 meters what people with normal vision see at 60 meters (i.e., 2/60 to 6/60 vision), have a field of vision between 5 and 20 degrees, or both.
- People classified as B4 can recognize objects between 2 and 70 meters away. They can see at 2 meters what normal vision looks like at 70 meters (i.e., 2/20 to 2/70 vision). Their visual field is larger than 20 degrees in the best eye with the best practical eye correction.

You might choose to use another form of classification not specific to sport. This is referred to as a classification of blindness and is sometimes used by school districts to identify students' disabilities.

- Legally blind: 20/200 vision, or seeing at 20 feet (6 m) what someone with normal vision sees at 200 feet (60 m).
- Travel vision: 5/200 to 10/200 vision, or seeing at 5 to 10 feet (1.5 to 3 m) what someone with normal vision sees at 200 feet (60 m).
- Motion vision: 3/200 to 5/200 vision, or seeing at 3 to 5 feet (1 to 1.5 m) what someone with normal vision sees at 200 feet (60 m).

- Light perception: Less than 3/200 vision, or the ability to distinguish a strong light at a distance of 3 feet (1 m) from the eye. A person with this classification cannot detect hand motion 3 feet from the eye.
- Total blindness: The inability to recognize light shone directly into the eye.

Equipment

The official goals, which resemble soccer goal nets, are 30 feet wide (9 m) and 4 feet (1.2 m) high and are positioned on the goal line. If you decide to construct your own goals with PVC pipe or lumber, make sure that the corners and edges are padded. Goals are not needed to play the game in your physical education classes.

The ball is approximately the size of a basketball and is made of very durable rubber. Inside the ball are a set of bells, similar to jingle bells, that roll freely when the ball is rolled from one end of the court to the other. The sound of the bells helps the player track its location. For information about purchasing a goalball, contact the USABA (see appendix B).

Players must wear eye shades any time they are on the court. During official competition, players are not allowed to touch or adjust their eye shades while on the court. If eye shade adjustment is needed, players must ask the referee for permission to do so.

Hip, elbow, and knee padding is recommended for all players because the method of blocking a thrown ball is to execute a dive-and-block movement. Players must be taught how to position their bodies in preparation for such a move to avoid injury. Because blocking is an aggressive movement, only players with appropriate padding will be able to block with minimal risk of injury. You might be able to secure hip pads from your school's football program and elbow and knee pads from the wrestling team. You might also be able to construct your own padding using foam padding and elastic athletic bandages.

Starting the Game

A coin toss decides which team will be awarded the ball and which team will defend a chosen goal. All players on the court must wear eye shades and should be familiar with their location on the court. A brief period of court orientation is allowed prior to the start of an official game.

Game Objective

The objective of the game is to throw the goalball past the opponents' back line, or end line, into the goal net. All players start in a standing position commonly referred to as a basic athletic stance (i.e., feet shoulder-width apart, slight bend at the hips, weight evenly distributed, arms relaxed with slight bend at the elbow). There are three player positions on the court: a center and two wings. The center position must cover from sideline to sideline within the team area and stands about 2 to 3 feet (0.6 to 1 m) in front of the wings. The two wings must cover a smaller area, usually one body length from the sideline to their playing positions. Player movement is limited. When the ball is thrown, the players must be able to move quickly to block the ball by dropping down and sliding to the side of the sound made by the oncoming ball.

Basic player positions for throwing.

Blocking a goalball is made from a horizontal position on the floor. Players blocking a thrown ball must be able to rise to their feet as quickly as possible to return the ball. Once the player has secured a block, the ball must be returned to the opponents' end of the court within 10 seconds. Throwing the ball, whether on an attack or following a block, cannot occur more than two consecutive times by any player. It is possible for the same player to block a ball two consecutive times and return the ball with two consecutive throws, but a third consecutive block cannot be followed by a third consecutive return throw. Because no player is allowed to throw a ball more than two consecutive times, passing is very important.

Passing among teammates is allowed and should be practiced. If a ball is blocked by the right winger, that teammate may pass it to the left winger or center player for a return throw. Passes are made by rolling the ball across the floor to a teammate quietly enough so as not to tip off the new position of the goalball to the opponents. Passing becomes a very strategic offensive maneuver as one team tries to attack the other's court by throwing the ball at the opponents' end of the court.

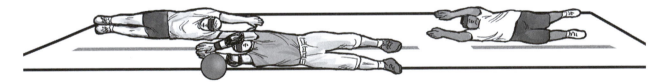

Basic player positions for blocking.

Game Length

The USABA has established an official game length of two 10-minute halves, or 20 total minutes. In the case of an overtime, the teams play two additional three-minute halves. A second coin toss is used to determine which team will throw first in the overtime.

General Rules and Penalties

Because the sport of goalball does not have a corresponding sport for people without disabilities, the rules discussed in this chapter are all specific to the sport.

Rules Specific to Goalball

Coaches or teachers may escort starting players or substitutes to their playing positions. Once the game has begun, however, players are responsible for maintaining their playing positions throughout the game. Players should use the tactile lines on the court to help with court orientation.

The ball must touch the floor in the team area and be rolling as it enters the neutral area. The ball cannot be airborne over the neutral area; if it is, the throw is ruled a high ball, and the ball is awarded to the opposing team.

If the ball rolls to a stop in the neutral area and no player makes an attempt to control it, it is considered a short ball. Short balls are awarded to the defending team at the time of play. If a ball rebounds off a player from a block and rolls to a stop in the neutral area, the ball is returned to the throwing team. This rule applies when a ball rebounds off a goalpost and rolls dead into the neutral area. Players may not enter the neutral area to retrieve a dead ball during play.

If a player throws a ball in such a manner as to not have floor contact in the neutral area, it is considered a long ball and the throw counts but cannot be scored. The ball is then turned over to the defending team.

During play, if a player attempts to pass to a teammate and the pass goes out of bounds, the play is considered an infraction. All infractions result in turnovers to the defending team.

The two types of penalties enforced in goalball are personal and team penalties. When a penalty is enforced, a penalty shot is awarded. During a penalty shot, all players from the penalized team must clear the floor with the exception of one player. The ball is awarded to the nonpenalized team for a penalty shot. The penalized team can only defend the goal with one player. The player that remains to defend against the penalty shot is determined by the type of penalty committed. In the case of a personal penalty, the player committing the penalty must defend the goal single-handedly. In the case of a team penalty, the last player to throw from the penalized team must defend the goal single-handedly. Once the penalty shot is completed, play is stopped and the penalized team is allowed to return to the court.

The following are examples of personal penalties:

- *Illegal touch of the eye shades while on the court.* No player is allowed to use vision to detect the thrown ball. Once the players are on the court, they are not allowed to adjust their eye shades or blindfolds. Feel free to modify this rule based on your teaching situation.

- *Throwing the ball for a third consecutive time.* Remember, no player is allowed to throw more than two consecutive times.

- *Some form of illegal defense.* Players must remain at their playing positions when defending and must remain in the team area of the court.

- *Unfair play or delay of play.* Players must remain relatively quiet during competition. Any loud, inappropriate verbal calls from players to their teammates on the bench could be considered unfair play.

The following are examples of team penalties:

- *10-second delay.* Teams have only 10 seconds to return a throw once they have gained possession.

- *Team delay.* Teams not prepared to start play on time, or player substitutions made without notifying the referee are considered team delays.
- *Unfair play.* Similar to the ruling of unfair play mentioned for personal penalties.

Summary of the Sport

Table 10.1 includes the basic information you will need to conduct a goalball game. Use this table as a quick reference in your physical education classes.

Table 10.1   Overview of Goalball

Field of play	Volleyball court: 60 by 30 ft (18 by 9 m) Goal width: 30 ft (9 m) center on the back line; goal height: 4 ft (1.2 m) Team area and throwing area: 30 by 10 ft (9 by 3 m); neutral area: 30 by 20 ft (9 by 6 m)
Players	Maximum allowed on court is three per team.
Equipment	Goalball (specially made; contact the USABA national office in Colorado Springs, CO) Goals (to include netting) are not needed for teaching in physical education class. Eye shades or blindfolds, knee pads, elbow pads, hip pads
Legal start	The game is started with a toss of a coin. The winner can choose to throw first or defend a favored goal.
Ball movement	A player may use only the hands to move the ball; no kicking is allowed. A player may throw only two consecutive times when attacking. Passing is allowed within the team area; however, once the team has established control of the ball, players have 10 sec to return a throw. Balls passed out of bounds are awarded to the opponents.
Infractions	All infractions result in turnovers to the defending team. Examples: • Premature throw: Throwing the ball before referee signal • Stepover: The whole foot stepping out of bounds during a throw • Passout: Passing the ball out of bounds to a teammate • Ball-over: Balls blocked into the neutral area and considered dead are awarded to the throwing team.
Penalties	All penalties (personal or team) result in a penalty shot. Personal penalties: • Long ball throw: A thrown ball not touching the neutral area • High ball: An offensive throw that does not touch in the neutral area • Eye shades: Players touching or adjusting their eye shades while on the court • Third time throw: Throwing a ball more than two consecutive times • Illegal defense: Defensive contact by a player outside of the team area • Unfair play: Ruled by the referee as behaving inappropriately Team penalties: • 10 seconds: Taking longer than 10 sec to return a thrown ball • Team delay of game: Team not ready to play at the start; any actions to prevent play • Unfair team play: Similar to personal unfair play • Illegal coaching: Coaching from the bench area during the competition (coaching from the bench is allowed during time-outs)

SKILLS TO BE TAUGHT

Three basic skills are addressed for goalball: throwing, blocking, and passing. These three skills should be adequate to help you teach students with visual impairments or who are blind. Students who are not visually impaired or blind will enjoy the athleticism involved in the sport. Goalball is a team game that requires players to work together during offensive and defensive phases of the game.

Although the skill is called throwing, the execution is generally considered a one-handed roll of the ball across the court to the opponents' goal area. The goalball should be thrown rapidly and with enough force to carry it the length of the court. The speed and accuracy of the throw will be determined by the skill level of the players. You have the option of adjusting court dimensions to better suit your students' levels of performance. You also can start new players with a two-handed throw.

Blocking a thrown ball is the heart of the defense. Students must listen closely for the sound of the ball rolling toward them and move quickly to block as the ball nears their location. To execute the block, students must dive to the floor and lie on their sides facing the oncoming ball. In the block position students should have their arms and legs extended, attempting to make their bodies as long as possible. They need to work to keep the legs together so that the ball does not pass through their legs while they are on the floor. As both arms are extended overhead, the top arm should be dropped low enough to cover and protect the student's face. Once the ball is blocked, the student must gain control of the ball for a return throw or pass it to a teammate.

Throwing

This explanation is for a right-handed student using a one-handed delivery and a simple three-step approach. The stance and approach to throwing a goalball are similar to those of delivering a bowling ball. To execute the throw, the student takes a left, right, left step approach. The first step (left) should be short and quick, followed by a second (right) and third (left) step with longer strides.

During the first step, the student swings the goalball back while supporting it from underneath with the right hand. On the second step, the student brings the goalball forward with force as the body is lowered close to the floor. On the third

Basic throwing stance.

Swing the goalball back during the approach for throwing.

Low body position upon release and follow-through.

step, the student slides on the left foot with the body in a low release position. The ball is released on the slide forward as the student plants the left foot, lifting the throwing hand for the follow-through.

Blocking

Students start in a basic athletic position, which means that the feet are shoulder-width apart, body weight is evenly distributed on both feet, knees are slightly flexed, arms are held forward, hands are about at waist height, and elbows are slightly flexed. For a ball approaching from the right, the student takes a short jab step to the right and begins to lower the body into the path of the oncoming ball. The student continues facing the ball as it approaches and must avoid turning his back to the ball. As the ball nears the body, the student makes initial contact with the floor with hands and arms to cushion floor contact. Once the hands and arms are in contact with the floor, the student quickly lowers the knees and hips on the right side of the body. As the entire body reaches the floor, the student strives to make himself as long as possible, keeping the arms stretched out over the head and protecting the face with the top arm. The final blocking position is lying on the right side with arms extended, legs together, and the left arm across the face.

This technique works for a ball approaching from the left. To block a ball approaching head-on, the student eliminates the first jab step and simply tries

Basic athletic position in preparation to block.

Short step to the side of a block.

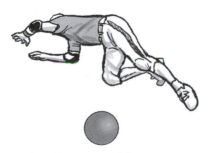

Hands, elbows, and knees contact the floor early.

Side-lying position: arms extended, legs together, face protected during block.

to assume the blocking position as quickly as possible. Most students attempt to block goalballs thrown directly at them by just dropping directly to the floor on their dominant sides.

Passing

Passing is accomplished by rolling the ball from teammate to teammate in a more controlled fashion, with the ball traveling less than 20 feet (6 m). Passes can be executed with one or two hands. The key to passing is to move the ball so that a teammate, and not an opponent, hears the ball. To accomplish this, the student faces a teammate and lifts the ball from the floor about 4 to 5 inches (10 to 13 cm). With the ball held slightly off the floor, the student swings and releases it toward a teammate so that it drops to the floor loudly enough to rattle the bells inside. If the ball is not lifted and dropped to initiate the pass, the bells inside will not make enough noise to help a teammate locate the oncoming pass.

Locating a teammate to execute an accurate pass must be accomplished as discreetly as possible. Because it is not advantageous for teammates to use frequent verbal communication, a system of tapping on the floor is recommended to request or receive a pass. Students might establish a numbering system to help identify one another—for example, one tap is the right wing player, two taps is the left wing, and three taps is the center, or whatever combination you design.

Teams could work together to execute two passes (e.g., right wing to left wing, left wing to center, ending with a center return throw) before returning a throw at the opponent. Keep in mind that such a maneuver needs to take place within the 10-second limit.

Face teammate and lift the ball in preparation to pass.

Locate a teammate to execute an accurate pass.

FUNCTIONAL PROFILES AND GENERAL MODIFICATIONS

The functional profiles for students who are blind or have a visual impairment are not related to their disability, but rather to their ability. The sport of goalball requires all players to wear eye shades or a blindfold, thus equalizing the disability. As a result, a player classified as having minimal vision is equal to a player who has no vision. The difference in the players' performance is related more to their ambulatory skills and level of independent movement.

Student Functional Profiles

To play the sport of goalball, students must be able to hold, throw, and block the ball independently. These skills require that they have sufficient levels of physical fitness and motor coordination to move laterally, drop to the floor, and rise to their feet without assistance. Functional profiles for this sport focus on levels of assistance needed to move on the court, rise from a blocking to a throwing position, or lower from a throwing to a blocking position and not on levels of visual acuity or field of vision.

Table 10.2 suggests student profiles that might fit your teaching situation. After determining your students' levels of ability, consider the activity modifications listed in table 10.3.

General Modifications

Table 10.3 suggests general modifications to the three skills necessary to play goalball. Notice that these modifications are suggested according to student functional profiles. You can decide how to apply these general modifications to your specific student population.

Table 10.2 Student Functional Profiles for Goalball

Functional skill level	Student profile
Low	Unable to hold a goalball, move to locate a thrown ball, lower the body to the floor, or rise to stand from a blocking position independently.
Moderate	Able to hold a goalball independently with two hands; has moderate physical fitness level; able to lower the body to the floor and assume a blocking position, but needs minimal assistance to rise from a blocking position.
High	Able to hold a goalball with one or two hands, lower the body to the floor and assume a proper blocking position, and rise to stand from a blocking position independently.

Table 10.3 General Modifications for Goalball

Skill level	Skill	Activity modifications
Low	Throwing	Use a lighter ball that is tethered for support. Practice pushing the ball to simulate the throwing action.
	Blocking	Block a thrown ball from a kneeling position while supported from behind.
	Passing	Push a heavier ball (medicine ball) on a tabletop while seated.
Moderate	Throwing	Receive assistance with the hand-over-hand technique while attempting a one-handed throw.
	Blocking	Block from a kneeling position. Use a folding chair to assist movement from kneeling to standing after blocking.
	Passing	No modifications: Execute pass with current level of two-handed throw.
High	All skills	No modifications: Used with highest-functioning students.

GAME PROGRESSIONS

The games listed in the remainder of this chapter use the same class formats as in previous chapters (one on one, small group, large group). Keep in mind that you are trying to address all three learning domains (psychomotor, cognitive, and affective).

GAMES-BY-SKILL-LEVEL INDEX: LOW-FUNCTIONING STUDENTS

The index in table 10.4 will help you choose games according to the skill you want to teach and the ability level of your student with a visual impairment. This first index is for low-functioning students who require a high degree of assistance. Very low-functioning students will need to begin with one-on-one games and may progress to small or large group situations as their skills improve. The index is followed by descriptions of the games listed.

Table 10.4 Games-by-Skill-Level Index for Low-Functioning Students—Goalball

Skills	One on one	Small group	Large group
Throwing	Up It Goes	Throw It Out I	Throw It Out II
Blocking	Don't Go There I	Don't Go There II	Don't Go There III
Passing	Here I Am	Remember Me I	Zigzag Relay

GAME DESCRIPTIONS

Each game description in this section includes class format, organizational pattern, equipment, description, extensions, and inclusion suggestions. You may select any game that you believes matches the ability level of your students who have a visual impairment.

Skill ▶ Throwing

UP IT GOES

Class format: One on one

Organizational pattern: Individual with teacher or peer assistant

Equipment: Basketball, medicine ball, or goalball

Description: The student with a visual impairment is seated on the floor with the ball positioned between her legs. The student lifts the ball with two hands and holds it up for a count of 10 seconds.

Extensions: Increase the time of the lift by five-second increments. A teacher aide or student from the class can sit behind the student and use a hand-over-hand technique to assist with the lift. The student can also change from a seated position to a kneeling position every three lifts.

Inclusion suggestion: Witnessed by you, the student can verbalize her accomplishment to two friends in class.

THROW IT OUT I

Class format: Small group

Organizational pattern: Students with and without disabilities wear blindfolds and sit in a circle formation on the floor.

Equipment: Basketball, medicine ball, or goalball; blindfolds or eye shades

Description: Students throw the ball (i.e., roll it) around the circle while seated using two hands as needed. On your signal, the student with the ball tries to throw it out of the circle. Students must become familiar with the position of everyone in the circle so they can determine the best direction to throw the ball out. Likewise, students can be working on early blocking skills by listening carefully to the roll of the ball and attempting to block it from exiting the circle.

Extensions: Have students play one game from a seated position and then move to a kneeling position. Increase the size of the circle as students' skill levels improve.

Inclusion suggestion: Rotate new students without visual impairments into the circle, and have the student with a visual impairment explain the rules of the game.

THROW IT OUT II

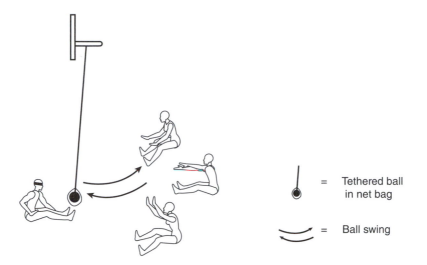

= Tethered ball
  in net bag

= Ball swing

Class format: Large group

Organizational pattern: Three sighted students sit in a semicircle around a student with a visual impairment.

Equipment: Basketball, goalball, or medicine ball; net for hanging the ball from a basketball rim

Description: All students are seated the first one or two times they play this game. After some experience, allow all students to stand and conduct the game as described. The ball hangs all the way to the floor from the basketball rim. The student with a visual impairment holds the tethered ball in the starting position (previously described for throwing). You will need to provide hand-over-hand assistance, placing your hand over the student's hands as he initiates movement, to help balance the ball. Three sighted teammates are in front of this student in a semicircle formation. From a standing position, the student with a visual impairment steps and throws the ball according to the skill sequence described for throwing to each teammate. The student is working on the step sequence, release, and follow-through. Because the ball is tethered, it will swing out and will not roll on the floor; the student should be ready to catch the ball on the return swing from each teammate. The objective is to work around the semicircle throwing to all teammates, who are using an auditory cue (floor tapping) to request the throw. Remember to keep the ball rolling on the floor throughout the game.

Extension: Widen the distance between the students in the semicircle.

Inclusion suggestion: The student with a visual impairment can demonstrate the activity to the entire class.

Skill ▶ Blocking

DON'T GO THERE I

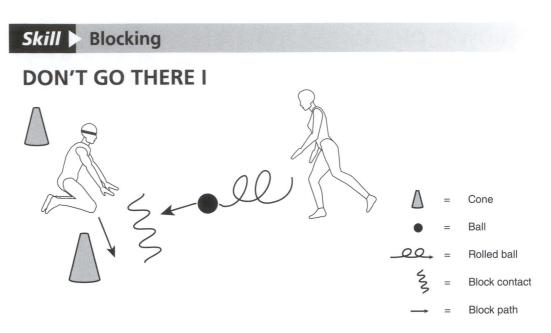

▲	=	Cone
●	=	Ball
↝	=	Rolled ball
↯	=	Block contact
→	=	Block path

Class format: One on one

Organizational pattern: Individual with teacher or peer assistant as needed

Equipment: Basketball, medicine ball, or goalball; two traffic cones

Description: The student with a visual impairment kneels between two cones placed 3 feet (1 m) apart. A sighted partner attempts to roll the ball past the student and between the cones. The objective for the student with a visual impairment is to block the ball from passing between the cones. Use a partial hand-over-hand technique to assist the student with blocking.

Extensions: Increase the distance between the cones, or increase the distance between the kneeling student and the one releasing the ball.

Inclusion suggestion: The student with a visual impairment can determine the distances for throwing once her skill level has improved.

DON'T GO THERE II

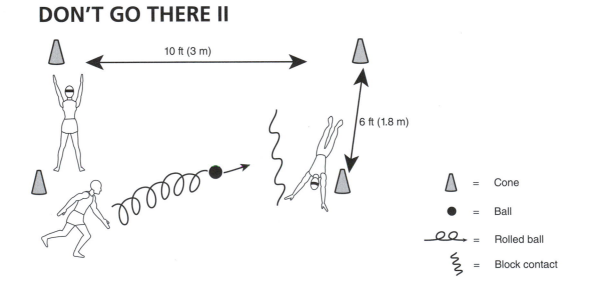

▲	=	Cone
●	=	Ball
↝	=	Rolled ball
↯	=	Block contact

Class format: Small group

Organizational pattern: Three students, two blindfolded and one without a blindfold, positioned within a small area 10 by 6 feet (3 by 1.8 m)

Equipment: Basketball, medicine ball, or goalball; blindfolds; four traffic cones

Description: Create a small rectangular working area (e.g., 10 by 6 ft; 3 by 1.8 m) using four traffic cones. A blindfolded student is at each end of the area, lying down between the cones. Their objective is to block a thrown ball while lying on the floor at each end. The sighted student alternates throws, keeping track of how many blocks were made.

Extensions: Increase the distance of the rectangle, or rotate the students.

Inclusion suggestion: The student with a visual impairment can decide which end should block first.

DON'T GO THERE III

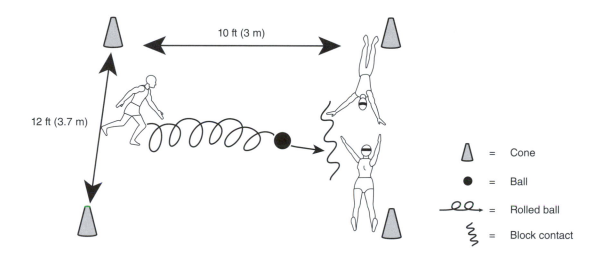

Class format: Large group

Organizational pattern: Three students, two blindfolded and one sighted, within a rectangular area

Equipment: Basketball, medicine ball, or goalball; blindfolds; four traffic cones

Description: Increase the rectangle from Don't Go There II to a 10- by 12-foot (3 by 3.7 m) area. The blockers are at the same end of the rectangle across the opening between the cones. As the ball is rolled at the opening, the two blockers must work together to stop the ball.

Extension: Once students have blocked the ball, they may stand up with the ball; assist as needed.

Inclusion suggestion: A student with a visual impairment can report the number of blocks made.

Skill ▶ Passing

HERE I AM

Class format: One on one

Organizational pattern: Individual with teacher or peer assistant as needed

Equipment: Basketball, medicine ball, or goalball

Description: Seated or standing, the student with a visual impairment holds the ball (provide assistance as needed). A sighted student approximately 6 feet (1.8 m) away taps on the floor until the student with a visual impairment passes the ball correctly.

Extension: The student without a visual impairment can change locations after each successful pass; have them work for three consecutive successful passes before changing locations.

Inclusion suggestion: The student with a visual impairment can decide how many successful passes should be made before the sighted student changes locations.

 # REMEMBER ME I

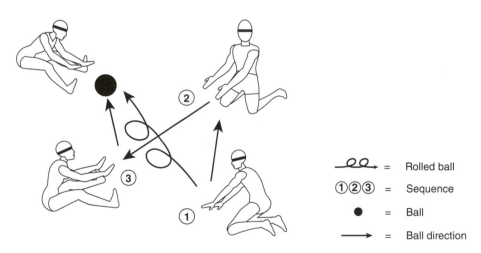

‿‿�	= Rolled ball
①②③	= Sequence
●	= Ball
⟶	= Ball direction

Class format: Small group

Organizational pattern: Students with and without visual impairments are wearing blindfolds and sitting in a small circle on the floor.

Equipment: Basketball, medicine ball, or goalball; blindfolds

Description: On a signal, the students pass the goalball back and forth across the circle. The objective of the activity is to pass the ball around the circle in the same sequence as the original pattern, meaning that once the ball has been passed around the circle and everyone has touched it, the second time around should follow the same pattern, with students passing to the same people each trip. Each pass is preceded by a tapping on the floor by the receiver.

Extensions: Work for minimizing physical assistance for the student with a visual impairment. Have the group alternate positions: first seated, then kneeling, then standing. Vary the diameter of the circle with each round.

Inclusion suggestion: The student with a visual impairment can determine the sequence of passing positions (e.g., seated-kneeling-standing or kneeling-seated-standing).

ZIGZAG RELAY

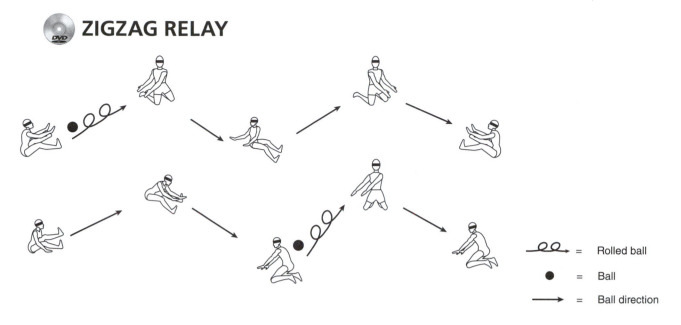

= Rolled ball

= Ball

= Ball direction

Class format: Large group

Organizational pattern: Students are seated on the floor in two lines ready for a passing relay. Stagger teammates about 6 feet (1.8 m) apart so that the pattern of passing the ball will be zigzag.

Equipment: Basketball, medicine ball, or goalball; blindfolds

Description: All students wear blindfolds. On a signal the ball is passed to the next person, who is using a tapping signal to receive the pass. The first team to pass the ball to the opposite end wins.

Extension: Students can move from a seated position to kneeling, and then to standing.

Inclusion suggestion: The student with a visual impairment can determine the order in which their teammates are positioned and be allowed to change those positions with each race.

GAMES-BY-SKILL-LEVEL INDEX: MODERATE-TO HIGH-FUNCTIONING STUDENTS

The index in table 10.5 will help you choose games for your students with visual impairments or who are blind, with moderate to high skill levels.

Table 10.5 Games-by-Skill-Level Index for Moderate- to High-Functioning Students—Goalball

Skills	One on one	Small group	Large group
Throwing	Step to Throw I	Step to Throw II	Step to Throw III
Blocking	Slide Over	Block It	Four Square
Passing	Here I Am	Remember Me II	Work It Across

GAME DESCRIPTIONS

The following games are suggested for students you consider to be more mobile. As always, feel free to modify them as needed.

Skill ▶ Throwing

STEP TO THROW I

Class format: One on one

Organizational pattern: Individual with teacher and peer assistant as needed

Equipment: Basketball, medicine ball, or goalball

Description: This activity requires the student to concentrate on footwork while throwing. Using the teaching points from the skill description presented earlier in this chapter, have the student hold the goalball with one hand and work on taking a one-step slide delivery as she releases the ball to a sighted partner about 10 feet (3 m) away. The sighted partner should make some type of noise (whistle, floor tap) to give the student a reference for throwing.

Extensions: Move the sighted partner to various locations within the 10-foot (3 m) radius. Have the sighted partner roll the ball back, and have the student with a visual impairment work on blocking the return throw from a kneeling position. Rotate the sighted partners from the members of the class. Have the sighted partners wear blindfolds after several rotations through the activity.

Inclusion suggestion: The student with a visual impairment can call out the location of the sighted partner before throwing using the partner's name (e.g., "Tom, you are on the right side"). Once the student has identified where the partner is standing, she can redirect her partner to establish a new target location.

STEP TO THROW II

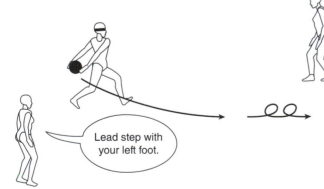

Lead step with your left foot.

= Rolled ball

● = Ball

⟶ = Ball direction

Class format: Small group

Organizational pattern: The same basic formation as Step to Throw I, except that there are three target partners and one partner assistant

Equipment: Basketball, medicine ball, or goalball

Description: The student with a visual impairment works on the one-handed throw, this time incorporating a three-step approach. The student assistant stands next to the student throwing and verbalizes the appropriate cues as the student throws—for example, "Ready, lead step with your left foot, quick step with your right foot, bring the ball back, now slide forward on your left foot, plant your foot, and release." The three target partners provide feedback on the throw—for instance, "Great throw, Sally, that was right at me." The distance should be at least 30 feet (9 m).

Extension: Add an orientation line for the student to find before each throw. For example, cut a small piece of cord, tape it to the floor with floor tape, and have the student throw from the line each time. To help with orientation, have the student locate the line each time after throwing by bending over and feeling for the line. This line simulates the orientation line on the official court.

Inclusion suggestion: The student with a visual impairment can determine the sequence of throws.

STEP TO THROW III

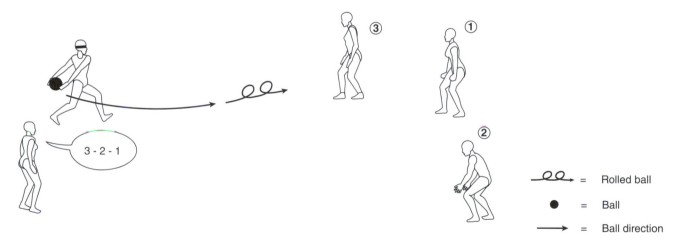

3 - 2 - 1

⟳ = Rolled ball

● = Ball

→ = Ball direction

Class format: Large group

Organizational pattern: The same basic formation as Step to Throw II

Equipment: Basketball, medicine ball, or goalball

Description: Each target partner has a number: 1, 2, 3, and so on. The student with a visual impairment throws three balls in succession according to the sequence of numbers provided by the partner assistant. For example, if the partner assistant says, "3-2-1," the student must throw the ball first to the student worth 3 points, then to the student worth 2 points, and finally to the student worth 1 point. Target partners should provide verbal feedback on the success of the throw.

Extensions: Play a math game with the student throwing (e.g., "Throw the ball to the student whose number represents 3 minus 2"). Create two teams and have a math challenge.

Inclusion suggestion: The student with a visual impairment can determine the math challenge (e.g., "What are two numbers that add up to 5?").

Skill ▶ Blocking

SLIDE OVER

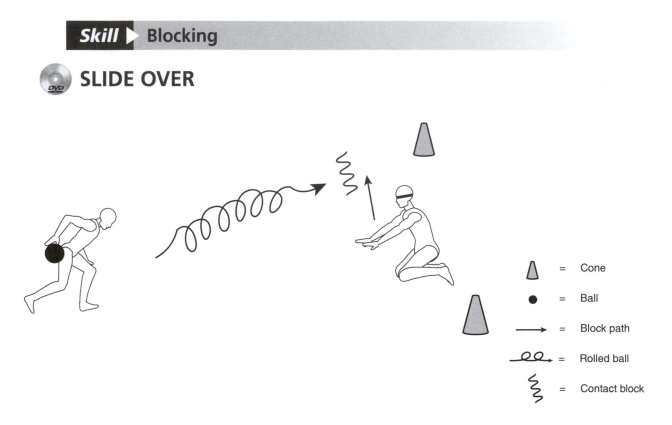

= Cone

= Ball

= Block path

= Rolled ball

= Contact block

Class format: One on one

Organizational pattern: Individual with teacher or peer assistant as needed

Equipment: Basketball, medicine ball, or goalball; traffic cones; blindfolds

Description: The student who is blocking starts in a kneeling position. A sighted partner stands about 6 feet (1.8 m) in front of the student with a visual impairment. The student with a visual impairment must wear a blindfold. The sighted partner rolls three balls to the left and three to the right, allowing enough time between throws for the student with a visual impairment to return to the starting position. The objective is to have the student with a visual impairment block the rolled balls while defending a space marked between two cones at least 13 feet (4 m) apart.

Extension: Move the student from a kneeling position to a standing position.

Inclusion suggestion: The student who is blocking can demonstrate to the class; then verbalize all the points to remember to block a rolled ball (e.g., "I have to listen carefully for the ball. Then I have to move quickly to the right or left and lead with my hands and arms. Then I have to dive to the floor and make my body long to block").

BLOCK IT

"Tap"

● = Ball

----➤ = Attempted roll

Class format: Small group

Organizational pattern: Six students in a circle formation (15 feet, or 4.6 m, in diameter) and a student with a visual impairment in the center wearing a blindfold

Equipment: Basketball, medicine ball, or goalball; blindfolds

Description: The objective of the game is to get the ball across the circle without having it blocked by the student in the middle. If the ball is blocked three times, a new student (wearing a blindfold) plays the middle position, and the student with a visual impairment joins the others in the circle. The student in the middle should start in the basic athletic position. The students in the circle should tap the ball to the floor one time prior to throwing it across the circle to provide some type of auditory cue for the blocker.

Extensions: Change the number of times a ball should be blocked—once, twice, and so on. Alternate the student blocking the ball between a kneeling and a standing position.

Inclusion suggestion: The student blocking can determine the diameter of the circle.

FOUR SQUARE

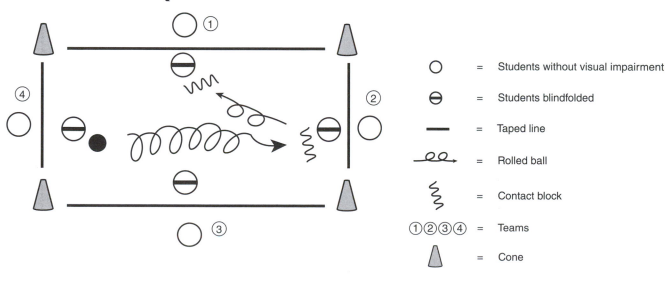

○ = Students without visual impairment

⊖ = Students blindfolded

— = Taped line

ᥱᥱ➤ = Rolled ball

Ꮓ = Contact block

①②③④ = Teams

▲ = Cone

Class format: Large group

Organizational pattern: Four traffic cones mark the corners of a square about 25 by 25 feet (7.6 by 7.6 m). A taped orientation line, about 3 feet (1 m) in length, is centered on each side of the square.

Equipment: Basketball, medicine ball, or goalball; traffic cones; blindfolds

Description: There are four 2-person teams (each side of the square hosts a team): one student wearing a blindfold on each of the orientation lines and one sighted person behind that student to serve as a ball retriever following errant throws or goals. The objective of the game is to throw the goalball across the square at an opponent in an attempt to get it past the blocker. If the ball is blocked, the blocking student should recover, find the orientation line, and return a throw. The throws may be at opposite or adjacent sides of the square. Blockers should be standing in the "up and ready" position.

Extensions: Increase the size or number of the squares. Rotate all students as blockers.

Inclusion suggestion: The student with a visual impairment can keep score and report it at the end.

Skill ▶ Passing

HERE I AM

Class format: One on one

Organizational pattern: Individual with teacher or peer assistant as needed

Equipment: Basketball, medicine ball, or goalball; traffic cones

Description: The student with a visual impairment should be paired with a sighted partner, and both students should be standing in a ready position. The sighted student stands approximately 10 feet (3 m) away, facing the student with a visual impairment. To work on passing, have the student without a visual impairment tap on the floor to indicate where he wants the pass to travel. Both students need to work together to establish smooth, coordinated passing.

Extensions: The student without a visual impairment can change locations after each successful pass; have them work for three consecutive successful passes before changing locations.

Inclusion suggestion: The student with a visual impairment can decide how many successful passes should be made before the sighted student changes locations.

REMEMBER ME II

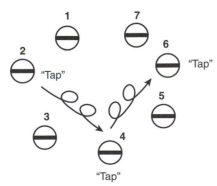

⊖	=	Students blindfolded
"Tap"	=	Signal for pass
⎯⎯	=	Rolled ball

Class format: Small group

Organizational pattern: Six or seven students with and without visual impairments are in small circles (approximately 25 ft, or 7.6 m, in diameter) wearing blindfolds and standing in the ready position. Each student has a number.

Equipment: Basketball, medicine ball, or goalball; blindfolds

Description: On a signal the students pass the goalball back and forth across the circle using an "odd" or "even" call. For example, if the call is "odd," the pass can travel only to students with odd numbers, and vice versa for the "even" call. To help with the passing, receivers tap on the floor before each pass.

Extension: Create math problems for the group and have them complete the number of passes derived from the math problem. If you ask, "How much is 10 plus 2?" the group should complete 12 successful passes.

Inclusion suggestion: The student with a visual impairment can create the math problem.

WORK IT ACROSS

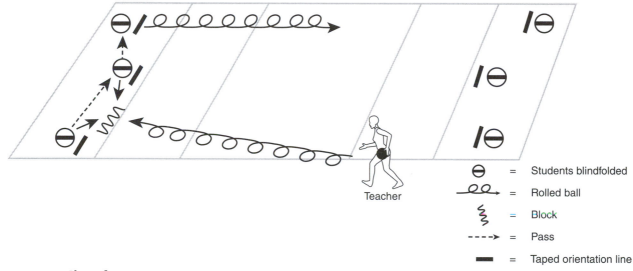

⊖ = Students blindfolded

eℓ = Rolled ball

ⓢ = Block

- - -> = Pass

▬ = Taped orientation line

Class format: Large group

Organizational pattern: Students are standing in a ready position in regulation positions on the court (i.e., center, right wing, left wing). An orientation line exists for each position.

Equipment: Basketball, medicine ball, or goalball; blindfolds; thin rope; floor tape

Description: Players (all blindfolded) are in their court positions and have located their orientation lines. You or a designated student throws a ball from the opposite end of the court to simulate an actual game. The players respond to the thrown ball by blocking it, securing it, and then passing it across the court to each other. The passes must be made to all players before a return throw can occur. For example, if the opposition throw is blocked by the right winger, that player must pass it to the center and then the center must pass it to the left winger before a return throw can occur.

Extensions: Increase the number of passes to be made; call out a sequence in which to make the passes (e.g., right wing, left wing, center).

Inclusion suggestion: The student with a visual impairment can determine the sequence of passing.

Remember that blank forms for assessments, IEPs, and unit and lesson plans are located on the DVD.

Chapter 11

Slalom

The slalom is a track and field event for athletes with cerebral palsy (CP) created by the Cerebral Palsy International Sports and Recreation Association (CPISRA). This event is for people with moderate to severe physical limitations due to some cerebral injury. Participants can use a manual or power (use of battery) wheelchair; this chapter focuses on those using power wheelchairs. The slalom offers an alternative track event for people who are unable to sprint race in their wheelchairs. The event is part of track competition, but it has a much broader application within your physical education class. Those with conditions such as muscular dystrophy, spinal cord injury (quadriplegia), and spina bifida who cannot manually propel their wheelchairs can participate in this event. In addition, students without disabilities can be challenged by the slalom with minimal modifications such as participating on scooter boards.

DESCRIPTION OF THE SPORT

The slalom must be conducted on a hard, level surface. Although competition has been conducted indoors, traditionally it is held outdoors. Outdoor surfaces with sufficient room include tennis courts, high jump areas near tracks, and staging areas for sprinters. Perhaps the best location is a blacktop surface near a track or gymnasium.

Students competing in the slalom must race their wheelchairs through six obstacles as fast as possible. Each obstacle presents a challenge for the student to control the wheelchair without accumulating penalty points or seconds. Each time a student makes a mistake at an obstacle, he accumulates penalty seconds, which are added to his total time.

The slalom course must be clearly marked and taped with directional arrows that indicate the order in which to attack the course. Students and teachers (coaches) are permitted to walk the course once prior to competition, but they are not permitted to practice the obstacles during the walk-through. During official competition, the course is closed 15 minutes prior to the event.

Field of Play

The slalom course is set up on a hard, level surface. There should be 13 feet (4 m) between obstacles with enough room for a straight sprint at the end of the course. See figure 11.1.

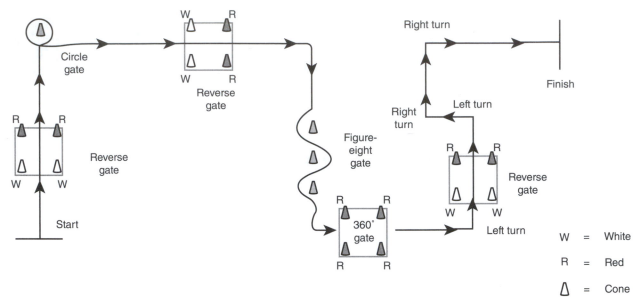

Figure 11.1 The slalom course.

Players

Official competition is conducted for people who have CP or other disabling conditions that require the use of a power wheelchair.

Equipment

To set up the slalom event, you need several rolls of floor tape to mark the direction of the course and placement of the obstacles. You also need 26 markers. Official markers are cut from PVC pipe and stand 16 inches (41 cm) high with a 4-inch (10 cm) diameter. You are free to use alternatives for your situation (e.g., plastic bowling pins) as long as the markers are white. You need red ribbon or cloth, cut into short strips, to tie around six markers, and white flags to place inside four of the markers. The colors white and red have significant meanings to participants; each color indicates a change in the direction of travel while moving through the markers.

The markers are used to form gates that participants must maneuver through. There are three reverse gates, one 360-degree gate, a circle gate, and a figure-eight gate. Reverse and 360-degree gates are approximately 3 feet (1 m) square and are marked with floor tape. It is important to mark the boundaries of each gate with tape, because participants are penalized for touching the lines during each pass through the course. The final section of the slalom is a series of turns (one to the left and two to the right) before finishing with a straight sprint. This final segment is also marked by directional arrows made of the floor tape. Participants are penalized only for touching lines that mark the gate obstacles, not for touching directional arrows.

Starting the Game

The participant must position the wheelchair so that the front tires are on the starting line. The start of the slalom is from a stationary position. The starter uses a starter's pistol and says, "Take your mark, set," and then fires the pistol. The participant's recorded time starts when the front tires of the wheelchair cross the finish line.

Game Objective

The objective of the slalom event is to complete the course as fast as possible without accumulating penalty points or being disqualified. The participant must follow the arrows and pass through the obstacles (gates) in the correct order. Penalty seconds are assessed if the participant completes the course out of sequence or skips an obstacle.

In an official event, three officials and two recorders are on the course to judge infractions. The participant is assessed additional seconds for marker and line infractions. Any participant who cannot finish the course as a result of mechanical failure is disqualified.

Participants must pay attention to the direction of travel. As they enter a reverse gate, they must be able to turn their wheelchairs 180 degrees to exit the opposite side of the gate. In other words, they enter forward and exit backward. As they exit traveling backward, they again must turn their wheelchairs 180 degrees to travel forward into the next gate. Reverse gates are marked by white markers at the entrance and red markers at the exit. The circle marker is a single marker that the participant must encircle completely before moving on to the next gate. The figure-eight gate has three markers set 3 feet (1 m) apart in a straight line. To successfully complete the figure-eight gate, the participant must weave among all three markers before moving to the next gate. The 360-degree gate is marked by four red markers, indicating that a complete turn must be executed inside the gate before exiting. The participant enters and exits the 360-degree gate traveling forward.

Game Length

In an official competition, the only time constraint is enacted prior to the start of competition. The slalom is officially closed 15 minutes before the first race.

General Rules and Penalties

The slalom is a race against time. The participant is penalized additional time for the following infractions: (a) missing an obstacle, (b) knocking over a marker, (c) touching a line with a tire, and (d) touching a marker with the wheelchair or a body part.

If a participant fails to follow the correct sequence of the course design, she must correct her mistake prior to entering the next obstacle. The participant must correct this fault without assistance from coaches or teammates. Failure to correct this fault will result in a disqualification. For example, if a participant skips an obstacle and realizes her mistake, she must return to the skipped obstacle prior to finishing the course.

Knocking over a marker results in a five-second penalty. The marker may not be replaced from where it was knocked down until the next participant is ready to run through the course. If a marker gets caught underneath a wheelchair, it is up to the participant to free the marker from the wheelchair. The participant must remove the trapped marker by using wheelchair movements. No event official, coach, or teammate may assist in the removal of a trapped marker.

If the tire of the wheelchair touches a line of either the reverse or 360-degree gate, a three-second penalty is assessed. All maneuvers must be completed within the boundaries of each gate without touching the lines.

Touching a marker results in a three-second penalty added to the participant's total time. As the participant moves into and out of each gate, she must concentrate on keeping her body position as stable as possible. If a participant strikes a fallen marker, no additional penalty time is added.

Summary of the Sport

Table 11.1 will help you set up a slalom event for your students considered severely disabled. Although this event is designed for students with disabilities who use power wheelchairs, students using manual wheelchairs can also participate.

Table 11.1 Overview of the Slalom

Field of play	Any hard, level surface—for example, tennis court, playground, track high jump takeoff area
Players	Students using power wheelchairs—for example, those with severe CP, muscular dystrophy, spinal cord injury (quadriplegia), spina bifida, or other like conditions
Equipment	Floor tape; PVC pipe cut 16 in. (41 cm) tall by 4 in. (10 cm) diameter (26 pieces) or plastic bowling pins; strips of red cloth
Legal start	Stationary position at the starting line; front tires behind starting line; starter pistol is fired
Completing the course	Participants must pass through the course as fast as possible, paying attention to the direction of travel and the type of obstacle (reverse gate, single-pin circle gate, 360-degree gate, figure-eight gate). Participants must avoid body and wheelchair contact with taped lines and markers as they pass through the course.
	All reverse and 360 gates are 3 ft (1 m) square, and the figure-eight gate has three markers set 3 ft (1 m) apart.
Penalties and disqualifications	Skipping an obstacle (or not reentering in the correct order): Student is disqualified.
	Knocking over a marker: 5 sec
	Touching a line with a tire: 3 sec
	Touching a marker with the wheelchair or a body part: 3 sec

SKILLS TO BE TAUGHT

The slalom has four gate types that require specific maneuvers to negotiate: the reverse gate, the 360-degree gate, the figure-eight gate, and the circle gate. Only three maneuvers are used, however, because the circle gate requires the same wheelchair movement as the 360-degree gate, only with a tighter turning radius. The three maneuvers require the student to control body position and the speed of the wheelchair, and accelerate and decelerate appropriately while negotiating an obstacle. Competition is traditionally conducted on a hard, flat, level outdoor surface, but students can practice these skills inside the gymnasium during your general physical education class.

Reverse Turn

Students should learn to identify a reverse gate before executing a reverse turn. The entrance to a reverse gate is marked with white markers indicating that the student must enter in a forward direction. The exit is marked by red markers, which requires the student to exit in a reverse direction. To negotiate this obstacle successfully, the student must have complete control of the wheelchair both entering and exiting.

To complete the reverse gate successfully, the student should enter in a forward direction and initiate a 180-degree turn as soon as possible once inside the gate, being careful to avoid line or marker infractions. The student should position the wheelchair directly in the center of the obstacle before turning. The student must know the length and width of the wheelchair and must maintain control. Once the 180-degree turn is complete, the student must exit the obstacle from the opposite side of entry. The student should look for landmarks or focal points to help with positioning and align the wheelchair before attempting the reverse exit. Once the reverse exit has taken place, the student must again turn the wheelchair to a forward direction to continue through the course; another 180-degree turn is required to head for the next obstacle.

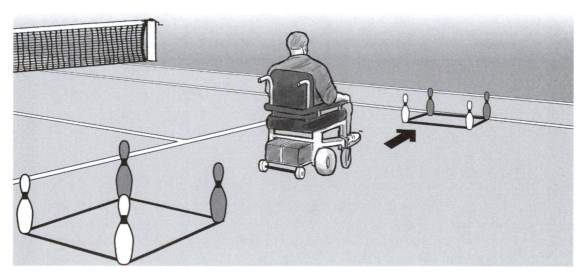

Entering the reverse gate with white markers.

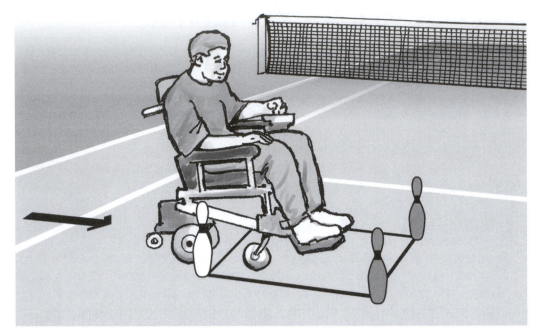

Inside the reverse gate.

Execute a 180-degree turn within the reverse gate; then exit backward.

360-Degree Turn

The 360-degree turn is marked by four red markers at each corner. The student enters the gate with the same control as described for the reverse gate and positions the wheelchair in the center. To conduct the 360-degree maneuver, the student must have proper sitting posture and control of the toggle switch or joystick on the wheelchair. The student must turn the wheelchair one complete turn and exit from the opposite side of the point of entry facing in a forward direction. Remember, while turning the wheelchair within the obstacle, the student must avoid touching the lines and markers.

Enter a 360-degree gate facing forward.

Maintain body position; execute a complete turn within the gate.

Exit facing forward.

Circle Gate

This figure shows a single-pin circle gate. The objective is to circle this single pin without touching the pin. There are no lines or boxes to address. If the student knocks over the pin, it is a five-second penalty.

The single-pin circle gate.

Figure-Eight Turn

The student approaches the figure-eight gate in a forward direction and must weave through each of the three markers before moving to the next gate. The student should approach each marker ready to turn in the direction of most wheelchair control. For example, students who have more control turning to the right should approach the left side of the marker. Students who turn their wheelchairs with more control to the left should approach the marker from the right side.

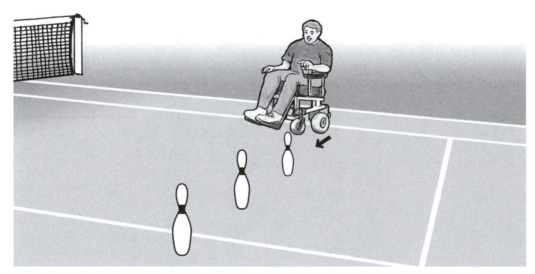

Approach the figure-eight gate with control.

Pass through, maintaining good sitting position.

Avoid touching markers.

FUNCTIONAL PROFILES
AND GENERAL MODIFICATIONS

The purpose of including the slalom in this book is to provide suggestions for your students with severe physical disabilities in at least three extremities. Therefore, there is no section included for moderate- to high-functioning students. All activities in this chapter are written for the student who uses a power wheelchair independently.

General Modifications

Table 11.2 offers suggestions for how you might apply general modifications to the three skills necessary to complete the slalom. As always, the students in your class and your teaching situation will determine your choice of modifications.

Table 11.2 General Modifications for Slalom

Skill level	Skill	Activity modifications
Low	Reverse turn	Enter the obstacle and back straight out without a reverse turn.
	360-degree turn	Enter the obstacle and change the direction of travel to exit (not necessarily a full 360-degree turn; e.g., a quarter turn).
	Figure-eight turn	Weave around one marker rather than all three.

GAME PROGRESSIONS

Because of the independent nature of this event, it is difficult to create small group and large group activities. Nevertheless, some small group and large group activities are suggested to address motivation and practice for students with severe disabilities. These games also address the three domains of learning in physical education: psychomotor, cognitive, and affective.

GAMES-BY-SKILL-LEVEL INDEX

This chapter has only one games-by-skill-level index (table 11.3) because the functional profile for this sport is low/severe. You should still cross-reference the skill by the class format you desire (one on one, small group, large group).

Table 11.3 Games-by-Skill-Level Index for Low-Functioning Students—The Slalom

Skills	One on one	Small group	Large group
Reverse turn	Tap and Go	Grand Reverse	Reverse and Go
360-degree turn	Circle Up	Ring Masters	Reverse, Turn, and Go
Figure-eight turn	The Weave	Giant Slalom I	Giant Slalom II

GAME DESCRIPTIONS

The games are arranged according to skills and class formats. Each game description includes class format, organizational pattern, equipment, description, extensions, and inclusion suggestions. You are free to decide the application of these games to your teaching situation.

Skill ▶ Reverse Turn

🪩 TAP AND GO

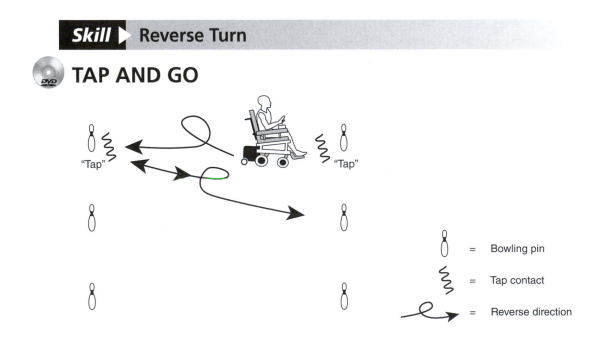

Class format: One on one

Organizational pattern: Individual with teacher or peer assistant as needed

Equipment: Six plastic bowling pins

Description: Create two rows of three plastic bowling pins approximately 15 feet (4.6 m) apart. Bowling pins in each row should be 10 feet (3 m) apart. The student starts in the middle of the two rows facing the first pin of row 1. On command, the student moves the wheelchair forward, under control, and taps the first bowling pin (if it falls, that's OK). As the tap is made, the student reverses direction and spins 180 degrees to face the first pin of the second row. Again under control, the student moves forward and taps the pin, does a reverse spin, and moves on to the second pin of the first row. The student continues tapping and going until all pins have been tapped. Emphasize wheelchair control and reversing direction.

Extension: Shorten the distance between the two rows of bowling pins, which will require additional control of the wheelchair.

Inclusion suggestion: The student can demonstrate to the class his ability to accomplish the task.

GRAND REVERSE

Whistle blow

= Scooter

= Travel direction

Class format: Small group

Organizational pattern: Small groups of three or four students with and without disabilities in a circle formation

Equipment: Scooters, whistle

Description: Students are in three or four small groups in circle formations around the gym. Students without disabilities use scooters. The objective of the game is to have all the groups moving in a circular direction while facing the same direction (e.g., forward). On the first whistle and subsequent whistles, everyone changes the direction they are facing but not the direction of travel. Make sure to allow enough space between students using scooters and students using power wheelchairs.

Extensions: Vary the activity by changing the frequency of the signals to change directions. Change the size of the circle. Include a ball in the activity and have students pass the ball when they change direction.

Inclusion suggestion: The student with a disability can initiate the change of direction.

REVERSE AND GO

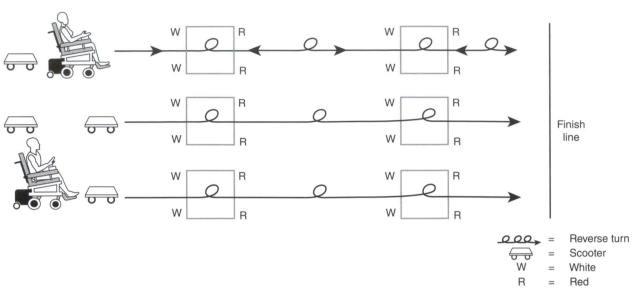

ℓℓℓ↗ = Reverse turn
🛹 = Scooter
W = White
R = Red

Class format: Large group

Organizational pattern: The class is divided into three teams in preparation for a relay race.

Equipment: Plastic bowling pins (or equipment to make markers), floor tape, stopwatch, scooters

Description: Using the diagram from the official competition, set up six reverse gates (two per team) using red and white markers. Each reverse gate should measure 1 meter square and be marked with floor tape. Position each reverse gate 13 feet (4 m) apart and allow 33 feet (10 m) for a finishing distance. Line up each team behind its set of reverse gates and place students without disabilities on scooters. On the command "Go," students travel (in turns) to the first gate and perform a reverse movement inside the gate without touching any of the boundary lines. Once they have completed a reverse movement, they exit and continue to the next gate to repeat the movement. After they have completed the second reverse gate, they exit and sprint to the finish line. Students who touch a gate line have penalty seconds added to their total times.

Extensions: Change the position of the students without disabilities on the scooters; for instance, they can complete the first trip seated, then change to a prone and then a kneeling position. Increase the number of reverse movements to be performed by those without disabilities (e.g., two reverses within each gate).

Inclusion suggestion: The student with a disability can decide the students' positions on the scooter for travel.

Skill ▶ 360-Degree Turn

CIRCLE UP

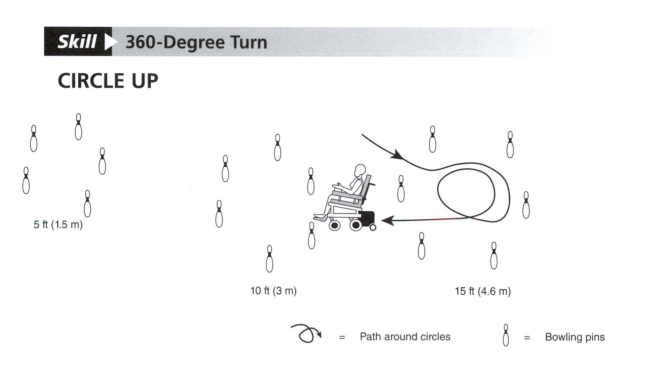

5 ft (1.5 m)

10 ft (3 m)   15 ft (4.6 m)

⟲➘ = Path around circles   ᳀ = Bowling pins

Class format: One on one

Organizational pattern: Individual with teacher or peer assistant as needed

Equipment: Plastic bowling pins or traffic cones, floor tape

Description: Create three circles using plastic bowling pins or cones as boundaries. Each circle has a different diameter (e.g., 15 ft, 10 ft, and 5 ft, or 4.6 m, 3 m, and 1.5 m). Use the floor tape to mark the entrances and exits to and from the circles. The student moves her wheelchair forward into the largest circle and executes a complete 360-degree turn inside. Once she has completed the turn, she must find the exit arrow (floor tape) and exit the circle. The student must master one circle size before moving to the smaller size.

Extension: Challenge the student to move in succession from the 15-foot (4.6 m) circle to the 10-foot (3 m) to the 5-foot (1.5 m) circle without stopping.

Inclusion suggestions: The student can decide which circle to start with. Also, a student without disabilities can join using a scooter.

RING MASTERS

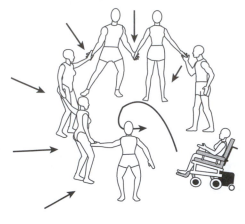

→ = Students making circle smaller

⟲ = Path of student inside circle

Class format: Small group

Organizational pattern: Small groups of three or four students with and without disabilities in a circle formation

Equipment: None

Description: Small groups of students create several circle formations around the gym. Students forming the circle should hold hands. The student with a disability is in the center of one circle (or more depending on the number in your class). On the signal to move, the student in the center of the circle moves his wheelchair around the inside circumference of the circle. On each pass around the circle, the students move inward to create a smaller circle. The objective is to get the student in the center of the circle to turn 360 degrees in the smallest circle possible for his skill level.

Extension: At a signal to change direction, the student turns 360 degrees in the opposite direction as the circle continues to get smaller.

Inclusion suggestions: The student with a disability can decide the starting circumference for each of the circles. Students without disabilities can participate by performing some form of locomotor movement around the circle (e.g., hopping on one foot, sliding sideways, or bear or crab walking).

REVERSE, TURN, AND GO

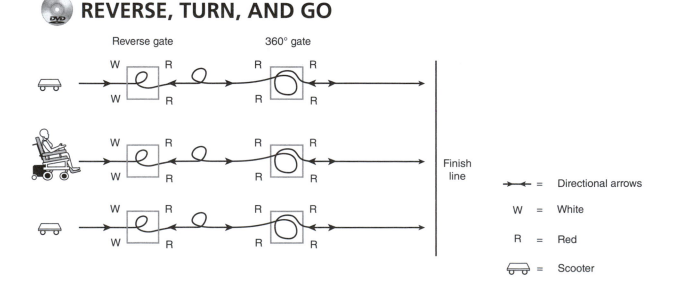

Reverse gate   360° gate

Finish line

➤← = Directional arrows

W = White

R = Red

🛹 = Scooter

Class format: Large group

Organizational pattern: The class is divided into three teams in preparation for a relay race.

Equipment: Plastic bowling pins (or equipment to make markers), floor tape, stopwatch, scooters

Description: Using the diagram from the official competition, set up three reverse gates and three 360-degree gates (one each per team) using red and white markers. Each gate should measure 1 meter square and be marked with floor tape. Position gates 13 feet (4 m) apart, and allow 33 feet (10 m) for a finishing distance. Line up each team behind its set of gates, and place students without disabilities on scooters. On the command "Go," students travel, in turns, to the first gate and perform a reverse movement inside the gate without touching any of the boundary lines. Once they have completed a reverse movement, they exit and continue to the next gate to complete a full 360-degree turn inside the gate. They then exit and sprint to the finish line. Students who touch a gate line have penalty seconds added to their total times.

Extensions: Change the position of the students without disabilities on the scooters; for example, on their first trip they may sit, then change to a front-lying or kneeling position. If scooters are not available for students without disabilities, have these students perform various locomotor movements as they participate in the relay race, such as hopping on one foot or jumping with two feet.

Inclusion suggestion: The student with a disability can decide the order of the course (e.g., the 360-degree gate first, then the reverse gate).

Skill ▶ Figure-Eight Turn

THE WEAVE

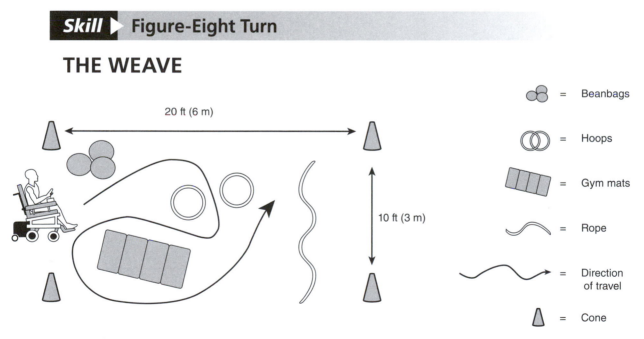

Class format: One on one

Organizational pattern: Individual with teacher or peer assistant as needed

Equipment: Various pieces of equipment scattered about the game area, such as beanbags, hoops, gym mats, and rope

Description: Scatter several pieces of equipment randomly on the floor within a small game area (e.g., 10 by 20 ft, or 3 by 6 m). On the signal, the student begins moving within the game area, avoiding contact with the equipment. The student should move left and right while weaving through the game area in figure-eight patterns.

Extensions: Increase the number of pieces of equipment within the area. Challenge the student to move from one end of the game area to the opposite end as fast as possible.

Inclusion suggestions: A classmate without a disability can move on a scooter through the course at the same time as the student with a disability. The student with a disability can scatter the pieces of equipment and adjust the distances between pieces. The student with a disability can also decide the scooter position for the student without a disability (e.g., kneeling, sitting, prone).

GIANT SLALOM I

= Weave

= Run direction

= Pins

Class format: Small group

Organizational pattern: Students stand in small groups around circles of bowling pins. A student with a disability is in the center of each circle.

Equipment: Plastic bowling pins or small traffic cones

Description: Students are in small groups of three or four. The student with a disability is in the center of a circle of bowling pins (at least 12 pins about 6 ft, or 1.8 m, apart). Students without disabilities stand outside the circle of bowling pins. On a signal, the student with a disability moves from the center and begins weaving in and out of the bowling pins as the students without disabilities move around the circle. After one trip around the circle, the student returns to the center and calls out a classmate's name. The student who is called moves to the center of the circle, tags the first student, and then moves around the circle, weaving in and out of the bowling pins. The game continues until all students have completed a turn around the circle. Once each group has had an opportunity to practice, repeat the game for time, remembering to enforce any penalty times for touching or knocking over the bowling pins.

Extensions: Increase the number of bowling pins or traffic cones, or decrease the distance between cones for the weave. Set up the same game using a straight-line formation.

Inclusion suggestion: Students without disabilities can use scooters or some form of alternative locomotor movement, such as skipping or hopping on one foot.

GIANT SLALOM II

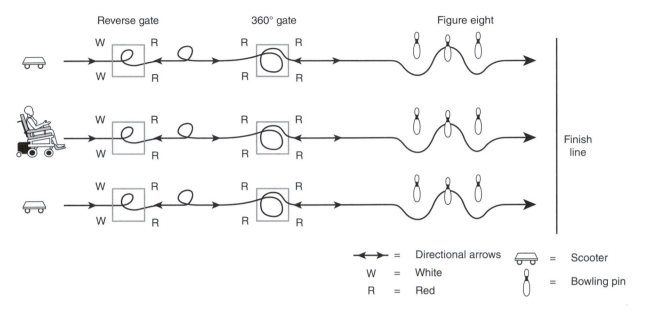

←→ = Directional arrows	⬚ = Scooter	
W = White	🎳 = Bowling pin	
R = Red		

Class format: Large group

Organizational pattern: The class is divided into three teams in preparation for a relay race.

Equipment: Plastic bowling pins (or equipment to make markers), floor tape, stopwatch, scooters

Description: Using the diagram from the official competition, set up three reverse gates, three 360-degree gates, and three figure-eight gates (one each per team) using red and white markers. Each gate should measure 1 meter square and be marked with floor tape. Each of the three markers for the figure-eight gate should be 3 feet (1 m) apart. Position gates 13 feet (4 m) apart, and allow 33 feet (10 m) for a finishing distance. Line up each team behind its set of gates, and place students without disabilities on scooters. On the command "Go," students travel, in turns, through the course, completing passes through the reverse, 360-degree, and figure-eight gates as fast as possible. You may want to enforce penalty seconds to the total times of students who touch a gate line.

Extensions: Change the position of the students without disabilities on the scooters; for instance, on their first trip they may sit, then change to a front-lying or kneeling position on subsequent trips. If scooters are not available for students without disabilities, these students can perform various locomotor movements as they participate in the relay race (e.g., hopping on one foot or jumping with two feet).

Inclusion suggestion: The student with a disability can decide the order for completing the course (e.g., reverse gate first, then the figure-eight gate, and finishing with the 360-degree gate).

Remember that blank forms for assessments, IEPs, and unit and lesson plans are located on the DVD.

Chapter 12

Boccia

Boccia is a throwing sport that can be played indoors or outdoors. It was adapted for people with disabilities and first played internationally at the 1984 International Games for the Disabled in New York. This sport is now played within the Paralympics and does not have an Olympic counterpart. The Cerebral Palsy International Sports and Recreation Association (CPISRA) conducts international boccia competitions for athletes with cerebral palsy or other severe locomotor dysfunction. According to the International Boccia Committee, the game is played in over 40 countries by those with and without disabilities. This chapter focuses on the rules for those with disabilities who play *indoors on a court or gymnasium floor.*

DESCRIPTION OF THE SPORT

Boccia has its roots in Italy in the 16th century. The object of the game is to throw (roll) leather balls as close as possible to a target ball called the jack ball. The jack ball is thrown into play and must remain on the court within the playing area. Individual players, pairs, or teams (called sides) throw their balls to see who can get closest to the jack ball. The order of play is determined by the "close rule." The side that is *not* closest must throw until they are closer to the jack ball. Once that occurs, then the opponent throws trying to get closer to the jack. This is determined each time with the side that is not closest throwing the next ball. The play proceeds until all balls are played. Once all the balls have been thrown, that completes an *end.* Individual matches consist of four ends with six balls per player per end; pairs competition has four ends and six balls per pair (or three balls per player); and team competition has six ends with six balls per team (or two balls per player per end).

The activities in this chapter use only individual competition. You may elect to conduct pair or team competitions in your physical education classes. Remember that this sport can address those with severe disabilities and those without disabilities (e.g., the multilevel and modified curriculums mentioned in chapter 3).

Field of Play

The game is played on a court measuring 41 by 20 feet (12.5 by 6 m) (approximately the size of a badminton court) with the throwing area divided into six throwing boxes and the target area marked with a V line (see figure 12.1). The jack ball must clear the area between the throwing line and the V line to be considered in play before the match can begin.

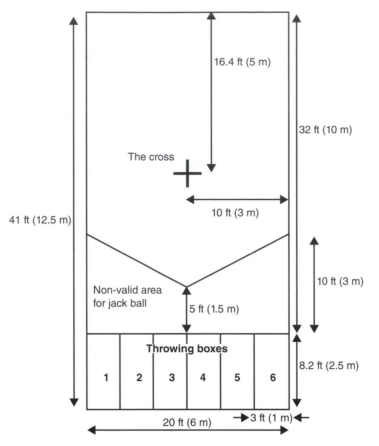

Figure 12.1 Boccia court.

Players

Players use wheelchairs and can range in ability from needing assistance to hold and throw, to using an assistive device (ramp or chute), to being able to independently grasp, release, and throw. Competition is arranged for individuals (one member), pairs (two members), or teams (three members); each arrangement is called a side. If you include this game in your general physical education class, have typically developing students use folding chairs. This is a great class management tool because students can recognize who is playing the game and who is waiting a turn.

Equipment

Players may bring their own boccia balls to a competition. A set of boccia balls consists of six red balls, six blue balls, and one white jack ball. Official indoor boccia balls are made of leather and designed to roll smoothly on the floor. In international competition the balls are always inspected for cuts or deformities that could compromise performance and are weighed and measured prior to and during competition.

Starting the Game

The game starts with a coin flip to determine the player, pair, or team's color choice. The red side initiates the first end and is responsible for throwing the jack ball into play. The match begins with the jack ball being thrown into play; it must cross the V line and remain within the court boundaries. The court has a throwing area which is divided into six throwing boxes and players must be positioned inside the throwing boxes. During individual play, the players must start in box 3 (red) and box 4 (blue); pairs competition has players throwing red balls in boxes 2 and 4 while players throw blue balls in boxes 3 and 5. Team competition allows three boxes for each team to be occupied (boxes 1, 3, 5 [red] and boxes 2, 4, 6 [blue]). Read about serving rotation in the next section.

Game Objective

The objective of the game is to throw the colored ball closest to the jack ball. The red side throws first, and then the blue side throws; the side farther from the jack ball is the next side to throw. If the blue side is farther from the jack ball, that side throws again and continues to throw until the players secure a closer position or throw all their balls. As soon as the blue side positions a ball closer than the red side, red throws until that side is closer to the jack ball. The play continues with the side that is farther throwing until all balls are played.

At the conclusion of each end, the referee measures the distance of the balls to determine which ball is closest to the jack ball, and awards points: 1 point for each ball that is closer to the jack ball than the opponent's closest ball. If two or more balls of different colors are equally distant from the jack ball, and no other balls are closer, then each ball that is equidistant is awarded a point. The player, pair, or team receives the points for that end. In subsequent ends, the jack ball is served by the next player. In individual play, serving rotates, whereas in team and pair play, it moves down the line from left to right as players face the court. (An example in team play: box 2 would be serving jack in the second end, box 3 would be serving in the third end, and so on.)

After the correct numbers of ends are played, the side with the most points wins the game. In the case of a tie score at the end of a game, a tie-break end is played; this is played as a normal end. In a tie-break, the winner of the coin toss chooses to throw first or second; the jack is placed on the replacement jack cross position (see figure 12.1), and play proceeds as in a normal end. A second tie-break end could be played if needed.

In individual competition, the side throwing red balls throws from box 3, and the side throwing blue throws from box 4 (see figure 12.1). In pairs competition, the side throwing red throws from boxes 2 and 4, and the side throwing blue does so from boxes 3 and 5. In team competition, the red team throws from the odd-numbered boxes, and the blue team throws from the even-numbered boxes.

Game Length

Time limits are determined by the composition of the sides (individual throwers have five minutes per player per end; individual players using ramps to assist have six minutes per player per end; ramp pairs have eight minutes per pair per end; and throwing pairs have six minutes per team per end).

General Rules and Penalties

The official competition rules by CPISRA are extensive and in-depth, far beyond the scope of this book and its intended audience. To better address the needs of students studying to be physical educators, or those currently employed as physical educators, a modified version of the rules is presented here. To view the official rules for boccia according to CPISRA, go to www.cpisra.org.

No jack ball or colored ball may be thrown prior to the referee's signal. All players, coaches, and sport assistants (SA) must be in their designated areas. SAs are leaders who assist the player(s) during competition only, such as placing a ball on a ramp, positioning a ramp, or positioning a wheelchair prior to the release of the ball. Any equipment needed to assist the player in rolling the ball (a ramp or chute) must remain within the throwing box and may not touch any lines at the moment of throwing. The player must be seated with at least one buttock in contact with the seat when releasing the ball. The player cannot touch the court outside of the throwing box upon release. If a ball bounces off the player who threw it, the opposing player, or any equipment, it is considered in play. All thrown balls that touch or cross the boundary lines are consider out, and all-out-of-bounds balls are removed from the court and placed in a dead ball container.

If the jack ball is knocked off the court during a match, it is repositioned on the replaced jack cross marking on the court (see figure 12.1). When the jack ball is replaced, the side farther from the replacement mark throws next. If two or more balls of different colors are equally distant from the jack, the side that threw last throws next. Play continues normally. If a player accidently drops a ball, and it is not considered an intentional throw, the referee can allow the player to rethrow the ball. After all balls have been thrown, the referee scores the end. If the score is tied, a tie-break end is conducted, which is simply a normal end.

Players must remain in their throwing boxes during the match. A player who wants to come onto the court during her time, to check the positions of the balls, must ask permission of the referee.

Violations during play lead to the award of penalty balls—two additional balls awarded to a side, which are thrown at the conclusion of an end. Penalty balls result from the following: failing to ask permission before moving out of the throwing box; in the case of an SA, turning to watch the court during play; inappropriate communication between players or with SAs or coaches; and, in the case of an SA, moving the wheelchair or ramp or rolling the ball without the player's direction. The following actions lead to the awarding of penalty balls as well as retraction of a thrown ball: releasing the ball while the athlete, SA, or equipment is touching a throwing box line; releasing the ball without appropriate contact with the seat; releasing the ball when it is touching the court outside of the throwing area; moving the ramp forward or backward (it can be moved only left to right); and having the ramp overhang the front throwing line upon release. SAs may not turn to look during the preparation of the shot. A retraction-only penalty results from releasing the ball prior to the referee indicating which color to play, throwing the ball out of turn, and throwing a colored ball before the jack ball has been thrown into position. Warnings and disqualifications can occur during competition for the following actions: unreasonable delay of a match, leaving the court area between ends, and displaying poor sporting behavior toward the referee. One time-out is allowed per side during pair and team play for up to two minutes.

General Considerations for Throwing

The only motor skill addressed in this chapter for boccia is throwing. The underhand throw is suggested when longer throws are needed, and the overhand throw is suggested when shorter, softer throws are needed.

Students with low functional ability can use an assistive device to help them throw. One such devise is a ramp for propelling a ball down onto the court after release by the player. Peer students serving as sport assistants (SA) are allowed to place the ball on the ramp, but the release must come from the player. Some students with low functional ability use a pointer device attached to head gear, which allows them to hold the ball steady on the ramp until release. The SAs are allowed to assist only with aiming the ramp and ball placement; they may not turn to watch the competition and the results of the throw during the execution of the throw; they must face the opposite direction from the court during all throws. Communication systems must be established between the player and the SA (e.g., short voice signals, head nods, blinking, shoulder shrugs) to determine where to place the ramp for each throw. The ramp may never be moved forward or backward to adjust aiming, only left or right within the designated throwing area.

Summary of the Sport

Table 12.1 provides an overview of boccia. This quick reference will help you learn how to play the game.

Table 12.1   Overview of Boccia

Field of play	The game is played on a court measuring 41 by 20 ft (12.5 by 6 m) with the throwing area divided into six throwing boxes and the target area marked with a V line. A replacement jack cross is marked with tape in the playing area for a replacement during tie-breakers or in case the jack ball is knocked off court.
Players	The game can be played between individuals, pairs, or teams (of three), each of which is called a *side.* Substitutes are allowed in team and pair play.
Equipment	A set of boccia balls consists of six red, six blue, and one white jack ball. Official indoor boccia balls are made of leather and designed to roll smoothly on the floor. Assistive devices are allowed for those with severe disabilities (e.g., ramps, chutes, or an aid attached directly to a player's head, mouth, or arm) to help throw or propel the ball on the court.
Legal start	A coin is flipped, and the winning side chooses a ball color. The jack ball is presented to the red side; a player from that side throws the jack into play on the referee's signal and then follows up with the first red ball when signaled.
Game objective	The objective of the game is to throw the colored ball closest to the jack ball. At the conclusion of each end, the referee measures the distance of the balls closest to the jack ball and awards points. Each division of play has a specific number of ends assigned per game. At the end of the game, the side with the most points wins.

(continued)

Table 12.1 (continued)

Tie-break ends	In the case of a tie score at the conclusion of the specified number of ends, a tie-break end is played; this is played as a normal end. A coin is tossed, and the winner chooses to throw first or second. The jack is placed on the replacement jack cross, which is marked on the floor in the playing area; a second tie-break end could be played if needed.
Game length	Time limits are determined according to the composition of sides (individual throwers have 5 min/player/end; individual ramp players have 6 min/player/end; ramp pairs have 8 min/pair/end; and throwing pairs and teams have 6 min/team/end).
Penalties, retractions, warnings, and disqualifications	Penalties result in two extra balls awarded to the opposing side. Penalty balls are played at the conclusion of the end when all balls have been played. Retractions result in the removal of a ball when a violation occurred. Yellow cards indicate warnings. Red cards indicate disqualifications. Penalties: Two penalty balls and a retraction: **Award of penalty balls:** Touching a throwing box line (or outside of the box) upon release of the ball; moving the ramp forward or backward between shots; having the ramp overhang the front line upon release; releasing the ball without appropriate contact with the seat of the chair; a ramp sport assistant looking onto the court during the preparation of the shot **Two penalty balls:** Failing to ask permission before moving out of the throwing box; a sport assistant moving the wheelchair or ramp, or rolling the ball without the player's directions; a ramp sport assistant looking onto the court; a sport assistant communicating with a player during the end; team and pair players communicating when it is not their side's turn to play; preparing for a shot during an opponent's time **Retraction:** Throwing the jack ball or a colored ball prior to the referee's signal; throwing a ball out of turn; throwing a colored ball before the jack ball has been thrown into position Warnings and disqualifications: Unreasonable delay of a match; leaving the court area between ends; displaying poor sporting behavior toward the referee
Sport assistant (SA)	A sport assistant is a member of the team other than the coach who is designated to assist the player on the court. SAs working with players using a chute or ramp may not turn to view the court during play or reposition the chute or ramp at their own discretion. The player must decide on the position of the ramp or chute and communicate that position to the sport assistant.

SKILLS TO BE TAUGHT

Players have to execute the skill of throwing with any of three techniques: use of a ramp, underhand, or overhand. They must be able to throw long (or deep onto the court) or short with more accuracy. Using any of these throws helps them execute the game strategies of blocking, defeating a block, and playing the circle.

Throwing With Ramp

Players must position their bodies and wheelchairs so they are facing the jack ball; this provides alignment for an accurate shot. The ramp should be centered in front of the player's body to facilitate aiming straight down the ramp to the target area. The player will need to determine the incline of the ramp to address the length of throw required (i.e., generally a ramp positioned with a steep incline to the floor will generate a faster roll to help carry the ball a greater distance; whereas a flatter incline can be used for shorter throws).

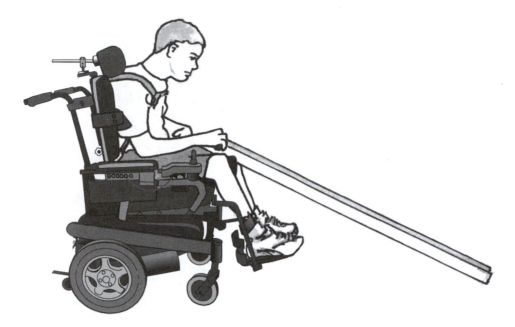

Position ball on ramp and prepare for release.

Throwing Underhand (Long)

Players who can independently grip and release boccia balls often use an underhand motion to throw with more force. To throw the ball underhand, a player must open his hand wide enough to grip the ball, close his fingers around the ball with enough pressure to hold the ball independently, establish a good balanced position (seated), swing the throwing arm backward then forward keeping the elbow slightly extended, and release the ball in a forward motion

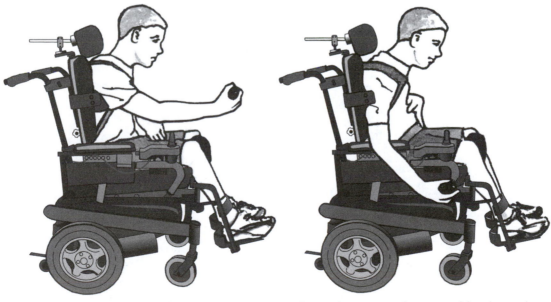

Throwing underhand: Arm forward in preparation for down swing.

Arm movement down and backward.

Arm back and prepare for forward swing.   Forward swing, prepare for release.

Ball forward, release, and follow-through.

by opening the grip in a controlled manner. Once the ball is released, the throwing arm should continue lifting upward for follow-through and in line with the target.

For throws needed to reach the back of the court, make sure the player throws hard using the hardest ball (remember that official boccia balls are made of leather, and some are firmer than others). If the player is using a ramp, make sure to set the ramp at a steep incline and have the player release the ball near the top of the ramp. Some ramps have extensions for use on long shots; make sure to use the hardest ball for these shots.

Throwing Overhand (Short)

To deliver a short court shot, players must throw softer; they can change their arm position for an overhand throw. In using an overhand throw, the player should focus on lofting the ball higher to result in a softer landing with minimal roll. If using the ramp, the slope of the ramp should be flatter, and softer balls should be used in short throws.

The target area for practicing short throws should be the midcourt cross (see figure 12.1). Players should practice stopping the ball on the cross at midcourt.

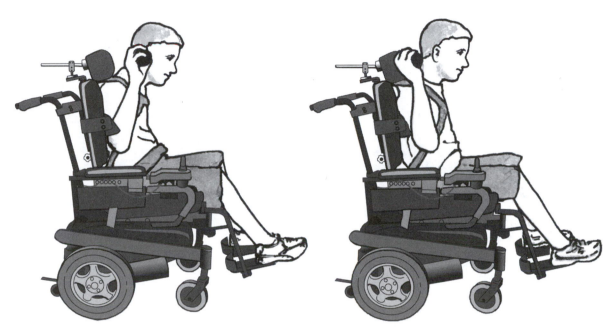

Boccia overhand throw: Raise ball in preparation.

Pull ball back, ready to extend elbow.

Move ball forward, extending elbow.

Release ball with elbow extension and arm follow-through.

During practice sessions, players should keep notes of the arm or ramp position that works best for soft throws to midcourt.

The following are strategies within the game of boccia that utilize ramp, underhand, or overhand throwing. You have the choice to match the throwing type to your students' skill levels.

Blocking

The idea behind blocking is to set up a wall of balls, a blockade, between the jack and the opponent. During blocking practice, players attempt to stop their colored balls between the jack and the line of their opponent's throws. Players should address blocking by looking at the opponent's line of attack from all angles (this is similar to lining up a putt in golf). To do this, a player should request and be granted permission to move onto the court; once permission is granted, the player should position behind the jack ball so as to look back at the opponent's throwing box. From behind the jack ball, the player should imagine a spot on the court between the opponent's throwing box and the jack ball that will block a throw. As the player returns to her throwing box, she should focus on the spot established to block the opponent's throw and complete the blocking throw. Not all blocking throws require movement onto the court.

Defeating the Block

If a player is blocked by a ball from his opponent, he should be able to bounce one of his balls into the ball that is blocking him, resulting in defeating the block. Players should practice defeating the block to create a clearer path to the jack or rebound their ball closer to the jack. These are similar strategies to those used in billiards, curling, or shuffleboard to gain better playing positions.

Playing the Circle

To assist with aiming, attacking, or blocking, players should consider playing the circle. To score, they need to be closer to the jack than their opponent is. They should keep in mind that they may ask for permission to go onto the court during their throwing time. Once on the court, they can ask the referee to show them the opponent's closest ball. They can then mentally draw a circle at that distance all the way around the jack ball and return to their throwing area. The circle they created is their scoring area.

FUNCTIONAL PROFILES
AND GENERAL MODIFICATIONS

The functional profiles presented in table 12.2 are meant to help you address students that might be in your general physical education class. These functional profiles are operationally defined for this book and are not to be considered official profiles of the game. Read the table to see if you have students that might fit these profiles, and then consider the activity modifications listed in table 12.3.

Student Functional Profiles

Functional profiles for this sport focus on the levels of assistance needed to throw the boccia balls. These functional profiles are operationally defined using a variation of the classification from CPISRA (www.cpisra.org). They will help you decide how to plan, assess, implement, teach, and evaluate your lessons for students with disabilities in your classes.

General Modifications

Table 12.3 presents general modifications you might consider using to teach boccia in your classes for students with and without disabilities. These suggestions are offered as overviews and include equipment modifications.

Table 12.2   Student Functional Profiles for Boccia

Functional skill level	Student profile
Low (wheelchair with ramp)	Severe disabilities in all four extremities; uses a power wheelchair; must use an assistive device (ramp) to propel the ball and needs a sports assistant (SA) for placement and aiming.
Moderate (wheelchair)	Severe to moderate disabilities in the upper extremities or minimal paraplegic (two lower) or hemiplegic (one side) disabilities; can push a manual wheelchair continuously for a moderate distance (at least 30 ft, or 9 m) or uses a power wheelchair; able to grasp and release the ball to throw without assistance; can position in the throwing area without assistance; has good independent sitting balance.
High (sitting)	No neurological or physical disability in the upper extremities or trunk; has minimal disability in at least one lower extremity; able to stand or sit independently; able to grasp and release the ball to throw without assistance; can position in the throwing area without assistance; maintains sitting balance following the throw.

Table 12.3   General Modifications for Boccia

Skill level	Skill	Activity modifications
Low	Throw (propel) using an assistive device	Use a folded gym mat placed in the lap as a ramp.
		Push a 12 in. (30 cm) playground ball toward a colored traffic cone (target) placed 5 ft (1.5 m) away.
		Bump a large cage ball with a power wheelchair toward a colored traffic cone (target) placed 5 ft (1.5 m), 10 ft (3 m), and 15 ft (4.6 m) away.
Moderate	Throw independently using an underhand or overhand motion	Push a large cage ball with the upper body toward colored traffic cones (target) placed around the court.
		Roll 12 in. (30 cm), 14 in. (36 cm), and 18 in. (46 cm) playground balls toward designated areas on the court.
		Roll 12 in. (30 cm), 14 in. (36 cm), and 18 in. (46 cm) playground balls toward a large cage ball (jack ball).
High	Throw independently using an underhand or overhand motion while sitting in a standard chair	No modifications: Used with highest-functioning students. Have students play using boccia equipment.

GAME PROGRESSIONS

The games listed in this chapter use the same class formats that previous chapters use (one on one, small group, large group). Keep in mind that you are trying to address all three learning domains (psychomotor, cognitive, and affective).

GAMES-BY-SKILL-LEVEL INDEX: LOW-FUNCTIONING STUDENTS

The index in table 12.4 will help you choose games according to the ability level of your student(s). This first index is for low-functioning students who require a high degree of assistance—in this case, a ramp. Very low-functioning students might need to begin with individual games and may progress into small or large group situations as their skills improve.

Table 12.4 Games-by-Skill-Level Index for Low Functioning Students—Boccia

Skills	One on one	Small group	Large group
Throwing (ramp, long, and short)	Crossing the Atlantic	In the Zone	Ramp Attack
Blocking	Build a Fort	Not in My House	Block Party
Defeating the block	Clearing the Way	Four Corners I	Four Corners II

GAME DESCRIPTIONS

Each game description in this section includes class format, organizational pattern, equipment, description, extensions, and inclusion suggestions. You may select any game that you believe matches the ability level of your students. Remember that students with low functional profiles use assistive devices (ramps) to throw in boccia (see appendix C).

Skill ▶ Throwing (Ramp, Long, and Short)

CROSSING THE ATLANTIC

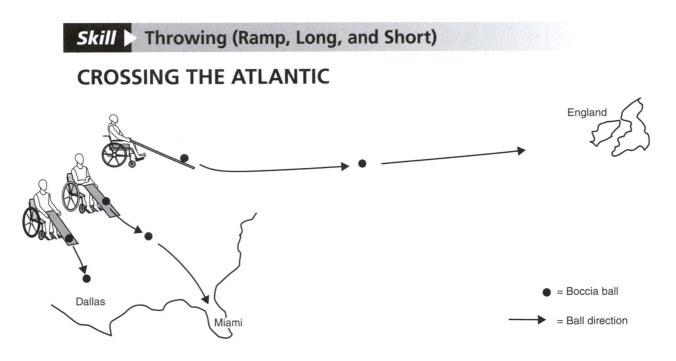

Class format: One on one

Organizational pattern: Individual with teacher or peer assistant

Equipment: Ramp, boccia balls or 6-inch (15 cm) slightly deflated playground balls

Description: The distance across the Atlantic from New York to London is approximately 3,470 miles (5,584 km). In this game, students pretend that each foot the ball travels during a throw equals 100 miles (e.g., 3 feet equals 300 miles), or that each meter equals 100 kilometers. Have the student release a ball down the ramp and measure and record the distance rolled; they should roll 10 balls and add their distances. The objective is to cross the Atlantic with the fewest throws (this may take several class sessions). The student should be experimenting with the best angle of release to propel the ball the greatest distance.

Extension: Change the distance by changing the location of the destination (e.g., travel from your town to Chicago, Miami, or Dallas).

Inclusion suggestion: The student can decide which trip to take for the day (e.g., Chicago, Miami, Dallas) and select one peer to join him. Students alternate throwing during the activity.

IN THE ZONE

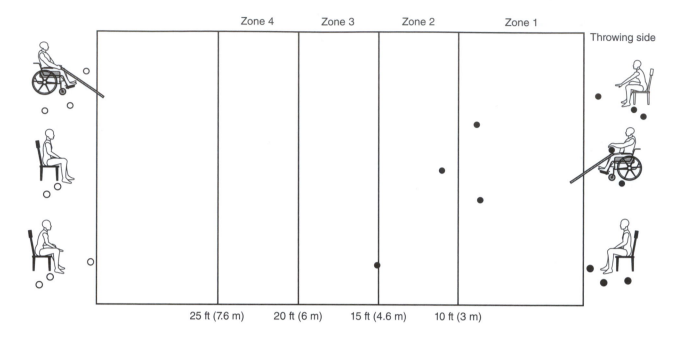

Class format: Small group

Organizational pattern: Students with and without disabilities are lined up on opposite ends of the basketball court (three to eight students on each end) facing each other. All students must be seated in folding chairs or wheelchairs. Make sure at least one ramp is used for throwing from each end.

Equipment: Ramp, boccia balls or 6-inch (15 cm) slightly deflated playground balls or tennis balls, folding chairs

Description: The court is marked off into four zones from the end of the court (e.g., at 10, 15, 20, and 25 ft, or 3, 4.6, 6, and 7.6 m) extending the width of the court. One group of students throws first and attempts to land one ball in each of the zones. The student using the ramp should attempt to reach one deep and one short zone during play. After two rounds, the sides switch and balls are rolled from the opposite end. The group with the most balls rolled into the correct zones after two rounds is declared the winner. More than one ball per zone is not allowed.

Extension: Have all students throw in an alternating position (e.g. standing, sitting, standing) as they are lined up on each end.

Inclusion suggestion: Allow the student with a disability to decide the order of throw for his side.

RAMP ATTACK

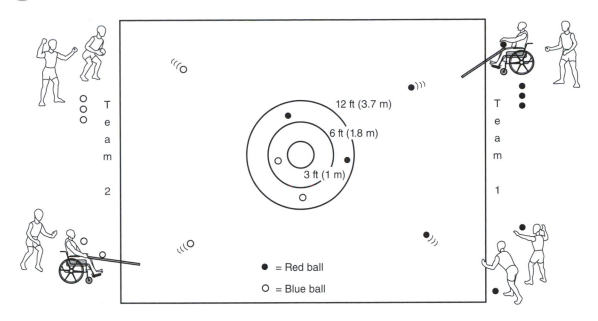

Class format: Large group

Organizational pattern: Divide students into two teams, each with a ramp for throwing, and place them in the four corners of the basketball court. The two corners diagonally opposite each other have ramps, and the remaining two corners do not have ramps.

Equipment: Ramps; boccia balls or 6-inch (15 cm) slightly deflated playground balls, tennis balls, softballs, or 6-inch (15 cm) Nerf balls

Description: Each team gets 10 balls, 5 balls per corner. Draw three concentric circles in the middle of the basketball court with diameters of 3, 6, and 12 feet (1, 1.8, and 3.7 m). On the signal, each team throws at the same time attempting to get their balls to stay in the innermost circle. At the end of eight minutes, the team with the most balls in the innermost circle wins the game.

Extensions: Allow one team to throw at a time; once all the balls are thrown, then allow the second team to throw. Alternate a ramp throw from one team and a nonramp throw from the other team until all balls are used. Score the game in the same manner.

Inclusion suggestion: This entire activity is designed to be played as an inclusive game.

Skill ▶ Blocking

BUILD A FORT

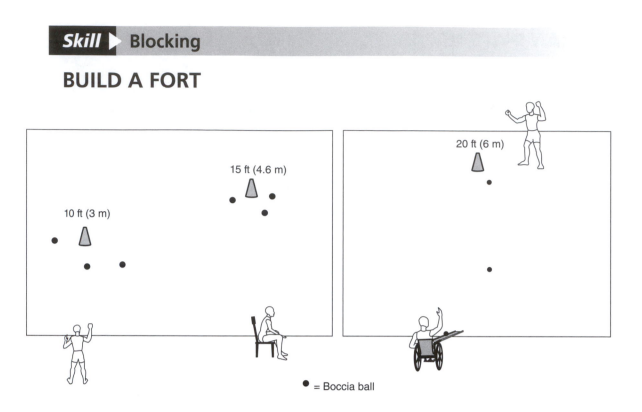

● = Boccia ball

Class format: One on one

Organizational pattern: Individual with teacher or peer assistant

Equipment: Ramp; traffic cones; boccia balls or 6-inch (15 cm) slightly deflated playground balls, tennis balls, softballs, or 6-inch (15 cm) Nerf balls

Description: Place three traffic cones as targets 10 feet (3 m) apart on the gym floor at 10, 15, and 20 feet (3, 4.6, and 6 m) from the baseline of the basketball court. Place the ramp on the court facing the target cones. The object of the game is for the student to throw three balls at each of the target cones so that the balls roll to a stop creating a block, or fort, around the cone. The student should throw three balls at the first cone before moving to the next one. The goal is to place the balls in such a formation as to surround the cone from several angles. The ramp can be moved to address the different throwing distances and angles to create the blocks.

Extension: Have the student use various size balls moving from larger to smaller.

Inclusion suggestion: Students without disabilities could try to roll a ball through the fort to challenge the block.

NOT IN MY HOUSE

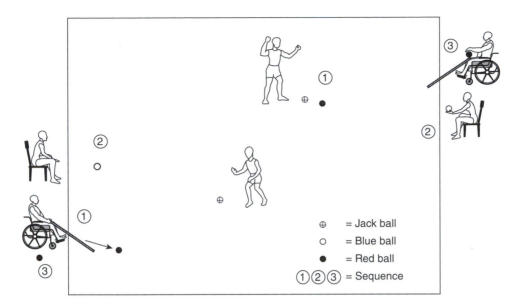

= Jack ball
= Blue ball
= Red ball
= Sequence

Class format: Small group

Organizational pattern: Students with and without disabilities work in small groups of three. The group will be throwing at a jack ball placed 12 feet (3.7 m) from a basketball baseline.

Equipment: Ramps; boccia balls or 6-inch (15 cm) slightly deflated playground balls, tennis balls, softballs, or 6-inch (15 cm) Nerf balls; chair

Description: Place a jack ball out on the court at least 12 feet (3.7 m) from the throwing area (baseline of a basketball court). Position a ramp on the baseline facing the jack ball. A student without a disability is seated on a chair next to the student using the ramp and positioned to throw at the jack ball. The student using the ramp has two balls, and the student seated in the chair has one. The student using the ramp throws first in an attempt to block the path of throw of the opponent in the chair. The student in the chair throws second and tries to beat the block and position closer to the jack ball. The student using the ramp throws third and tries to get closer to the jack than the student in the chair did.

Extensions: The activity can be played at various distances to the jack ball using various sizes and types of balls. Additional throws can be added as students' skills improve.

Inclusion suggestion: The game can be repeated in stations around the gym with all students using homemade ramps and folding chairs.

BLOCK PARTY

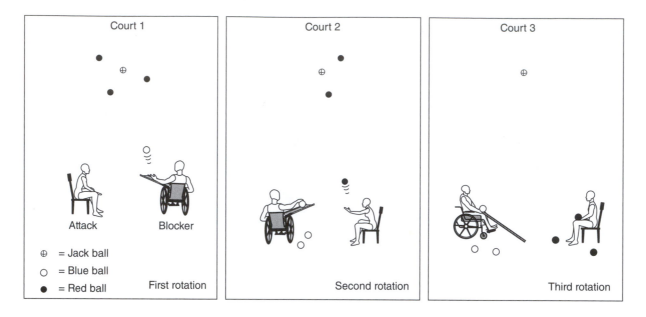

Class format: Large group

Organizational pattern: Students are arranged in two teams, red and blue, on three courts marked on the gym floor and each attacker has three boccia balls. Attackers use the red balls, and blockers use the blue balls. Ramps should be placed at each court and used as needed. Each team faces a jack ball that has been thrown into play for each court.

Equipment: Ramps; boccia balls or 6-inch (15 cm) slightly deflated playground balls, tennis balls, softballs, or 6-inch (15 cm) Nerf balls; chairs

Description: Place a jack ball on the court at least 12 feet (3.7 m) from the throwing area (baseline of a basketball court) on each of the three courts. Position a ramp on the baseline facing the jack ball in a throwing area for each court. Students without disabilities use the red balls and should be seated on chairs next to the students using ramps, who are throwing blue balls. If there is only one student using a ramp, that person will be considered a "team."

Players on the attacking team (red balls) throw at the jack ball consecutively (i.e., each attacker on each court throws a first red ball, then a second, and then a third without interruption) in an attempt to get as close as possible to the jack ball. Once all red balls are delivered, the blockers throw one blue ball in an attempt to block the path of the red ball closest to the jack. After throwing one ball on their starting court, all blocks rotate one court and repeat the blocking throw, finishing by rotating to a third court and throwing a final block. Attackers remain at the original court throughout the activity. The purpose of the game is to have blockers learn to read and block a variety of game situations.

Extension: Put a time limit on the blocking throw (e.g., the first throw must be made in two minutes, the second in one minute, and the third in 30 seconds). This will require the blocker to read the situation and react sooner.

Inclusion suggestions: Blockers and attackers can switch roles. Allow student(s) with disabilities to select the size of the ball to use for the jack ball. If you do not have an official boccia set and have to use alternative types of balls (e.g., playground, tennis, Nerf), the size of the jack ball does not matter.

Skill ▶ Defeating the Block

CLEARING THE WAY

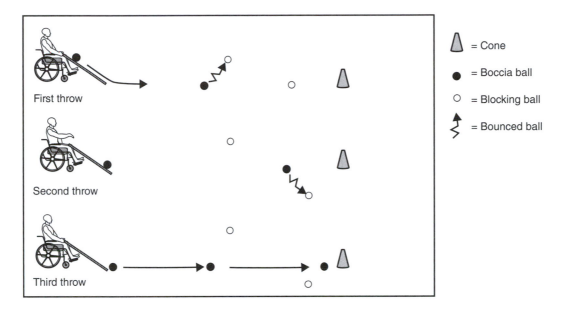

Class format: One on one

Organizational pattern: Individual with teacher or peer assistant

Equipment: Floor tape; traffic cone; ramps; boccia balls or 6-inch (15 cm) slightly deflated playground balls, tennis balls, softballs, or 6-inch (15 cm) Nerf balls

Description: Position a ramp on the court facing a cone that represents a jack ball (e.g., a traffic cone), which is at least 10 feet (3 m) away. Place two balls in a straight line 2 feet (0.6 m) apart between the student and the target. These balls serve as blocking balls. The objective of the game is to have the student throw a ball at the closer blocking ball and bounce it out of the way to clear the way for the second throw. The purpose of the second throw is the same: to bounce the blocking ball out of the way to clear a path to the target. Once a path has been cleared, the student throws at the target and attempts to get as close as possible.

Extension: Work from larger to smaller blocking balls as the student's skill improves.

Inclusion suggestion: Students without disabilities can join and alternate blocking and rebounding throws.

FOUR CORNERS I

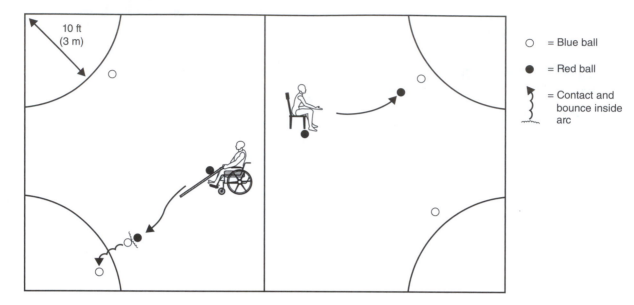

Class format: Small group

Organizational pattern: Students work in a small group using one attack position.

Equipment: Floor tape; ramps; boccia balls or 6-inch (15 cm) slightly deflated playground balls, tennis balls, softballs, or 6-inch (15 cm) Nerf balls

Description: Mark a 10-foot (3 m) arc in each corner of a basketball court using floor tape. Place one ball just outside the arc in each corner, and position the students at one attack location (i.e., midcourt on the sideline). The objective of the game is to throw an attack ball so that it bounces the ball from outside the arc to inside the arc in as few throws as possible. Students can alternate throwing (i.e., the student using a ramp throws first, then the student without a disability, then the student using a ramp). This activity is a great lead-up to Four Corners II.

Extensions: Have students work from larger to smaller blocking balls as their skill improves.

Inclusion suggestion: Students without disabilities should assist with positioning the ramp and practice serving as sport assistants (SAs).

FOUR CORNERS II

Class format: Large group

Organizational pattern: Student(s) work in large groups using multiple attack positions around the gym.

Equipment: Floor tape; ramps; boccia balls or 6-inch (15 cm) slightly deflated playground balls, tennis balls, softballs, or 6-inch (15 cm) Nerf balls

Description: Use the same markings as in Four Corners I (i.e., 10 ft, or 3 m, arc in each corner of a basketball court and one ball just outside the arc for each corner). In this activity, position students in multiple attack positions around the gym and allow them to attack the balls diagonally across the gym from their positions. The objective of the game is the same as in Four Corners I (i.e., throw an attack ball so that it bounces the ball from outside the arc to inside the arc in as few throws as possible).

Extensions: Have students work from larger to smaller blocking balls as their skill improves. Student attack groups can rotate to a new attack position after throwing all their balls.

Inclusion suggestion: Students without disabilities should assist with positioning the ramp and practice serving as sport assistants (SAs).

GAMES-BY-SKILL-LEVEL INDEX: MODERATE-TO HIGH-FUNCTIONING STUDENTS

The index in table 12.5 will help you choose games according to the ability level of your student(s). This index is for students who you believe have moderate to high functional ability and do not require a high degree of assistance. Students without disabilities should participate in these activities. Notice that these games also use the class formats of one on one, small group, and large group.

Table 12.5 Games-by-Skill-Level Index for Moderate- to High-Functioning Students—Boccia

Skills	One on one	Small group	Large group
Throwing (long and short)	Boccia Math	Around the World	Tic-Tac-Toe
Blocking	Carpet Blocker	Gate Blocker	Tic-Tac-Toe With a Block
Defeating the block	Side Pocket/Corner Pocket	Even or Odd	In or Out

GAME DESCRIPTIONS

The following games are designed to promote the skills of throwing (underhand and overhand) and using a ramp to throw a boccia ball. Activities to emphasize game strategies of blocking and defeating a block are also included. The information is presented according to class format, organizational pattern, equipment, description, extensions, and inclusion suggestions.

Skill ▶ Throwing (Long and Short)

BOCCIA MATH

Class format: One on one

Organizational pattern: Individual with teacher or peer assistant

Equipment: Five traffic cones; boccia balls or 6-inch (15 cm) slightly deflated playground balls, tennis balls, softballs, or 6-inch (15 cm) Nerf balls

Description: Randomly place five traffic cones in an open space at various distances (5 ft, 10 ft, or 1.5 m, 3 m). Mark each cone with a number (1 through 5; tape a sheet of paper on the cone with a number printed on the paper). In this activity you use four math functions—addition, subtraction, multiplication, and division. The student has three throws to solve the math problem you present. For example, if you say, "What is 4 + 1?" the student has three attempts to hit the cone with the number 5 on it. The activity can continue with additional math questions (e.g., "What is 10 – 7?" and the student would have three attempts to hit the cone with the number 3 on it).

Extensions: Work from larger to smaller balls as the student's skill improves. You could change the activity by saying "Using only three throws, your math total must equal 10," or "In two throws, your total must equal 5."

Inclusion suggestions: Students without disabilities could be used to suggest math problems and work with the student with a disability. The student with a disability could demonstrate her skill and math ability to her classmates.

AROUND THE WORLD

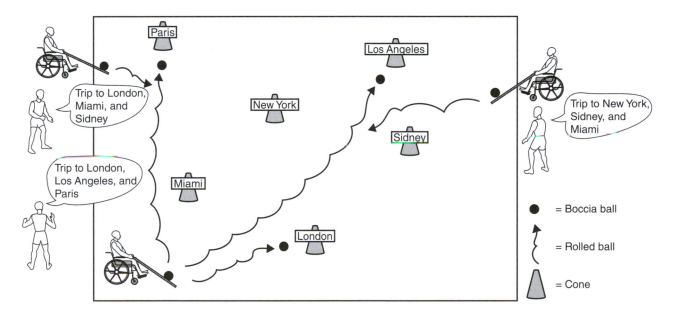

Class format: Small group

Organizational pattern: Students work in small groups using multiple attack positions around the court.

Equipment: Floor tape; traffic cones; boccia balls or 6-inch (15 cm) slightly deflated playground balls, tennis balls, softballs, or 6-inch (15 cm) Nerf balls

Description: Randomly place several traffic cones in an open space at various distances (5 ft, 10 ft, or 1.5 m, 3 m). Use as many cones as needed for students to complete a trip around the world. Mark each cone with the name of a famous city (e.g., London, Paris, Los Angeles, New York, Sidney). The objective of the activity is to take a trip around the world by throwing at, and hitting, the cones bearing the names of the cities you call out. For example, you might say, "I want you to travel from London to Paris to New York," and the students must throw at the cones in that order. Allow as many throws as you believe are necessary based on the skills of the students throwing.

Extensions: Have students work from larger to smaller balls as their skills improve. Have students complete round trips by saying, "I want you to travel round trip from Los Angeles to New York."

Inclusion suggestion: Students without disabilities could alternate throws and travel with the student with a disability.

TIC-TAC-TOE

Class format: Large group

Organizational pattern: Student(s) work in large groups using two attack positions on opposite sides of the court (use cones to mark off activity area). Students with and without disabilities should be in each group if possible.

Equipment: Floor tape; traffic cones; boccia balls or 6-inch (15 cm) slightly deflated playground balls, tennis balls, softballs, or 6-inch (15 cm) Nerf balls

Description: Create two throwing areas approximately 20 feet (6 m) apart, and mark each with a large tic-tac-toe grid at least 10 feet by 10 feet (3 by 3 m). Divide students into two groups and create two throwing teams within each group; one team uses blue balls, and the other team uses red balls. Throws occur on an alternative rotation (red throws first, then blue). The objective of the game is to be the first to get a tic-tac-toe (three in a row) on the grid. Have students focus on making long, medium, and short throws.

Extensions: Have students work from larger to smaller balls as their skills improve. Allow each team to throw at least one ball per player on each round; consider increasing the number of balls players are allowed to throw in each round based on their performances. Consider changing the type of ball (e.g., deflated playground balls, softballs, tennis balls).

Inclusion suggestion: Students without disabilities should alternate throws with students with disabilities on each attempt.

Skill ▶ Blocking

CARPET BLOCKER

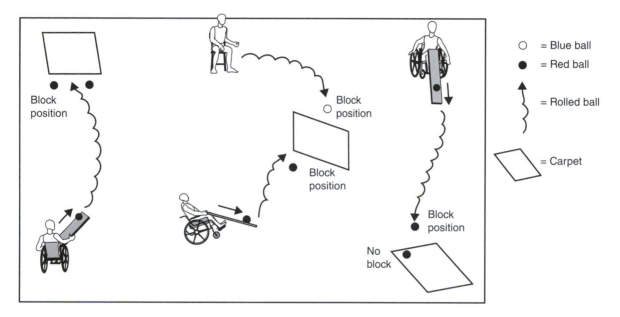

Class format: One on one

Organizational pattern: Individual with teacher or peer assistant

Equipment: Boccia balls or 6-inch (15 cm) slightly deflated playground balls, tennis balls, softballs, or 6-inch (15 cm) Nerf balls; carpet squares; folding chairs

Description: Place at least three carpet squares at various distances from the sideline of a basketball court (e.g., 10, 20, and 25 ft, or 3, 6, and 7.6 m). The objective of the activity is to have the student throw three balls at each carpet square that block the path to the carpet but do not touch the carpet. Each ball must roll up short of the carpet square and block access to it.

Extensions: Have students play the game using various size balls and moving from larger to smaller. Try varying the distances of the carpet squares.

Inclusion suggestion: Students without disabilities could sit in folding chairs when throwing.

GATE BLOCKER

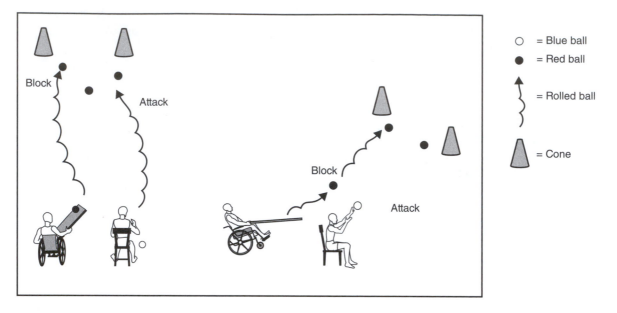

Class format: Small group

Organizational pattern: Students work in small groups using multiple attack positions on opposite sides of a basketball court.

Equipment: Traffic cones; boccia balls or 6-inch (15 cm) slightly deflated playground balls, tennis balls, softballs, or 6-inch (15 cm) Nerf balls; folding chair

Description: Place two traffic cones on the court approximately 2 feet (0.6 m) apart to create a gate. You can have students set up multiple gates around the gym. Next, divide students into small teams with equal numbers of blockers and attackers. The team throwing the block should be positioned on the edge of a basketball court at least 15 feet (4.6 m) from the gate. The objective of the game is to throw three balls in succession and block the entrance to the gate. The goal is to throw with control so the ball stops in front of the gate, but does not pass through the gate (practice using overhand throw). After all three balls have been thrown from the same blocker, three attack balls are thrown in an attempt to beat the block and pass through the gate from one attacker.

Extensions: You can set up multiple stations around the gym depending on the space available. The rotation of blocking and attacking can be changed to an alternative pattern (e.g., the first ball is thrown to block, the second is an attack, the third is a block, the forth is an attack). Keep in mind that the focus is to work on blocking the entrance to the gate. Practice throwing underhand and overhand.

Inclusion suggestion: Students without disabilities could throw from a seated position using a folding chair.

TIC-TAC-TOE WITH A BLOCK

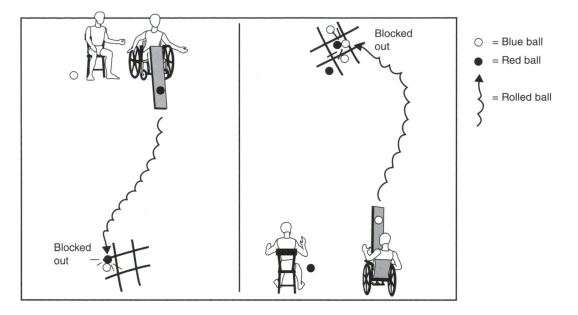

○	= Blue ball
●	= Red ball
↑	= Rolled ball

Class format: Large group

Organizational pattern: Use the same organizational pattern as the game Tic-Tac-Toe.

Equipment: Floor tape; traffic cones; boccia balls or 6-inch (15 cm) slightly deflated playground balls, tennis balls, softballs, or 6-inch (15 cm) Nerf balls; folding chairs

Description: The game is played the same as Tic-Tac-Toe with one change: now the teams are allowed to alternate with a blocking attempt. For example, the red team throws a ball into a tic-tac-toe square followed by the blue team throwing a ball to block or bounce the red ball out of the square. The focus of the game now shifts to blocking.

Extensions: Have students work from larger to smaller balls as their skills improve. Consider changing the type of balls to throw (e.g., deflated playground balls, softballs, tennis balls).

Inclusion suggestion: Students without disabilities sitting in folding chairs should alternate throws with students with disabilities on each attempt.

Skill ▶ Defeating the Block

SIDE POCKET/CORNER POCKET

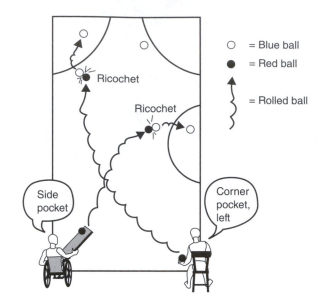

Class format: One on one

Organizational pattern: Individual with teacher or peer assistant

Equipment: Floor tape; boccia balls or 6-inch (15 cm) slightly deflated playground balls, tennis balls, softballs, or 6-inch (15 cm) Nerf balls

Description: Mark a rectangle area on the floor approximately 15 by 6 feet (4.6 by 1.8 m) using floor tape. Create three small target areas within the rectangle: two in the corners opposite the throwing end, and one at the midpoint along one side. Place a ball on the outside edge of each target area approximately 6 inches (15 cm) from the floor tape (which marks the area in which to serve a blocking ball). The student is positioned at the opposite end of the rectangle away from the target areas. The objective is to throw a ball so that it bounces off a blocking ball and ricochets into the target area, thus defeating the block. Before throwing, the student must announce the target area she is attempting to throw at by saying *Side pocket or Corner pocket.*

Extensions: Have the student use various size balls moving from larger to smaller. Try varying the distances of the throw depending on the student's skill levels.

Inclusion suggestion: Students without disabilities could join the activity by throwing the blocking ball in an attempt to position this ball to block the target area.

EVEN OR ODD

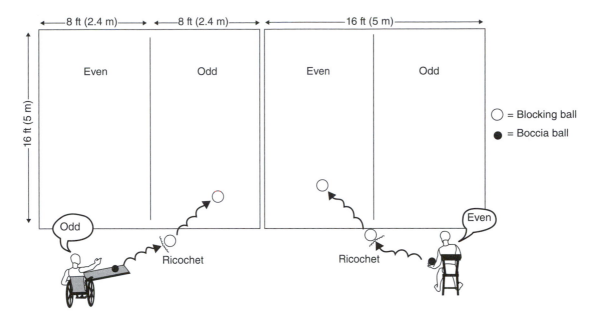

Class format: Small group

Organizational pattern: Students work in small groups using multiple attack positions on the same side of a basketball court.

Equipment: Floor tape; boccia balls or 6-inch (15 cm) slightly deflated playground balls, tennis balls, softballs, or 6-inch (15 cm) Nerf balls; folding chair

Description: Mark two large squares (16 ft, or 5 m, square) on the floor using floor tape; they should be approximately 20 feet (6 m) apart. Next, divide each large square in half using floor tape. Mark one of the 8- by 16-foot (2.4 by 5 m) squares as *Even* and the other as *Odd,* repeating this on the second large square. Place a blocking ball in front of and outside the large square at the 8-foot (2.4 m) line (i.e., at the midpoint of the large square). The students are positioned approximately 12 feet (3.7 m) away facing the squares. The objective is to throw a ball at the blocking ball and bounce the thrown ball into either the *Even* or *Odd* square. Prior to throwing, students must call out which square they are trying to bounce the ball into by saying *Even* or *Odd.* The focus of this activity is to learn how to control the thrown ball so it bounces into the correct square and defeats the block.

Extensions: You can set up multiple stations around the gym depending on the space available. You could consider using various size balls moving from larger to smaller or simple to complex challenges depending on the students' skill levels.

Inclusion suggestion: Students without disabilities could throw from a seated position using a folding chair.

IN OR OUT

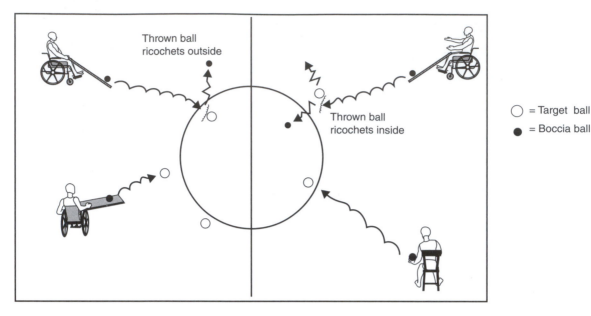

Class format: Large group

Organizational pattern: Students work in a large group format using multiple attack positions around a basketball court.

Equipment: Floor tape; boccia balls or 6-inch (15 cm) slightly deflated playground balls, tennis balls, softballs, or 6-inch (15 cm) Nerf balls; folding chair

Description: Mark a 15-foot (4.6 m) circle in the center of the basketball court (or use the smaller center jump circle). Place target balls around the circle, some just inside the circle and some just outside the circle. Place the students around the circle at least 12 feet (3.7 m) away in several throwing groups. Each group should throw three balls before changing positions or throwers. The objective of the game is to throw a ball so that it bounces off a target ball and lands either inside or outside the circle. For example, if the target ball is just outside the circle, the thrown ball should strike it at such an angle that the thrown ball rolls to a stop inside the circle. Players must announce their attempts by saying either *Inside* or *Outside* before completing the throw.

Extensions: Consider using various size balls moving from larger to smaller or simple to complex challenges depending on the students' skill levels.

Inclusion suggestion: Students without disabilities could throw from a seated position using a folding chair.

Remember that blank forms for assessments, IEPs, and unit and lesson plans are located on the DVD.

Wheelchair Selection and Fitting

Five sports presented in this book require the use of a wheelchair: wheelchair basketball, indoor wheelchair soccer, wheelchair tennis, slalom, and boccia. Students who use wheelchairs often know more than their teachers about the operation and maintenance of their wheelchairs. This section provides a brief overview of how to purchase and care for this important piece of equipment. Additional information is shared on how to measure or fit someone for a wheelchair. By knowing more about your students' wheelchairs, you will be in a better position to discuss this topic with your school district's physical or occupational therapists or to answer questions from parents. Remember that the wheelchair is an important piece of equipment for your students with disabilities. The more knowledge you have about it, the more informative you can be in your job. Increasing your knowledge of the wheelchair will also help normalize this piece of equipment for your students without disabilities. By demonstrating how much you know about the wheelchair, you help set the atmosphere and attitude for your classes. Learning more about the wheelchair also gives you an opportunity to teach others and reduce the stereotyping of students with disabilities who use this equipment to move.

The first step in selecting a wheelchair is to consult with the local physical or occupational therapist in your school district. These professionals are trained to conduct measurements for proper fit and selection. You may also follow the measuring tips suggested later in this appendix. Beyond proper fit, you should be able to determine the correct wheelchair type, frame design, and general size for your student.

WHEELCHAIR TYPES

Wheelchairs fall into two basic categories: manual and power. Manual wheelchairs are propelled by the person using it, whereas power wheelchairs are powered by a battery and motor. Only manual wheelchairs are discussed in detail because you are more likely to encounter these. However, should one of your students use a power wheelchair, make sure you have the student show you two key features: how to operate the on/off switch and how to disengage the clutch. Manufacturers do not put the on/off switch in the same location. Ask your student to show you where this switch is and how it functions. Do likewise for the clutch mechanism. Releasing the clutch allows you to move the power wheelchair when the power is off. This comes in handy when maneuvering in tight spaces or on pool decks. Always turn the power off and disengage the clutch when operating a power wheelchair on a pool deck.

Manual wheelchairs are offered in several designs: standard, ultralight (also known as sport competition), and racing. Standard wheelchairs are best described as those found in hospitals and are usually made of stainless steel, constructed for durability. The average weight of a standard wheelchair is approximately 50 pounds (22.7 kg) or more. These wheelchairs are usually equipped with removable armrests and footplates and have limited adjustments to seating. The tires are usually tubeless and made of hard rubber mounted on spoked wheels about 27 inches (69 cm) or more in diameter. The front tires, or casters, are generally 3.5 to 5 inches (8.9 to 12.7 cm) in diameter and are also made of tubeless, hard rubber. These wheelchairs can be used indoors or outdoors and can be maneuvered over many surfaces such as asphalt, cement, and wood floors.

Ultralights, or sport competition wheelchairs, are designed for activities that require quick response and fast-paced action. These wheelchairs are made of lightweight metal alloys and usually weigh between 15 and 20 pounds (6.8 and 9 kg). Many dimensions on these wheelchairs are adjustable, including the seat position, back height, foot carriage, seat angle, and camber of the mainwheels. They generally do not have armrests or footplates unless specially ordered. The camber is the "flaring out" of the mainwheels as you view the wheelchair from the rear. Camber is important for ultralight wheelchairs, because it contributes to maneuverability.

The front casters on ultralights are generally very small, approximately 3 inches (7.6 cm) in diameter, and often are the same wheels as those used on in-line skates. Because these wheelchairs are designed to be used indoors on a basketball court or outdoors on a tennis court, there is an increased likelihood of dirt and grime building up in the bearings of the front casters. The front casters should receive regularly scheduled maintenance, which includes cleaning the axles and bearings.

Another feature of the ultralight wheelchair is the pop-off wheels, which aid in repair issues and ease of transportation. A button at the center of the mainwheel axle, which is a solid piece of metal at the center hub, releases the wheel and tire assembly from the frame with one movement. When the button is pushed, the entire tire assembly can be removed and a backup tire assembly can be mounted. Once the tire assembly is removed from the wheelchair frame, the button can be pressed again to remove the axle from the hub for replacement or repairs. See figure A.1 for steps in removing the tire assembly from the wheelchair frame.

Racing wheelchairs are manufactured specifically for road races and track events. These wheelchairs are generally longer in the wheelbase and much lighter in weight than ultralight wheelchairs. Racing wheelchairs are custom fit for seating position. The person actually sits in a form-fitted cage, or bucket, area that has been precisely measured for hip width. Some models have a steering mechanism for the front casters to help negotiate road or track courses. Racing wheelchairs are a much greater financial investment than either of the other two models. It is not uncommon to pay over $3,000 U.S. for this type of wheelchair.

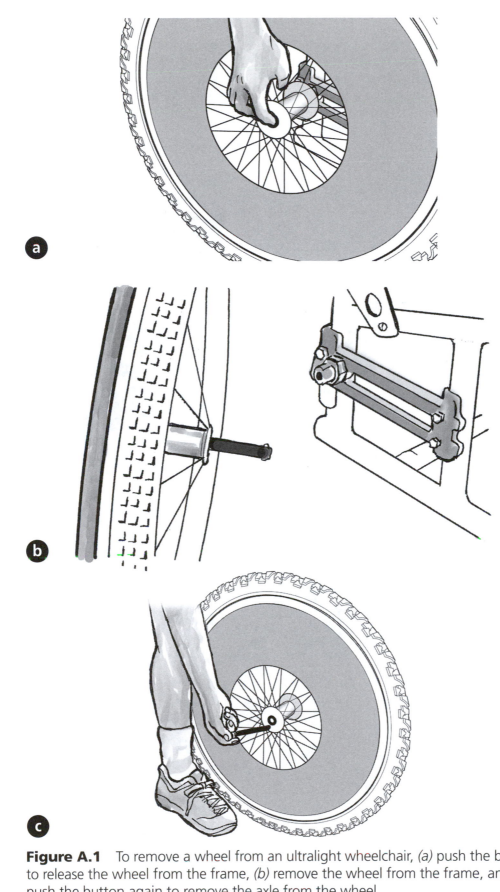

Figure A.1 To remove a wheel from an ultralight wheelchair, *(a)* push the button to release the wheel from the frame, *(b)* remove the wheel from the frame, and *(c)* push the button again to remove the axle from the wheel.

FRAME DESIGN

Wheelchair frames come in two basic models: folding and solid. Standard wheelchairs are manufactured to fold in half by collapsing down the middle. This feature allows for ease of portability; that is, it can be folded to fit into the trunk of a car. In addition to the folding frame style, most standard wheelchairs feature removable footplates, which can help with storage and transportation. See figure A.2 for the steps to follow in setting up a folding wheelchair.

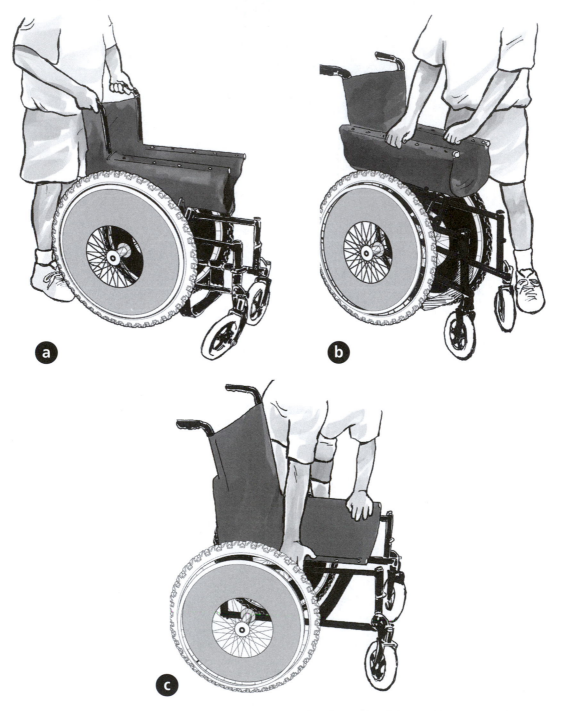

Figure A.2 Follow these steps to open a folding wheelchair: *(a)* position the folding wheelchair, *(b)* open the folding wheelchair, *(c)* and stabilize the folding wheelchair.

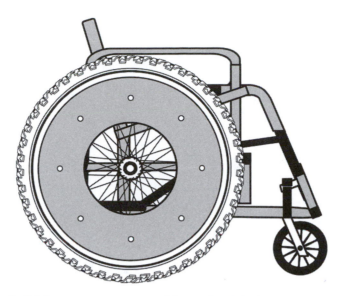

Figure A.3 Solid frame sport competition wheelchair.

Ultralight wheelchairs are of solid frame construction (see figure A.3). These frames are not designed to collapse for transportation or storage. The advantage of solid frame construction has to do with reaction forces. The solid frame wheelchair is better designed to "push back," or react, when a person applies a high degree of force, such as during manual propulsion. Because the frame is solid, it is less likely to absorb the force than a folding wheelchair. Think about sitting in a solid kitchen chair versus a soft couch. Which do you have an easier time rising from? The soft couch absorbs your forces as you push against it to stand, whereas the solid kitchen chair does not; in principle, it pushes back to help you rise more easily. You might simply ask your student, "Is that a solid frame or a folding frame?" These wheelchairs often come with a rear-mounted fifth wheel or antitip wheel for safety (not pictured).

WHEELCHAIR FITTING

Buying a wheelchair is as individualized as buying shoes. Each of us has unique foot characteristics that must be addressed when purchasing shoes: long and narrow, short and wide, short and narrow, and so on. The specific measurements of the person's body must be taken into account when fitting for a wheelchair. The basic anatomical measurements of the user must be taken regardless of whether you are purchasing a standard or an ultralight wheelchair.

The following are suggestions for measuring someone who is considering purchasing a wheelchair. Use these as guidelines, but seek the expertise of the school district therapist or a representative from a retail wheelchair distributor to help you with conducting the measurements. Remember to take all measurements with the person in a seated position.

- **Shoulder.** Measure from the top of the shoulder to the palm of the hand with the arm extended in front of the body (figure A.4a), and from the top of the shoulder to the seat (figure A.4b).
- **Leg.** Measure the length of the upper leg from the hip center to the knee joint (figure A.5a), and measure the lower leg length from the knee joint to the footrest (figure A.5b).

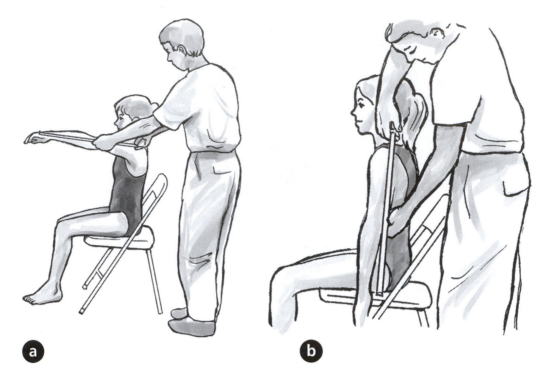

Figure A.4 *(a)* Shoulder measurement, arm forward. *(b)* Shoulder measurement, arm down.

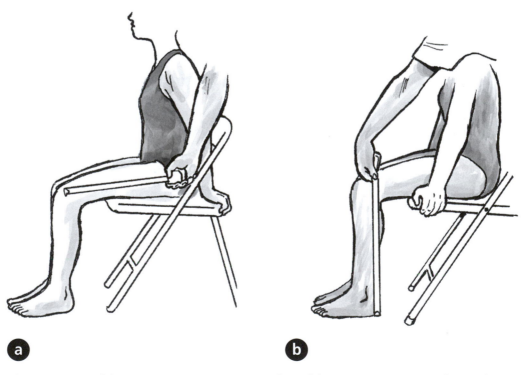

Figure A.5 *(a)* Leg measurement, upper leg. *(b)* Leg measurement, lower leg.

- **Hips (seat).** For seat length, or seat depth, measure from behind the knee joint to the back of the seat (figure A.6*a*), and for seat width, measure laterally from hip to hip (figure A.6*b*).

- **Back.** For back height, measure from the seat base upward depending on the type of disability (figure A.7). People with lower spinal cord injuries or injuries to the lumbar region will have lower seat-back heights, whereas those with injuries in the upper thoracic region will need higher seat-back support.

You may want to refer to table A.1 for an overview of how to fit a person to a wheelchair.

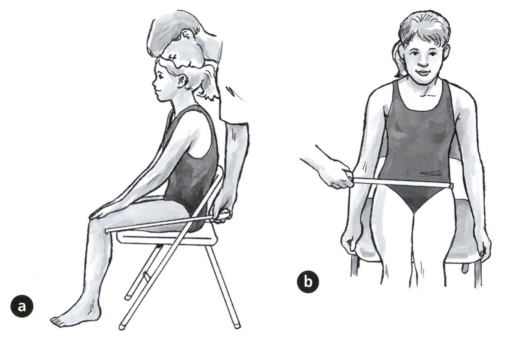

Figure A.6   *(a)* Seat-depth measurement. *(b)* Seat-width measurement.

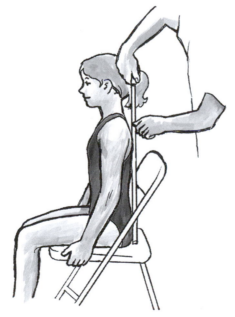

Figure A.7   Seat-back height measurement.

Table A.1 Measuring Guide for Fitting a Wheelchair

Body part	Measurements from a seated position
Shoulder	Top of shoulder to palm of hand with arm extended in front of body. Top of shoulder to seat.
Leg	Length of upper leg from center of hip to knee joint. Length of lower leg from knee joint to footrest.
Hips (seat)	Seat length or depth: Measure from behind the knee joint to the back of the seat. Seat width: Measure from hip to hip.
Back	Measure from seat base upward depending on type of disability. Individuals with lower spinal cord injuries (lower lumbar region) will have lower seat-back heights. Individuals with higher injuries (upper thoracic) will need higher seat-back support.

Adapted Sports and Activities Web Addresses

WEB SITES FOR DISABILITY SPORTS

Wheelchair & Ambulatory Sports, USA (formerly Wheelchair Sports USA)
www.wsusa.org/

Wheelchair Basketball: National Wheelchair Basketball Association
www.nwba.org

Indoor Wheelchair Soccer
www.cpisra.org

Sitting Volleyball: World Organization for Volleyball for the Disabled
www.sittingvolleyball.org

Wheelchair Tennis: International Tennis Federation
www.itftennis.com

Goalball: United States Association of Blind Athletes
www.usaba.org

Goalball Rules: United States Association of Blind Athletes
www.usaba.org/Pages/sportsevents/goalball.html

The Slalom
www.cpisra.org

Boccia
www.cpisra.org or http://usparalympics.org

Wheelchair Tennis: United States Tennis Association
www.usta.com/PlayNow/Wheelchair.aspx

World Wheelchair Tennis Academy (now part of Camp Deerhorn in Rhinelander, Wisconsin)
http://deerhorn.com

OTHER SPORT CONTACTS

American Association of Adapted Sports Programs
www.adaptedsports.org

Special Olympics
www.specialolympics.org

General Wheelchair Sports
www.wsusa.org

Deaf Sports
www.usdeafsports.org

Wheelchair Racquetball
www.usra.org

ADAPTED PHYSICAL EDUCATION WEB SITES

PE Central
www.pecentral.org

Adapted Physical Education National Standards
www.apens.org

PALAESTRA: Forum of Sport, Physical Education & Recreation for Those With Disabilities
www.palaestra.com

BlazeSports America
www.blazesports.org

Intercollegiate Tennis Association
www.itatennis.com

International Tennis Federation (ITF)
www.itftennis.com/wheelchair

National Paralympic Committee
www.usparalympics.org

National Recreation and Park Association (NRPA)
www.nrpa.org

Professional Tennis Registry (PTR)
www.ptrtennis.org

United States Professional Tennis Association (USPTA)
www.uspta.com

References

Block, M. (2007). *A teacher's guide to including students with disabilities in general physical education* (3rd ed.). Baltimore: Paul Brookes.

Collier, D. (2005). Instructional strategies for adapted physical education. In Winnick, J. (2005), *Adapted physical education and sport* (4th ed.). Champaign, IL: Human Kinetics.

Individuals with Disabilities Education Act of 2004 (IDEA) (PL 108-446), 20 U.S.C. 1400 (2004).

Kasser, S., & Lytle, R. (2006). *Inclusive physical activity: A lifetime of opportunities.* Champaign, IL: Human Kinetics.

Kelly, L., & Melograno, V. (2004). *Developing the physical education curriculum: An achievement-based approach.* Champaign, IL: Human Kinetics.

Morris, G., & Stiehl, J. (1999). *Changing kids' games.* Champaign, IL: Human Kinetics.

Mosston, M., & Ashworth, S. (1994). *Teaching physical education* (4th ed.). New York: Macmillan.

Newell, K.M. (1986). Constraints on the development of coordination. In M.G. Wade & H.T. Whiting (Eds.), *Motor development in children: Aspects of coordination and control* (pp. 341-360). Dordrecht, Netherlands: Nijhoff.

Thomas, K., Lee, A., & Thomas, J. (2008). *Physical education methods for elementary teachers* (3rd ed.). Champaign, IL: Human Kinetics.

United States Government Accountability Office (GAO). (June 23, 2010). Students with disabilities: More information and guidance could improve opportunities in physical education and athletics (GAO-10-519). *Report to Congressional Requesters.* Washington, DC: U.S. Government Accountability Office. www.gao.gov/new.items/d10519.pdf.

Suggested Readings

Many of the suggestions presented in this book have come from ideas generated by reading the following books. While much of the information found in *Teaching Disability Sport* is the result of professional experience, these suggested readings should offer you valuable support.

Auxter, D., Pyfer, J., Zittel, L., & Roth, K. (2010). *Principles and methods of adapted physical education and recreation* (11th ed.). Boston: WCB McGraw-Hill.

Cerebral Palsy International Sports and Recreation Association (CPISRA). (2010). *CPISRA sports manual* (10th ed.). www.cpisra.org/files/manual10p/CPISRA_Sports_Manual_10th_Edition_Final_Version_2010-04_Release_007.pdf.

Davis, R. (2010). Inclusive sports. In Human Kinetics (Ed.), *Inclusive recreation: Programs and services for diverse populations* (pp. 193-209). Champaign, IL: Human Kinetics.

Davis, R., Ferrara, M., & Byrnes, D. (1988). The competitive wheelchair stroke. *National Strength and Conditioning Journal, 10*(3): 4-10.

DePauw, K., & Gavron, S. (2005). *Disability and sport* (2nd ed.). Champaign, IL: Human Kinetics.

Hedrick, B., Byrnes, D., & Shaver, L. (1994). *Wheelchair basketball* (2nd ed.). Washington, DC: Paralyzed Veterans of America.

Jones, J. (1988). *Training guide to cerebral palsy sports* (3rd ed.). Champaign, IL: Human Kinetics.

Kasser, S., & Lytle, R. (2005). *Inclusive physical activity: A lifetime of opportunities.* Champaign, IL: Human Kinetics.

Kelly, L., & Melograno, V. (2004). *Developing the physical education curriculum: An achievement-based approach.* Champaign, IL: Human Kinetics.

Lieberman, L., & Houston-Wilson, C. (2009). *Strategies for inclusion: A handbook for physical educators* (2nd ed.). Champaign, IL: Human Kinetics.

Moore, B., & Snow, R. (1994). *Wheelchair tennis: Myth to reality.* Dubuque, IA: Kendall/Hunt.

Paciorek, M., & Jones, J. (2001). *Disability sport and recreation resources* (3rd ed.). Traverse City, MI: Cooper Publishing Group.

Shephard, R. (1990). *Fitness in special populations.* Champaign, IL: Human Kinetics.

Sherrill, C. (2004). *Adapted physical activity, recreation and sport: Crossdisciplinary and lifespan* (6th ed.). Boston: WCB McGraw-Hill.

Winnick, J. (Ed.). (2011). *Adapted physical education and sport* (5th ed.). Champaign, IL: Human Kinetics.

World Organization Volleyball for Disabled (WOVD). (2010). *Sitting volleyball rules.* WOVD Headquarters, Klein Heiligland 90, NL-2011 EJ Haarlem, Lindelaan 3: The Netherlands.

Index

Note: The italicized *f* and *t* following page numbers refer to figures and tables, respectively.

About the Author

Ronald W. Davis, PhD, is a professor of adapted physical education in the department of kinesiology at Texas Woman's University. He has almost 30 years of experience in higher education promoting professional development and advocating for people with disabilities. A former disability sport coach and referee, Davis was director of athlete classification for the 1996 Atlanta Paralympics. He has also served as project director for professional preparation training grants from the U.S. Department of Education, Division of Special Education (for students studying adapted physical education).

Davis has published extensively both nationally and internationally on injuries to elite athletes with disabilities, legal mandates for those with disabilities, training for people with disabilities, and related topics. He has been president of the National Consortium for Physical Education and Recreation for Individuals with Disabilities (NCPERID) and a member of the editorial board for the *Journal for Physical Education, Recreation and Dance.* He enjoys biking and spending time with his family.